THE CLASSIC SOCIAL CONTRACTARIANS

The Classic Social Contractarians

Critical Perspectives from Contemporary Feminist Philosophy and Law

JANICE RICHARDSON
University of Exeter, UK

ASHGATE

Published by

Ashgate Publishing Limited
Wey Court East
Union Road
Farnham
Surrey, GU9 7PT
England

Ashgate Publishing Company
Suite 420
101 Cherry Street
Burlington
VT 05401-4405
USA

www.ashgate.com

British Library Cataloguing in Publication Data

Richardson, Janice, 1961-
The classic social contractarians : critical perspectives from contemporary feminist philosophy and law.
1. Sociological jurispridence. 2. Feminist jurisprudence.
I. Title
340.1'15-dc22

Library of Congress Cataloging-in-Publication Data

Richardson, Janice, 1961-
The classic social contractarians : critical perspectives from contemporary feminist philosophy and law / by Janice Richardson.
p. cm.
Includes bibliographical references and index.
ISBN 978-0-7546-7017-9
1. Feminist jurisprudence. 2. Social contract. I. Title.

K349.R53 2009
305.4201--dc22

2009009820

ISBN 9780754670179 (hbk)
ISBN 9780754697206 (ebk)

Mixed Sources
Product group from well-managed forests and other controlled sources
www.fsc.org Cert no. SGS-COC-2482
© 1996 Forest Stewardship Council
FSC

Printed and bound in Great Britain by
TJ International Ltd, Padstow, Cornwall

Contents

Acknowledgements

I would like to thank Jon Rubin for his comments, sense of humour and his computer skills. I am also very grateful to Andy Schaap for his helpful comments on the book, to Beth Lord for her feedback on Spinoza and to Ian Law for commenting on an early draft of the Introduction and Rousseau before escaping into the Amazon jungle. Rousseau has that effect on some people.

List of Cases

UK

US

Introduction

Social contract theory, with its central image of free and equal persons who can create a society based upon rules that all can consent to, has been a major influence on political theory and ethics, from the Ancient Greeks and in particular from the seventeenth century through to today. These theories have varied widely in all aspects of the envisaged contract from the view of which parties take part, the aim of the parties and the role that the (usually hypothetical) contract plays in the argument. In their summary of the social contract tradition, Boucher and Kelly (1994) therefore argue that there is not one tradition but that social contract theories can be divided into broadly three areas: moral contractarianism, civil contractarianism and constitutional contractarianism, albeit that theories within these traditions may overlap. Moral contractarians attempt to ground moral principles by employing the idea of the social contract to ask questions such as: "would free and equal persons agree to this treatment?" In contrast, civil contractarians use the idea of a historical or hypothetical social contract either to legitimise coercive political authority or to provide some test of that authority's legitimacy (Boucher and Kelly 1994, 4). Constitutional contractarianism is a juristic conception of a contract between ruler and ruled that tends to be linked with civil contractarianism and has sources in Roman law jurists, the covenants of the old testament and the feudal contractual relations into which lords and vassals entered (Boucher and Kelly 1994, 10).

In this book I concentrate on the work of the classic social contractarians. Hobbes, Locke, Rousseau and Kant – along with the unusual addition of Spinoza – in order to consider different ways in which the "thought experiment" or "image" of the social contract is employed in argument and its implications for thinking about what it is to be an individual, along with the relationship between ourselves and others. This will be carried out through the lens of contemporary feminist philosophy. This interest in the different ways in which individuals can be envisaged prompts my controversial inclusion of Spinoza, who retells the story of the social contract to produce a different politics and conception of what it is to be human and our relations with others than is usually associated with the tradition.

One way in which political philosophy proceeds is by asking the question: "is government justified?", "is government worth having?", or "is the state a good bargain?" (John Simmons cited by Bittner 2007) in which the term "government" simply refers to state institutions (Bittner 2007). For legal theory, a similar question is asked with reference to obedience to the law. Any discussion of the social contractarians would then be framed by asking how their arguments serve to justify the law. This is not the approach of this book. Consider what happens when the question is changed to: "how can we live together without subordination or oppression?" or "how can we be free and equal?" This brings into light mundane areas of daily subordination, such as those that take place within the family and the workplace, which have a direct impact upon an individual's ability to have his or her voice heard. As feminists have argued, these are important political questions, which are obscured if the central question of politics or law is viewed as the relationship between an abstract individual and the state. The classic social contractarians, Hobbes, Locke, Rousseau and Kant, whilst their arguments were hardly feminist, did not limit their theoretical analyses to the question of the legitimation of the law or state institutions but raised broader issues about the operation of power in their attempts to theorise obedience and obligation. The way in which the story of the social contract is retold – and has increased in popularity since Rawls' *A Theory of Justice* was published in 1971 – also produces very different images of the individual and his (and sometimes her) relationship to both society and state.

Feminist readings of the social contact theory have made such an impact that they can now be viewed as part of mainstream political theory. There has also been recognition of the arguments made by female contemporaries of the earlier contractarians who raised many feminist objections to their work (Smith 1998). There is a large body of work that could be classified as contemporary feminist theory as well as the ground-breaking analysis of feminist philosophers, such as Carole Pateman, Susan Moller Okin, Jean Hampton and Drucilla Cornell on the social contract. My aim is not to attempt to outline all the many and varied ways in which feminists have either critiqued or employed contractarianism. Instead, it is to use contemporary feminist insights as a set of tools with which to examine aspects of the social contractarians' arguments and conversely look at the points at issue between such feminist political theorists: such as the usefulness of contractarian arguments for feminist politics today and the relationship between such political, legal and moral analyses.

Whilst contemporary feminist theory, especially the parts influenced by continental philosophy, may appear very abstract, it is always focused upon questions that have a practical goal: the prevention of the subordination, exploitation and lack of freedom of women. This includes issues of race, class, sexuality and disability. There is a particular treatment of women by the social contractarians that applies to all women by positioning those with female bodies in a particular (often contradictory) manner within their frameworks. To express feminist concerns more positively: feminist theory is concerned with equality and freedom – a focus shared by the social contractarians, who replaced arguments for political legitimacy based upon the divine rule of Kings with those that started with the assumption that all men (or, in the case of Hobbes, all men and women) were both free and equal.

Feminists have opened up different ways of thinking about the meaning of the political; highlighting that women's position had been viewed as "natural" and hence their subordination defined as non-political, for example. Political philosophers have not been monolithic with regard to their views on women, for example, within the social contract tradition, Carole Pateman (1988; 1989) points out that Hobbes was consistent in applying his individualism to women as well as to men. As a result, he views all women and men as equal in the state of nature because all individuals are able to kill each other and hence natural domination cannot occur. She argues that it is only with Locke that the social contractarians assume that women's subordination within the family is itself natural, despite their radical claim that government is a human construction.[1]

Similarly, Okin (1982) argues that there was potential for women to benefit from the individualism that became dominant in the seventeenth century because of the obvious contradiction between the attack upon natural hierarchy and the continued subordination of women. This opportunity was lost with the rise of the ideal of the "sentimental family", which increased the split between an intimate private sphere of family life and public life. This, she argues, undermined women's political claims in a number of ways. Firstly, it divided "women's sphere" of dependency and the domestic life more fully from the outside world than previously; secondly, the image of women became characterised by sentiment rather than the rationality required for citizenship; and finally, it reinforced the idea that a husband could represent his wife's interests, a position even reflected as late as Rawls' *A Theory of Justice* in 1971. She traces the switch from the individualism of Hobbes's *Leviathan* published in 1651 through to the pinnacle of the sentimental family, which is used to argue that women were to be educated to "submit themselves to the will of others", according to Rousseau's *Emile* published in 1762 (Rousseau 1993, 332). The history of individualism is of interest today when women have greater options and the tendency within the West may be towards greater individualism, at least amongst middle class white women (Beck 1999). I will explore the different meanings of individualism below but, in this context, Beck refers to the increase of opportunities for women to pursue individual interests outside of the family.

There are also a number of reasons for feminists to continue reading and critiquing the social contractarians today. They represent a turning point away from the assumption of natural hierarchies and into modernity. The question of how their progressive ideas failed to apply to everyone and the extent to which different aspects of their thought can be reinterpreted is still important. The idea of persons as free and equal whose political obligations arise from consent is no less as progressive today than it was in the seventeenth century. The issue of consent has been interrogated by feminist thought, which has highlighted different and historically contingent ways in which women's consent has been problematic for political and legal theory (for example O'Neill 1989; O'Donovan 1997; Pateman 1995). The idea of an autonomous self, whose exercise of will provides the ground for consent is troubled by the way in which women have been positioned historically as economically (and sometimes psychologically) dependent upon men. I look at the ways in which the social contractarians' subject matter continues to inform our

1 For arguments that Pateman's treatment of Locke is too harsh see Scholet (1998) and Waldron (2007).

view of what it is to be an individual and the way we are envisaged as relating to others. In the final chapter, I demonstrate this by considering a particular type of legal case that impacts upon the way in which autonomy is understood today. I will also compare the different ways in which Hobbes, Locke and Kant envisage the self as bounded and defined in opposition to others and contrast this with Rousseau and Spinoza, who in different ways employ but radically rework Hobbes' vision of individuals coming together in civil society.[2] Feminist philosophy has explored the meaning of what it is to be a self. This is a central theme of this book, which examines different conceptions of what it is to be an individual, person or self (and the way in which we are envisaged as coming together with others) that are employed in diverse ways by the social contractarians. This involves considering how, what Hampton (2002, 382–383) refers to as the "picture" of free and equal persons, within the "fiction", "device" or "thought experiment" of the social contract, is reworked within each conceptual framework. My concern is not to employ a purely textual (or "deconstructive") analysis as such but, taking my cue from Pateman, to focus upon the political implications of such work; to consider what constructive theoretical positions emerge when the position of women as well as men comes into view. Broadly, I want to ask: what is a useful way of thinking about the individual in a way that does not simply take men as the norm but also applies to women? For example, Hobbes starts with a view that individuals are unproblematically separate from each other and derives his political arguments from the psychological characteristics of being competitive, selfish but also rational. It has been argued that Hobbes discusses the psychological characteristics of his own market society and assumes that they are natural (Macpherson 1962). Importantly, Pateman (1988) illustrates the way in which this fails to detail the anomalous position of women, which involves an analysis of how the marriage and employment contracts grew up together to regulate subordination. A further move is also to question the naturalness of this conception of the individual as well as the individual's psychological traits; to ask how we come to see ourselves as individuals in modernity. When it is not assumed that such an image of individuals is natural then the question is raised about the historical conditions that made such an image possible. This history includes the work of the social contractarians, which continues to shape current political debates of libertarians and Rawlsians.

Whilst Pateman is understandably worried by political theorists who focus upon ethical concerns at the expense of the political question of "who has a voice", I will also be considering some of the work of feminists who wish to develop contractarianism, particularly Hampton, as well as Okin and Cornell,[3]

2 Whilst this is not the focus of my concern, it should be noted that this modern image of the self has much in common with postmodern images based upon Lacan, for example, in which there is a constitutive outside to the self, which is defined by its cut from the other (Battersby 1998, 81–102).

3 Cornell (1995, 242), in a brief footnote on Hampton, refuses the term "contractarian" but, as I will argue in the chapter 6 on Kant, I find it useful (and coherent) to read her as

to ask whether any progressive politics can be retrieved from the social contract tradition. I draw mainly upon feminist theory but also, in the next chapter discuss Charles Mills' work on race, particularly in *The Racial Contract* (Mills 1997), to examine some of his arguments, which he acknowledges owe a debt to Pateman, Hampton and Okin.

Chapter Summary

In the first chapter I will outline the main areas of contemporary feminist philosophy that are useful for thinking about the social contractarians and, conversely, why the questions addressed by the contractarians are relevant for thinking about freedom and equality today with reference to both men and women. This will introduce some of the conceptual issues and problems that are tackled throughout the book. These include the way in which the focus upon women (who are often situated within an anomalous position within a framework) can open up questions about a concept, thereby allowing it to be reworked in a constructive way. In addition, I introduce some of the debates within feminist philosophy regarding the way in which the image of the social contract is employed. Whereas Jean Hampton (2002; 2007) finds the image of the social contract useful as a heuristic device, it is vigorously attacked by Carole Pateman (1988; 2002; 2007). I am sympathetic to Pateman's analysis of the problems with the legal and political fiction of individuals as owners of "property in the person" (i.e. owners of their abilities that can be alienated) and the way in which this is informed by historical analysis. However, there are aspects of Hampton's work that are also useful; particularly the way that it informs legal analysis, to be discussed in chapters 6 and 7.

The fact that I find Pateman's historical analysis compelling means that I recognise limits in Hampton's analysis of morality. However, these can be supplemented by Pateman's own political analysis. In particular, Pateman demonstrates the way in which marriage contracts and employment contracts created, and can continue to create, relations of subordination that open the door to exploitation. This adds an important political dimension to the way in which Hampton's focus upon the psychology of individuals within her moral arguments appears to stress exploitation (being treated unfairly) as productive of the subjective belief that one is worth less than others as a person. Pateman accounts for Hampton's starting position by focusing upon subordination and accounting for it historically. There is, therefore, a parallel between the way in which Pateman's focus upon subordination allows her to account for exploitation in the home (which is Hampton's starting point) and exploitation in employment, which is the usual starting position of Marxists

reworking Kant, whilst recognising that I am downplaying her employment of Lacan and Derrida. (She was not raising the semantic question of whether the Kantian tradition should be referred to as "contractualist" nor whether the contract thought experiment is necessary for a consideration of personhood, which it is not, as discussed in chapter 1.)

(Pateman 2002). Attention to Hampton's work is also useful for demonstrating the way in which our gendered understanding of morality reaches its limits and requires a political analysis to account for it. Without a political analysis in the background Hampton cannot account for exploitation simply by an analysis of individuals, yet she does describe some gendered aspects of how moral issues can be experienced in a particular culture. I return to the genealogy of this morality and the way it becomes gendered in the final chapter.

I then consider each social contractarian in turn. In chapter 2, I look at the way in which Hobbes' view of the will, derived from his materialism – and his arguments against democrats (Skinner 2008, 140) – leads him to treat contracts under duress as valid. In contrast with the contemporary image of contract as a symbol of equality and agreement, Hobbes recognises contract as a way of establishing relations of subordination. I consider this in a legal context, which supports Pateman's reading of Hobbes. In addition, as Pateman points out, Hobbes is honest in drawing out the implications of his individualism. Hence, for Hobbes all hierarchies are socially constructed. Turning from politics to ethics, Hampton takes from Hobbes the warning that there is no obligation to make yourself the prey of another. There is no contradiction between this one element of Hobbes' thought that Hampton finds evocative in her moral theory and Pateman's analysis of Hobbes.

Finally, I defend Hampton against an argument made by Tom Sorell (2007). He argues that Hampton misinterprets Hobbes on what it means to be "prey to another". Hampton is clear how she is using this phrase. I use Sorell's point as a way of introducing a broader discussion of feminism and Hobbes' conception of freedom. There is an irony that Hobbes' analysis of freedom marks a break with the republican definition of freedom. In other words, by redefining freedom as the absence of any external impediment, he moves away from the idea of freedom as not being under the arbitrary will of another. The republican definition of freedom would appear to speak to Hampton's concerns about the position of women in the home in a way that Hobbes' definition does not. Nevertheless, republicanism was associated with the idea of natural status, which Hobbes rejects and it is this aspect of individualism that feeds into Hampton's concern that everyone should treat themselves (and not just others) as worthy of respect, otherwise they are simply "prey to others". The aim is not to promote selfishness but to recognise ethical problems with self-sacrifice that is borne of lack of self-respect. This approach to morality is not randomly sprinkled around the population and can only be understood within a social context, beyond the individual.

In chapter 3, I consider how Spinoza rereads Hobbes, such that his central themes, freedom and power, change their meaning. This, in turn, alters our understanding of what it is to be an individual and the way in which any associations, such as the family and the state are conceptualised. I look at the contradiction in Spinoza's work between his comments on women (as naturally unsuitable for citizenship) at the end of the unfinished *Political Treatise* and his metaphysics in the *Ethics*, Spinoza (2000a; 2000b). Given that Spinoza characterises the way in which bodies (and minds) come together to form any association in the same way, I draw upon the arguments that he gives in favour of democracy to discuss the position of women in the family. Spinoza argues that we enter into civil society in order to increase our freedom by improving our ability to reason, thereby increasing our knowledge of the world and our powers of acting in it. The most useful encounters we can have are therefore with others who are also rational and are pursing such knowledge. This applies to all associations, both within the polity and family, for example. Hence, I argue that, from a Spinozan perspective, it is against men's interests (i.e. irrational) to block women's rational development, i.e. their powers of acting in the world.

There is much interesting work which uses Spinoza as a starting point, particularly from feminists Moira Gatens and Genevieve Lloyd (1999) and by Susan James (2002; 2008). As part of their analyses they all examine the meaning of the imagination in Spinoza and put it to work in various ways, for example to think about social responsibility (Gatens and Lloyd 1999) and the imagination of judges (Gatens 1995). I point to the similarities (and important differences) between this emphasis upon the imagination and the work of Drucilla Cornell (1995; 1998; 2000; 2008), which draws upon both a Kantian and a psychoanalytic framework to produce legal arguments. This contemporary interest in the imagination is a thread that runs through the book (and is also considered in detail in chapter 6 on Kant). In an interview, Gatens points out that the imaginary[4] is doing some of the work that was previously performed by the term "ideology", but that Spinoza adds to the richness of the meaning of "ideology" (James, Lloyd, and Gatens 2000, 56). Spinoza views the imagination as the first type of knowledge, which is formed from our passionate responses to our encounters with other bodies. I agree that this is a very promising approach but also point out that Spinoza's emphasis is upon increasing knowledge by trying to understand why some encounters produce different passions. As well as producing a potentially useful view of imagination, he also produces a helpful way of thinking about reason, which is then neither a faculty nor merely calculative and is closely linked to the bodily imagination. The analysis of imagination and reason is central to explaining how he envisages the social contract as associations between individuals, who are never isolated from each other or the world of which they are a part. In addition, at a meta-level, Spinoza's view of the imagination has contributed to the way in which it is possible to understand how images and fictions which make up our social imaginary operate. This includes the fiction of the social contract itself.

4 The term "imaginary" is associated with a psychoanalytic framework derived from Lacan (2001), to be discussed in chapter 6, but can be used (in the sense of "social imaginary") simply to describe the self-image and ideas of a collectivity, communicated mainly through fictions and images. Gatens is relying upon the latter sense of the term. I will state if the psychoanalytic aspect of the term is doing any work and will otherwise assume this general meaning.

In chapter 4, I outline how Locke treats male domination within the family as natural rather than constructed, thereby dividing "political power" from "power within the family". This has allowed both political theorists and popular culture to marginalise women's subordination as non-political. This move was also associated with a conception of power as something that is held by the sovereign and that operates top-down through laws. As feminists have pointed out, this image of power ignores everyday subordination in the workplace and home. I detail the way in which Pateman highlights both this move and another fiction: property in the person, which still has a powerful influence upon our understanding of what it is to be an individual because it speaks to the way in which our society is organised. I demonstrate how Pateman supplements a Marxist approach by applying her reading of Locke to inform a discussion by Laslett (1999) on Locke's view of the self. In addition, I argue that her work is consistent with the useful examination of Locke on workmanship by Murphy (1992).

There is a common argument against Pateman that she views women's oppression as so strongly determined by contract in modernity that there is no escape. It is my argument that the complete opposite is true. Her work is concerned with increasing freedom and can even be read as fitting within and supplementing elements of Foucault's (1977; 1990) analysis. I realise that this is a controversial (and partial) reading, given Foucault's anti-humanism that is not shared by Pateman, but I am using it to drive home a point. Pateman does not assume that daily subordination is lived out through the dictates of contract but that contract produces "the role of" housewives and employees. The term "the role of" is in quotations because, as Foucault illustrates, such "roles" are more than an act but constitute a way of life; they constitute "who we are". Whilst Pateman (rightly) analyses the history of institutions of marriage and employment, the way in which she analyses the politics of everyday subordination means that she cannot be accused of having a view of power that simply focuses upon the laws and state in a top-down manner. The idea that the way of life (or meaning of what it is to be a housewife and employee) is created by contract does not imply that the contract can somehow dictate the nuanced details of daily routine and the ways in which these subordinate positions are negotiated, nor does it imply that they are inevitable. Pateman details the history of the fiction, "property in the person" and its relationship to contract, that "justifies" these ways of life. Foucault outlines the detailed bodily ways in which they are acted out, the techniques of power that operate so as to create individuals.

In chapter 5, I outline Rousseau's social contract, in which women are viewed as becoming unequal early in human development, within the second stage of the state of nature. Whereas Rousseau (1992) was concerned with inequality of wealth in his criticism of Hobbes and Locke, his work represents the high water mark of the sentimental family, linked with the claim that women are naturally subordinate to men and should be educated to "submit themselves to the will of others" (Rousseau 1993, 332). Rousseau's advocacy of the sentimental family as an ideal and his concerns about class inequality, raise the question of whether women's traditional position within the home could offer a positive exemplar of individuals who are not competitive within the market place; that they demonstrate an ethic of care, for example. However, Rousseau blocks this move by the way in which he positions women as susceptible to competition, to *amour propre*, particularly vanity. I examine how Rousseau places women in a double bind with regard to morality. They are expected to be concerned about their reputation and yet morality is associated with the exact opposite: the enlightenment ideal of being your own judge and thinking for yourself. Similarly, as Okin (2002) points out, women are positioned such that they do not fit within Rousseau's image of the "natural man" but nor are they citizens.

I explore Rousseau's position by tracing Althusser's (2007) careful reading of *The Social Contract*, which points to a series of linked discrepancies within Rousseau's text. At the end of the trail Althusser argues that theoretical discrepancies cannot be "ironed out" because they depend upon class differences that represent a practical problem. He scornfully comments that one of the routes left open to Rousseau is to write literature. I draw upon Okin's (2002) analysis of Rousseau's literature itself to show how the (political) question of the position of women produces practical problems. Women educated in accordance with Rousseau's views detailed in *Emile* and whose lives reflected those in his novels would exacerbate the inherent conflict between the two central institutions of Rousseau's thought: the patriarchal family and the civic republic. Rousseau does not register this conflict but instead views women themselves as naturally disruptive to the state, referring to "the disorder of women" (Rousseau 1968, 109).

In chapter 6, I examine the ways in which both Drucilla Cornell and Jean Hampton derive arguments from the Kantian social contract, despite the fact that he shares Rousseau's misogyny, such that he comments: "laborious learning or painful pondering, even if a woman should greatly succeed in it, destroys the merits that are proper to her sex ..." (Kant 1991a, 78). Kant views the social contract as an idea of reason. He changes the meaning of idea – for example, God or freedom – to differentiate it from concepts of the understanding. Cornell employs the Kantian derived test: "would free and equal persons agree to this?" to question the legitimacy of laws. Similarly, Hampton draws upon this image of free and equal persons to produce a test of fairness in everyday relationships, particularly between husband and wife.

Cornell draws a divide between personhood and selfhood. She argues for legal rights of persons not to be harmed in their self-development. The law is not responsible for self-development (and should not impose its idea of the good life). Its role is to protect against any harm to such self-development by others. For example, sexual harassment is understood as such a harm because it is the imposition of the harasser's imaginary in a situation of power differences, which can interfere with the openness of self-development of its victim, thereby "crowding out" more positive self-images. This classic liberal position is supplemented by the way that Cornell envisages the role of the imaginary, which is involved in a collective acting out of different ways of life.

This does not rely upon the Kantian conception of imagination as a faculty or the way in which Kant's analysis of the form (rather than content) of the imagination is part of reflexive judgement, discussed in terms of aesthetics in the *Critique of Judgement* (Kant 1987).[5] Therefore, I argue that she could employ the more promising Spinozan model of imagination without altering the way in which she employs Kant's social contract.

Finally, I conclude by illustrating the way in which some views of the individual, associated with Locke and Kant can be seen to arise in court cases today. By considering Battersby's (1995; 1998) reading of Kant's *Critique of Judgement* I explore Kant's image of a self, whose integrity is threatened but who is able to re-establish "his" boundaries against the outside. In this example, the boundaries are that of nature, which initially threatens as part of the experience of the sublime. A similar "bounded" image of the self is evoked by Locke in which freedom is viewed as taking place within the boundaries of one's property. Autonomy is conceived of as taking place within this property, from which one can exclude others and the state. Hobbes' isolated individuals evoke a similar image of "boundedness".

Nedelsky (1991) illustrates how Locke's image of the individual, in particular, is reflected in US law that sought to protect the property-owning minority from the majority. She contrasts this with the way in which children learn autonomy as a result of helpful intervention from others rather than by being left alone. This raises similar issues to those of Battersby who illustrates how a "female sublime" was created by women artists, for whom the sublime was viewed as an inappropriate subject of work. The work of these artists appeals to a dynamic image of a self that, like Kant's image, avoids being overwhelmed but neither is it isolated or defined by what is its outside. I consider the tensions within Rousseau on this issue of the relationship between self and others and then illustrate how Spinoza provides a model of the relationship between self and others that is not "bounded" and which, as a result, alters his understanding of autonomy. I end by looking at the role of images and fictions, such as the image of the social contract and my claim that whilst this is useful it is also necessary to rethink the way in which reason is envisaged.

5 This area of Kant's thought is being developed by political theorists, drawing upon Arendt (2001) to provide a model of a universal that does not rely upon concepts. See Ferrara (2008) and Beiner and Nedelsky (2001).

Chapter 1
The Social Contractarians and Contemporary Feminist Philosophy

The Anomalous Position of Women within Traditional Political Theory: The "False Universal" and Problems of Abstraction

The position of women is not only of concern as a practical issue; it can also provide useful resources for thinking about the historically contingent ways in which the relationship between individuals and others have been conceptualised. This is because women have not been treated as autonomous individuals or as (moral or legal) persons in the same way as men. Different ways in which the relationship between self and other are understood are also intimately related to our images of political organisation. Charles Taylor contrasts the social imaginary that, he argues, existed prior to the social contract theorists with today's social imaginary:

> Hierarchical complementarity was the principle on which people's lives effectively operated all the way from the Kingdom to the city to the diocese to the parish to the clan and the family. We still have some lively sense of this disparity in the case of the family, because it is really only in our time that the older images of hierarchical complementarity between men and women are being comprehensively challenged (Taylor 2004, 16).[1]

The historically contingent fact that hierarchical relations within the family have persisted raises interesting questions about the conceptual framework of the social contractarians, whose accounts rely upon their differing understanding of what it is to be an individual, complete with discussions about psychology, that will be examined in more detail in each chapter. There are different approaches to women's exclusion within alternative theoretical frameworks, such as those offered by the social contractarians. Often the claim in mainstream theory is that women can simply be added into the theoretical position without any change to that framework. However, more interestingly, feminist analysis has shown how – in some cases – the presumptions of the framework can be challenged by focusing upon and reworking the anomalous treatment of women.

---

1 The ways in which women have always challenged subordination are still coming to light, of course.

In thinking about the way in which feminist philosophy can impact upon traditional political theory a useful analogy can be drawn from Christine Battersby's (1998; 2007) work in the philosophy of aesthetics. She argues that the artistic canon often excluded women artists because they seemed not to fit exactly within a tradition. In addition, as women, these artists may have had certain types of art deemed unsuitable as an area in which to work. This "off-beat" position of women artists, which arose as a contingent result of particular historical circumstances, meant that they produced artwork that fits uncomfortably within the canon. When women artists are no longer marginalised, their artistic link with the canon can be reassessed and sometimes has the ability to disrupt and challenge the canon's boundaries, allowing it to be understood in a different way. Battersby (1998; 2007) illustrates this with a reassessment of the sublime in art.

Battersby's work can be viewed as containing a double move. It concerns a "paradigm shift" that can be viewed as analogous to challenges to a political framework made by feminist theorists, such as the view of power as more than simply the relationship between the state and citizen but as an issue that also arises within the home and workplace with the question: "who has a voice in this relationship?" However, this shift is not simply that of women artists/political philosophers of today reworking the canon, which can include revaluing and employing the work of earlier women that may have been dismissed (see Smith (1998) with regard to the social contractarians). The double move also includes an analysis of the historically contingent meaning of what it is to be female – for example how one's body[2] is positioned within networks of power – and how this contingency is reflected in the canon. The aim is not simply to point to anomalies but to add to the process of theory building; to re-frame current problems in a way that is useful for both men and women.

One tool that has been employed is the recognition that when philosophers have talked about men they often fail to register that they are simultaneously referring to a universal and have in mind only males, i.e. those with male bodies, which has meant that they are positioned in a certain way and associated with certain lifestyles historically. I will discuss the extent to which the classic contractarians, employing a quasi-anthropology, did consider the position of women and will also trace such ambiguities. However, this use of a "false universal" (appearing to talk about humanity but having males in mind as the "norm" or paradigm example of humanity) has also been disguised further within social contract frameworks such as that of Rawls. Following Kant in asking what free and equal persons would agree to, he initially employs the image (or thought experiment) of individual

2 I should be clear that Battersby (1989, 11) usefully distinguishes between "female" and "feminine". In art, the male genius was viewed as "feminine", having female characteristics, but it would be a category mistake to view him as "female". Hence those traits that were viewed as "feminine" were valued highly if exhibited by some males but not by females. The female body itself has consistently been devalued.

heads of household meeting under a "veil of ignorance" (meaning that none would know his position in society). Rawls then discusses which principles of justice could be agreed upon, relying upon the fact that those deciding would not know whether or not they would be in the position of the worst off in society. Okin (1989) highlights the problem of Rawls' assumptions that only the heads of household, assumed to be male, would be meeting under the "veil of ignorance" and that the current family structure is a just institution. Her argument then aims to improve upon Rawls, rather than abandoning his contractarian framework, by asking: what rules would those meeting under the "veil of ignorance" be willing to agree to if they knew that they risked being a woman in a patriarchal society?

Those feminist theorists (and critical race theorists, to be discussed below) who have employed the idea of a contract in such a manner have not been complaining of the abstraction employed in the contract *per se* but of what I have referred to as the "false universal" in which the historically contingent position of women (or non-white persons) has been subsumed within that of white men, who are then viewed as the neutral term. It was a conceptual blindness to women's historical position which, for example, allowed Rawls to assume that the family was a just institution and that its members had the same interests that could be represented by the (male) "head of household". However, there have also been different criticisms of the role of abstraction itself. I will detail these within the context of particular classic contractarians. It is worth making a broader point at this stage because this is an argument that has gained purchase within the humanities influenced by a line of thought with its antecedents in Nietzsche (2006).

To explain and develop this point, first I will outline the problem of the existence of concepts themselves as abstractions, as posed by Nietzsche. Nietzsche (2006, 117) uses the example of the concept of a leaf and argues that what is lost when this concept is used is the specificity of any single leaf. The use of concepts can therefore be viewed as a way of ignoring differences between leaves. So, does this matter? We develop concepts that are useful to us and would be unable to act in the world without such generalisations. The problem comes, not from abstraction *per se*, but from the way in which some abstractions operate to lose details that do matter – linked with the operation of power that is involved in doing the defining. As Battersby's work has illustrated, when the canon (of art and of political theory) operates so as to marginalise the contribution of women, women's artistic *oeuvres* can later be reassessed and the canon can be understood differently; its boundaries may be redrawn. The way in which we decide merit within the canon of art will differ from the way in which we assess whether political theory can be improved from being redrawn, of course. The aim is not simply to look at women's position just for its own sake but to clarify and improve the way in which political problems are understood and tackled. In some situations, the "adding in" of women to conceptual frameworks may make little difference but in others it may open up new ways of seeing old problems, with a view to facilitating social change. For me, the important point is not to be concerned about the need for theory to employ concepts and abstractions (because this is unavoidable) but to consider whether anything important has been lost by the abstraction. Inevitably, this involves a risk of wrongly excluding a particular viewpoint. It may be argued that to focus upon women will neglect issues of the intersecting concerns of race, class, sexuality and disability, for example. I hope to illustrate that social contractarians provide a fertile ground for thinking about the different ways in which political, moral and legal relations are envisaged in modernity in order to rethink how we envisage such relationships when the "blind spot" of women is brought to light, at a time when there has been a shift from the "sentimental family" to greater individualism in the West. This is not to ignore the fact that there are other areas of subordination. The focus of this book is upon contemporary feminist theory as a set of tools that may sometimes be useful for thinking about these other areas of subordination but that cannot stand in for the historical specificity of such analyses.

The different but related problem of abstracting an individual from the social context within traditional liberal theory is a central issue in this book. Whilst abstraction (of the individual from his/her social context in a thought experiment) has allowed the classic social contractarians to make their own conjectures about human nature, it has also opened up a discussion about non-ideal contracts, to which I now turn.

Non-Ideal Contracts

As illustrated by Okin, one strand of feminist thought has employed contractarian ideas, or images of how free and equal persons would behave. Amongst such theorists I draw upon the work of, not only Okin but also Hampton and Cornell, whose "contractarian" arguments therefore need to answer the strong criticisms of contractarianism raised by other feminists. I will examine these in detail within the context of the specific classic contractarians discussed in the book. However, one powerful critique, that of Carole Pateman, must be introduced early, not only because it was ground-breaking within this area but also because it provides such a strong argument against any use of contractarianism whatsoever. In addition, Pateman's work has been deeply influential (see for example Phillips 2008). Mills (1997) in *The Racial Contact* acknowledges his debt to Pateman. The disagreement between Pateman and Mills in their *Contract and Domination* (Pateman and Mills 2007) deals specifically with the question of whether the social contract can be of use to feminist and/or critical race theory. I will outline Mills' position, which also draws from Okin's analysis of Rawls, sketched above, and from Hampton. Then I will look at Pateman's analysis in detail so that her arguments can be considered throughout this book.

Mills (1997) points out that, in the influential work of Rawls, there is an image of an "ideal contract", used as a thought experiment in order to imagine the system of laws/political institutions persons would agree to if they negotiated "under the veil of ignorance" and hence did not know anything about their position in society. As outlined above, it is clear that Rawls had in mind a way of arguing against class and wealth privileges but not of gender, race, sexuality or disability, for example. Mill's argument is analogous to Okin's move of asking whether such "free and equal persons", who were meeting to decide upon issues of social justice, but did not know the position they would take up in the society they were to create, would risk being positioned as women in a patriarchal society. This involves importing some knowledge of the non-ideal contingent history of our society (the subordination of women) but still viewing them as ignorant of the position they would hold in any future society whose rules they are deciding. The thought experiment thereby forces us to imagine ourselves in the position of others, who are oppressed. Similarly, Mills poses the question: "would free and equal persons agree to be positioned as non-white in a racist society?" He uses this contractual framework to highlight issues of inequality, in this case racial oppression, which are marginalised within the influential contractarian tradition. He sees himself as having precursors in his shift from an "ideal contract", described by Rawls (in which no knowledge of historical subordination or oppression is considered within the thought experiment save for knowledge of wealth) to a "non-ideal contract" in which there is knowledge of other forms of subordination. Mills therefore positions his "racial contract" alongside what he characterises as earlier "non-ideal contracts": Rousseau's (1992) analysis of class inequality in his *Discourse on Inequality* as well as Pateman's (1988) analysis of women's position in *The Sexual Contract*, whilst noting, of course, that Pateman rejects any appeal to a hypothetical contract to support her arguments. This is a particular view of abstraction that – unlike some aspects of contemporary continental theory – does not aim to revalue what is repressed and marginal within language or emphasise "difference", or respect for "the other". Instead, Mills aims to employ an abstraction, the non-ideal contract, to draw attention to important historical issues that are neglected within mainstream political philosophy, by translating them into mainstream language in the terms of the social contract (Pateman and Mills 2007, 23).

I will examine how this is carried out in the work of Mills and of Pateman below. This element of Mills' argument makes his employment of the language of social contract sound purely pragmatic. He (rightly) wants to shock political theorists into recognising that the discipline is affected by a "blind spot" of racial subordination and oppression, in just the same way as feminists have shown how theory is affected by its gender blindness or its reliance upon the ambiguous treatment of women. As I will illustrate, such ambiguities include, for example, whether women/non-white persons are the subject or merely object of the social contract. However, in the body of his work Mills (1997) appears to want more from contract theory than simply this (worthy) pragmatic move. By analogy with Okin and Hampton, he wants to use the Kantian image of "free and equal persons" within the tradition in a manner that is productive, by evoking the social contract. Pateman rejects any use of the metaphor of contract as a model for free agreement because contracts – such as employment contracts and marriage contracts – are associated with subordination, to be discussed further below. The metaphor is consistent with a libertarian view of all social relations governed by contract. This vision of a "free society" is based upon the image of individuals owning their abilities as if they were commodities.

Both Pateman and Mills (2007) invite readers to ask whether their difference on this point is conceptual. For me, the answer is yes. There is a conceptual difference between them that, whilst at times appearing to be merely an issue of pragmatism (i.e. whether using this form of words, or this image, is politically useful), amounts to more than this. The difference between them derives from the different ways in which they read the contractarian tradition and, in particular, the centrality of Pateman's analysis of "property in the person", which I will sketch after an outline of Mills and examine in detail in chapter 4 on Locke. This arises as a result of the historical link that she illustrates between the employment and marriage contracts. This is eluded to, but not detailed, when Pateman and Mills comment that,

> One reason for [Mill's] optimism is that his use of "contract" is looser and more metaphorical than Pateman's; he sees "contract" as basically just a figure for representing the human creation of sociopolitical relations (Pateman and Mills 2007, 7).

In other words, Mills is drawing from the contractarian tradition to emphasise that sociopolitical relations are socially constructed; that there is no natural subordination. I use the phrase "drawing from" because, with the exception of Hobbes, of course, the social contractarians did view woman as naturally subordinate to men in the "private" realm, whilst arguing that public hierarchical relations between white men entailed no natural subordination.

Mills (2007, 85) explains this move by outlining the influence of Hampton upon his work. Hampton (2002, 382) refers to the way in which the classic contractarians (other than Kant) employed the social contract as a way of describing their existing society and prescribing a "new and more defensible form for such societies" (Hampton 2002, 382). Mills supports Hampton's argument that this "descriptive side", such as the stories of the state of nature, should be revived. It is important that this "description" (as illustrated by the sexual and racial contracts) is not mistaken for socio-political descriptions of how oppression actually emerged:

> For once we realize that contract is basically a matter of "imagery", a "picture", we should recognise that it is not vulnerable to standard literalist objections (for example that no promises are actually exchanged to support governmental structures), as it is essentially just expressing the insight that "authoritative political societies are human creations" [and] "conventionally-generated" (Pateman and Mills 2007, 85; quotations from Hampton 2002, 382–383).

The "descriptive side" of the social contract therefore works by a similar mechanism as that employed by Kant, when he says we should treat each other "as if" we were free and equal. The claim is that society works "as if" this fictional event had occurred. For Mills, it is not an empirical claim but a way of bringing historical oppression and its implications into focus in political theory. Pateman's response is that this dichotomy relies upon a fact/value distinction to separate "descriptive" from "normative" content. *The Sexual Contract* can be viewed as both descriptive (in the sense employed by Mills in that it provides a conjectural history to make a point) and also normative (in that she is arguing against libertarians and in support of participative democracy). This normative element is also present in the work of Rousseau and Mills, of course, and it may be that it is simply the fictional element that Mills is highlighting. I will return to Pateman's analysis below after describing the non-ideal contract.

Following Pateman, it is necessary to be careful in teasing out the complex linkages of different contracts involved in Mills and Pateman's approaches, both of which include reference to both hypothetical contracts and also to historical legal contracts. Mills states that he wants to return to the way in which the classic contractarians discuss the social contract by way of a "quasi-anthropology", i.e. their description of the (hypothetical) state of nature. So, there is an additional aspect to Mills' analysis in that he makes an analogous move to Okin, calling upon the reader to imagine free and equal persons entering into a hypothetical contract. Whilst they are still unaware of their future position in society, they now know something of the world's past racist history and the risk of being classified as non-white in a society with Jim Crow laws, for example. Mills therefore refers to actually existing historical racist laws and "white settler contracts", which will form part of their knowledge of history. He stresses that – by analogy with Pateman – he is not saying that all white individuals entered into a contract to agree to subordinate all non-white individuals but employs this idea (as a non-ideal) contract to illustrate our current position. It is this current position that must be acknowledged when employing the thought experiment of the social contract to ask if free and equal persons would risk being non-white in a racist society. The status of the historical racial contracts and how they link with the more abstract hypothetical contract is detailed in Pateman and Mills (2007). To consider this further it is necessary to turn to Pateman's work in detail.

The Sexual Contract: Freedom and Property in the Person

The Sexual Contract must be understood in the context of Pateman's *oeuvre*, the central focus of which is freedom and the hope of a genuine participative democracy. In particular, Pateman highlights the role that "property in the person" plays to disguise and justify subordination in the employment contract and traditional marriage contract, along with the way in which these contracts were developed together and can be juxtaposed with questions of citizenship.

In both *The Problem of Political Obligation* and *The Sexual Contract*, Pateman (1979; 1988) considers the work of the classic social contractarians to ask how an argument that was based upon the political ideal of consent of the governed (and depends upon an ideal of free and equal persons) could have become associated with the subordination of women. She illustrates the way in which, with the exception of Hobbes, the classic social contractarians positioned women as naturally subordinate to men, whilst also claiming equality for men in a separate public sphere outside of the "natural" household. To make this point, she rewrites the story of the social contract to also include an additional hypothetical "sexual contract" in which men are envisaged as entering into an agreement amongst each other to obey the law, which will then enforce the marriage contract and the subordination of women. This hypothetical rewriting is employed to illustrate a point and Pateman describes it in the following terms,

> [T]he way in which my argument in *The Sexual Contract* was developed was greatly influenced by the new techniques of theoretical analysis that were being used by deconstructionists and postmodernists in the 1980s (Pateman and Mills 2007, 219).

It is clearly not an attempt to explain women's subordination in socio-historical terms but is a way of saying that society works *as if* "the sexual contract" had occurred.

In contrast, the marriage contract and employment contract do have an actual legal history. One of the strengths of Pateman's work is the way in which she links a Marxist inspired critique of the employment contract, with the marriage contract to focus upon subordination rather than simply exploitation (Pateman 2002, 51). She points out that both types of contract allow workers and women to appear to give their consent to relationships that are actually characterised by their subordination and operate in situations in which they have had little choice but to enter into the contracts. In this context, the move of abstracting individuals from their social circumstances allowed liberal theory to ignore coercion. This can be illustrated with a legal example. Nineteenth century common law judges argued that workers could not make legal claims in negligence for unsafe working conditions because they were deemed to have consented to the risk, having chosen to work out of their own free will. It was only at the end of the century that the House of Lords in the UK recognised that in practice workers had little choice about their working conditions.[3] Similarly, there is much feminist work that illustrates the problematic manufacture of women's consent. As I will discuss in the next chapter, this issue of "coerced consent" is perhaps most stark in the way in which Hobbes redefines the will and freedom so as to produce an argument for obedience (Skinner 2008).

In *Capital*, Marx (1992) argues that, in the employment contract, there appears to be an equal exchange between a worker and his/her employer: work for wages. However, money is exchanged for labour power (the capacity to work). Labour power is not something that can be separated from the worker's body so to view it in this way (as a commodity) disguises the fact that the worker must actually go

---

3 *Smith v Baker & Sons* [1891] AC 625.

to work and obey the employer. The relationship is one of subordination, whilst at the same time, through the device of contract, the parties are both treated as "free and equal citizens". I have argued that it is useful to consider the way in which the meaning of contract within contract law has developed, along with the use of implied contractual terms (Richardson 2004a).

In his much debated and contentious work, Macpherson (1962) applies Marx's argument to Hobbes and Locke to argue that they illegitimately read into a state of nature a view of "human nature" that was not innate but reflected the way in which economic men were viewed within their emerging capitalist society. Pateman then develops Macpherson's /Marx's analysis to include women, who like workers, are positioned as entering into contracts of their own free will, whilst being denied other alternatives. However, wives were not viewed as exchanging their labour power for money but as providing "*consortium*", which included sex and housework, in exchange for "protection", i.e. financial support. Again, this can be illustrated with an example from the common law. As part of a civil action in tort, a man could claim for "loss of *consortium*" against a defendant who had negligently harmed his wife, preventing her from carrying out such "wifely duties".[4] I will return to this issue in the final chapter. Similarly, the consent to have sex was an implied term in the marriage contract so that it is only relatively recently that forced sex in marriage has been classified as rape – a position that pertained in the UK, for example, until 1991.[5]

Employment lawyers such as Deakin (2002) have illustrated the way in which such contracts developed together historically. Pateman situates her work historically:

> The patriarchal structures with which I was concerned have been considerably weakened, and the heyday of the worker/breadwinner was from 1840–1970 (Pateman 1996, 204).

She continues,

> Women and men alike are now being drawn into a global division of labour, and assessments of which women may gain or lose, and whether new forms of subordination are developing, are, necessarily, enormously complex and difficult when the restructuring is gathering pace. I believe my arguments in *The Sexual Contract* can throw light on the course of some recent developments, but to examine the issues would require another, very different, book (Pateman 1996, 205).

4 In the UK this survived until its repeal by the Administration of Justice Act 1982.

5 *R v R* [1991] 4 All ER 481.

Part of the current change involves the way in which what it means to be a "self", in particular the way in which we, in the West, construct individualism continues to alter with the change in family forms from the 1970s.

Whilst they may not have focused upon the issues of gender or race, a difficulty for the classic contractarians was to promote the idea of free and equal persons whilst not applying this move to women (or as Mills (1997) illustrates, to anyone non-white). Pateman points to the paradox that women were viewed as persons capable of consenting to enter into a marriage contract that then brought about their subordination through marriage. There are similar examples of such paradoxical treatment of women – as both persons and non-persons – in common law. For example, women brought a series of "persons cases" at the end of the nineteenth century up to 1930 to claim that where a statute referred to a "person" that this should include women. Cobden was elected to the London Country Council but it was held that she could not vote because she was not to be classified as a "person" under the relevant Act.[6] Nevertheless, she was prosecuted and penalised under an Act that made it unlawful for "any person" to act in corporate office without being qualified (Sachs and Hoff Wilson 1979, 26).

To illustrate the radical implications of Pateman's work, consider her argument in "Self-Ownership and Property in the Person: Democratization and a Tale of Two Concepts" (Pateman 2002). She clarifies the fact that discussions in political theory around "possessive individualism" (Macpherson's term) and "self-ownership" are in fact talking about the fiction of "property in the person". She prefers the latter term (to be discussed in more detail in chapter 4 on Locke) because it makes clear that the fiction involves treating aspects of a person as if they were property that could be alienated, i.e. it implies a stress on the "ownership" part of "self-*ownership*" (Pateman 2002). She considers possible societies that could emerge depending upon the extent to which the fiction of property in the person is accepted within law. If it is accepted that a worker can rent him/herself out for part of the day, then what is wrong with a slave contract, provided it is agreed upon by contract and not the threat of violence? As I will discuss further, the classic contractarians usually blocked this move. For Locke, to sell oneself into slavery would be to give someone else the right of life or death over oneself, a right that one did not own to give away because only God would have such a right. However, as I will discuss in chapter 4, there is nothing within his framework of viewing ourselves as owners of "property in the person", i.e. of having those rights over ourselves that would be held by a master over a slave in a slave owning society (Cohen 1995, 68), that precludes slavery. Locke's proviso is based upon a separate claim regarding the immorality of suicide.

To summarise, Pateman's thought experiment about an imaginary "sexual contract" describes a fictional contract made between men to subordinate women. Her rewriting of the classic contractarians was influenced by textual analysis, told to illustrate how their stories of an agreement to move from a state of nature to

6 *De Souza v Cobden* [1891] 1 QB 687, at 691; 60 LJQB. 533.

a state with laws appears to work by simultaneously instantiating both a social contract and a hidden sexual contract. We can provide socio-historical analysis of how women's subordination may have occurred but Pateman's move is employed simply to say "it works as if this hypothetical contract had been entered into by men". (I will describe this as a hypothetical "exclusionary contract". The term "exclusionary contract" will be a short hand way of denoting a contract that is entered into by one group of persons, which involves treating others, who are not parties to the contract, as merely objects of the contract. So, slave contracts would be so classified, provided the slave him/herself had not entered into such a "civil slave contract".)

Importantly, along with this thought experiment of a hypothetical sexual contract, Pateman employs an analysis of actual marriage contracts, along with employment contracts, to show how central the fiction of exchange of "property in the person" has been to subordination. She illustrates how it operated by disguising subordination as a fair exchange: labour power for money (for workers) and *consortium* for "protection" (for traditional wives) in contracts that developed historically together based upon a particular image of the family, which has now changed in the West. It is this element that makes Mills' analysis different from (whilst, as he acknowledges, influenced by) Pateman's position. Pateman's emphasis upon the role of property in the person in marriage contracts, employment contracts (and also in those of prostitution and surrogacy) mean that she is critical of any project that attempts to work within a contractarian framework. She views such an approach as antithetical to freedom because it smuggles in an image of an exchange of "property in the person" and/or evokes the classic contractarian image of individuals who give up their right to self-government. In contrast, Mills draws upon the "feminist contractarianism" of Hampton to argue for the need to distinguish between Hobbes' view of contract in which your value is simply your price and that of Kant for whom personhood entailed equality that could not be diminished (setting aside the problem that Kant was also dubious about whether women or anyone non-white were to be viewed as persons).

Therefore, the difference between Mills and Pateman may derive from the importance of "property in the person" to Pateman's argument, which arises from her analysis of women's position and that of workers. In contrast, when Mills or Pateman (Pateman and Mills 2007, 35–79) consider the "white settler" contract which is an exclusionary contract, envisaged as only made between white men, the exchange of property in the person does not arise because slaves are treated as objects of the contract. Whilst in Pateman's reading, women were not parties to the social and sexual contracts; they were parties to traditional marriage contracts. In contrast, slaves were treated as a type of property, whose coerced "consent" was not required. This white settler "exclusionary contract" is a fiction if viewed as a contract between all white (men) to exploit all non-white persons but the analysis also involves historical detail about slavery, along with the actual contracts and law relating to it. It may be that the centrality of property in the person for Pateman derives from her analysis of the interrelationship of citizenship, marriage and employment as opposed to slavery, so she (correctly, in my view) draws out the fiction of property in the person. There is more to this difference, however, as Mills (Pateman and Mills 2007, 19) appears to have a more positive reading of Locke; a point I will discuss in detail in the Pateman section in chapter 4.

As a further argument against the use of the fiction of contract for progressive politics, Pateman is critical of the way in which political philosophy has become dominated by moral theory, arguing that this closes down the space for analysis of subordination and how to challenge it, which are *political*, not ethical, questions (Pateman 2002, 22). This objection is aimed at the dominance of "methodological Rawlsianism". It would appear that both of these powerful criticisms: of the way in which talk of contract often smuggles in the fiction of "property in the person" and of the elision of political problems by moral theory, may also be directed at Jean Hampton's work. Hampton's interest is moral philosophy and she tries to use contractarianism for feminist ends. In the next section I will briefly outline Hampton's broad position and point out where it is compatible with Pateman's analysis and where Pateman's position can be viewed as supplementing Hampton's approach. Whilst, as explained in the introduction, I find Pateman's argument compelling, there are elements of Hampton's view of the equal worth of personhood – that rely upon a detailed discussion about daily subordination and psychological reactions to it – that are useful but could not be understood fully without the political analysis that Pateman provides. The limits of Hampton's position can be illustrated by the question of what happens if everyone fails her test of fairness in relationships, as I will discuss below. There has been much feminist critique of Kant's person as paradigmatically male, to be discussed in chapter 6. However, Hampton's reading of Kant illustrates the way in which he provides an image of the individual that is not based upon the fiction of "property in the person". As I will discuss in chapters 6 and 7, it may be that – just as Pateman is concerned that all references to contract will evoke the fiction of property in the person – images of what it is to be an individual in our society are also haunted by that of the possessive individual, owner of property in the person, because, as Pateman is clear, such fictions are not free floating but speak to us because of the power structures that exist, with specific genealogies. This does not mean that they are fixed and cannot be altered, in part by tracing their contingent histories. I will illustrate this point in chapter 7 by considering different contemporary images of child care in an area of current litigation. Pateman does not specifically reject the use of personhood that is employed by Hampton, her attack is upon the image of the contract *per se*, as I will discuss further in the next section.

One point should be noted regarding Pateman's work before discussing Hampton. Pateman emphasises that she is criticising political institutions and not the reaction of particular employers and husbands, who may not use the powers that they have been given by laws and social mores. This can be illustrated by considering the position of John Stuart Mill, who as a Victorian had many legal rights over his wife. He recognised that, whilst he could promise not to use these rights, he could not lose the power it gave him, despite wanting an equitable relationship. This again raises issues about the meaning of freedom that is central to Pateman's work. Whereas liberals, following Hobbes, have a view of freedom as negative freedom – that we are free if we are not subject to "external impediments" – Pateman comes closer to the republican tradition, with its definition of freedom based upon non-domination, in arguing that without the ability to have a voice in such relationships, women and workers are not free. (For Pateman's criticisms of republicanism see Pateman 2007.) They may be left alone by husbands like John Stuart Mill, whose behaviour would pass Hampton's test of fairness in relationships (to be outlined below) but they are not free whilst the institutions are such that genuine democratic participation cannot emerge. I will return to this in the chapter on Hobbes. (For the argument that Pateman cannot be viewed as a radical liberal, based upon her analysis of freedom, see Mansbridge 2008.)

Jean Hampton's Feminist Contractarianism

Before discussing Hampton's paper "Feminist Contractarianism", it is worth considering in more detail the important distinction drawn by Hampton (1991a) between the position of Hobbes and Kant that is central to her work. In her criticism of Hobbes as a moral theorist, she describes his image of individuals who co-operate only in order to further their self-interest as "mimicking" actual moral behaviour. For Hobbes, the only reason that we co-operate with others is because we need them. If we had the ability to be self-sufficient there would be no motivation for such co-operation. This is made plain in the work of Gauthier (1987) and others who develop Hobbes' analysis in terms of game theory – a logical analysis of when we should co-operate and when we risk losing to (or being exploited by) others, that assumes self-interest. Additionally, for Hobbes, whilst individuals in a state of nature are each able to kill each other and hence are equal, "self-worth" is defined in terms of your price or value to others, which can alter with others' evaluations. So, it is possible that your worth can drop if you are ill and viewed as less useful. For example, Hampton contrasts Hobbes with Kant for whom personhood denotes equal moral worth, which is derived from respect for persons as ends in themselves and cannot therefore be diminished. For Hampton, as for Kant, moral behaviour is to be persued out of duty and respect for persons and not out of self-interest.[7] Hampton's "Feminist Contractarianism" also points to the problem of individuals who "mimic" morality. She cites Carol Gilligan's analysis of children's reaction to moral dilemmas to point to different errors that are committed by boys and girls. This is exemplified by Jake and Amy

7 Darwall (2003) draws this distinction referring to the Hobbesian view as "contractarian" and Kantian as "contractualist" to denote the distinction. Given the importance of Hampton's influential article "Feminist Contractarianism", which draws mainly on Kant and under this rubric would be viewed as "contractualist", I have retained Hampton's usage of contractarian for both types of contract to avoid confusion.

in Gilligan's empirical research. When asked the question: "when responsibility to oneself and others conflict, how should one choose?"(Gilligan 1982, 36) eleven year old Jake confidently replies that,

> You go about one-fourth to the others and three-fourths to yourself.

Amy, another eleven year old, replies that:

> Well it depends upon the situation. If you have responsibility with some body else (sic) then you should keep it to a certain extent, but to the extent that it is really going to hurt you or stop you from doing something that you really, really want, then I think that maybe you should put yourself first. But if it is your responsibility to someone really close to you, you've just got to decide in that situation which is more important, yourself or that person, and like I said, it really depends upon what type of person you are and how you feel about the other person or persons involved (Gilligan 1982, 36).

Hampton points out the problems in the response of both Jake, who is too selfish, and Amy, who is the mirror image of Jake, being too selfless. Amy is dubious about putting herself first even when potentially hurt and, Hampton argues, risks being exploited because of the way in which she has been socialised. Hampton draws from Kant to argue that everyone has equal worth and so it is a mistake for Amy to treat *herself* as less worthy of respect than others. Interestingly, she argues that this is not the traditional approach of moral philosophy because Jake is viewed as the paradigm case and so morality is seen as a way of discouraging his selfishness rather than recognising a problem with selflessness, which is contingently linked with women's role. In addition, aside from any gender blindness, selflessness may not be perceived as a problem because it "mimics" good behaviour. In both "Feminist Contractarianism" and "The Wisdom of the Egoist" Hampton (2002; 1997) discusses how women (and men) can be socialised in terms of self-sacrifice and explores why this is so morally problematic, being based upon a lack of self-worth rather than respect for equal personhood.

Hampton describes in subtle detail particular situations in women's lives when they are put in a position in which self-sacrifice is demanded. For example, she considers a simple situation (possibly too easily dismissed as petty, yet recognisable) of a woman who is asked to ignore rudeness from her father-in-law for the sake of family peace. If she is to apply an ethic of care that focuses only upon holding together relationships such small scale self-sacrifice may be encouraged and viewed as "noble". However, Hampton argues that there is a price to be paid for such behaviour because it serves to undermine the woman's perception of her own (objectively equal) self-worth. More seriously, in criminal law, rape must be recognised by the state as an act that fails to accord a woman respect for her equal worth as a person. This equal worth cannot objectively be diminished but it can be subjectively undermined if the attack on her self-worth goes unrecognised. I will apply this point more broadly in law in the final chapter.

Hampton's position can be described only as "broadly Kantian" because, whilst she derives her arguments from the Kantian view of equal self-worth, there is one aspect of Hobbes that Hampton does employ: the argument that, "we are not under any obligation to make ourselves prey to others" (Pyle and Hampton 1999, 236). Whilst Hampton highlights a problem with "women's position" regarding morality, she describes a situation that can only pertain whilst women are socialised into subordination and, as Pateman underlines, this requires a political solution. Hampton also recognises that there are men who can take up this position. It is only contingently gendered. I will outline Hampton's contractarian move and then return to the issue of morality compared to politics.

Drawing from within the contractarian tradition, Hampton suggests a test that is to be applied to all social relationships, including husbands and wives or sexual partners, to serve as a guide as to whether the relationship is a just one:

> Given the fact that we are in this relationship, could both of us reasonably accept the distribution of costs and benefits (that is, the costs and benefits that are not themselves side effects of any affective or duty based tie between us) if we were the subject of an informed, unforced agreement in which we think of ourselves as motivated by self interest (Hampton 2002, 351).

There is an interesting mix of Hobbes with Kant here, because – whilst she draws upon the Kantian idea of equal worth, discussed above and believes in respect for persons out of duty – she is employing the idea of self-interested individuals (emphasised in Hobbes) to supplement the Kantian position (Richardson 2007a; Richardson 2007b). Hampton references Gauthier's use of Hobbes when he argues that,

> The contractarian need not claim that actual persons take no interest in their fellows; indeed we suppose that some degree of sociability is characteristic of human beings. But the contractarian sees sociability as enriching human life; for him, it becomes a source of exploitation if it induces persons to acquiesce in institutions and practices that but for their fellow feeling would be costly to them. Feminist thought has surely made this, perhaps the core form of human exploitation clear to us. Thus the contractarian insists that a society could not command the willing allegiance of a rational person if, without appealing to her feelings for others, it afforded her no expectation of net benefit (Gauthier 1987, 11).

It is important to consider to whom this argument is addressed. If Hampton's audience is to be those working in analytic or political philosophy then she could be viewed as making the same move as Mills in trying to bring issues of subordination and exploitation and their implications, including its psychological effects, into mainstream consideration. However, I think that Hampton, as a contractarian, is going beyond this to suggest a genuine test. In Kantian terms, this would be applied by individuals, for example, women who are making up their minds about whether to leave a relationship. I have argued (Richardson 2007a) that Hampton's feminist contractarianism is an attempt to protect those in the position of Amy from their own socialised self-sacrifice but that the way in which her thought experiment works could be better viewed as part of a collective discussion (such as consciousness-raising) rather than performed by an isolated individual.

Whilst I agree with Pateman's analysis of the history of the marriage contract and employment contracts, along with the point that it did not depend upon the actual behaviour of those involved (in that men like Mill may not have used their rights against their wives but they nevertheless existed and could therefore affect a wife's behaviour), some aspects of Hampton's description of the psychology of subordination and its implications are useful. This is taken further than Hampton's analysis of morality when it is transplanted into a political analysis that attends to both the ways in which subordination is justified by fictions that are part of the social imaginary (such as Pateman's analysis of the work of the fiction of property in the person in contract) and also pays attention to the habits that inculcate subordination, both of which contribute to the ways we learn to view ourselves. This is highlighted by Pateman when she points out that the workplace can become a training ground for subordination because workers are not expected to have a say in the organisation, which then makes it more difficult for them to gain the confidence and social skills necessary to take part in democracy more generally. Here, Pateman's attention to psychology is similar to Hampton's analysis of relations of subordination, whilst Pateman also supplies a broader historical background that informs this psychological analysis of both theorists.

To illustrate the way in which Hampton's work can be informed by Pateman's political analysis, imagine what happens to Hampton's test in a hypothetical society in which all sexual relationships fail because both men and women have been socialised into believing in a family form in which male domination is viewed as natural. From a Hobbesian position, developed by a game theoretic viewpoint, if women in such a dystopia were socialised to want such families then they would be in a weak bargaining position and would simply have to make the best bargain. From my reading of Hampton's "Kantian position", it would be (objectively) wrong to enter into a relationship in which the test failed because you would be allowing yourself to be treated as less than a person and owe yourself a duty to avoid this (in exactly the same way as a duty is owed to treat others with respect as persons). The only solution in such circumstances is a political solution – which is Pateman's point (and with which I doubt Hampton would have disagreed).

Hampton (2002, 357) makes clear that her central move is to use Kant to think about extending respect for equal personhood to everyone. The social contract is therefore only employed as a thought experiment in order to help imagine respect for free and equal personhood. Hampton is clear that, strictly, it is not the idea of entering into a contract (as an agreement) that is doing the work in her test but the image of free and equal personhood itself, a point is recognised by Pateman (2007, 22).

Hampton's understanding of the meaning of the social contract can be highlighted by considering Gauthier's criticism of it (Hampton and Gauthier 2007, xii). Gauthier points out that in "Feminist Contractarianism", Hampton states that,

> Every contract theory ... has used the idea of a contract as a heuristic tool that points us towards the correct form of moral reasoning and has not relied on the notion of contract in any literal way to do any justificatory work (Hampton and Gauthier 2007, xii).

Gauthier takes issue with this point as "selling contractarianism short". He claims that the contract does do work:

> Only by determining what rational persons would agree to in a suitable pre-moral situation can we give content to and a rationale for moral principles. Proposed or alleged moral principles can be put to the contractarian test – might they be agreed to by rational persons seeking principles to govern their interactions? I leave to the reader to decide if this is merely a heuristic tool (Hampton and Gauthier 2007, xii).

This is a curious criticism because it is initially unclear where he differs from Hampton on the function of the hypothetical contract. Gauthier is clearly not trying to claim that the contract does the usual work of legally binding the parties to what they have promised for consideration. As Dworkin points out, "A hypothetical contract is not simply a pale form of an actual contract; it is no contract at all" (Dworkin 1989, 17). Surely this would be the "literal way" it would do the justificatory work that Hampton is rejecting? For her, the contract is a heuristic tool because it forces someone to try to put themselves in another's position as a thought experiment in contrast to a contract that binds by agreement. This is illustrated by Hampton's comment on Hobbesian moral theory that,

> [T]he notion of contract does not do justificational work *by itself* in the Hobbesian moral theory – this term is used only metaphorically. What we "could agree to" has moral force for the Hobbesians not because make-believe promises in hypothetical worlds have any binding force but because this sort of agreement is a device that (merely) reveals the way in which the agreed-upon outcome is rational for all of us ... Thus the justificational force of this kind of contract theory is carried within but is derived from sources other than the contractor agreement in the theory (Hampton 2007, 11).

So, for Hobbesians, the contractual device is heuristic in helping us to decide what is rational for anyone to agree to, based upon what serves his or her best interests. Similarly, Kant does not appeal to an agreement but, to the process itself – of thinking from the position of others – that is "morally revealing" (Hampton 2007, 13). For Kantians, the contract device is heuristic because the move of being forced to put yourself in the position of others allows you to act in such a way that respects their equal personhood.

It may be that Gauthier's argument that the contract is more than a heuristic device (i.e. that it is doing more work) derives from his Hobbesianism in contrast to Hampton's Kantianism. For Gauthier, the contract is being used as a type of game to decide how a rational individual should act to maximise his or her interests on the basis of others' behaviour. To view the contract as a game (within game theory) does mean that it is doing more work than simply forcing us to respect others as persons (which is its role for Kantians). Gauthier does not expand further upon why he describes Hampton as "selling contractarianism short" and so this is speculation as to his position that relies upon the different roles they view for contract.

Hampton (2007, 25) briefly engages with Pateman, on this issue, by arguing that the contract is a device to bring out the Kantian idea of intrinsic non-instrumental value. So, she concludes, the contract image does not imply that those contracting parties or their services are commodified. I think that this is too quick a dismissal of Pateman's complex analysis. As Pateman points out, theories of original contracts are not merely devices for moral reasoning, they are,

> *political* theories devised to throw light onto societies of the time and to justify a particular form of political order (Pateman and Mills 2007, 208).

Mills argues that there is compatibility between Pateman's position and that of Hampton and Okin on the theoretical use of contract (Pateman and Mills 2007, 84–92). There is clear agreement regarding their feminist politics and to the extent that they rely upon empirical analysis about women's lives but Pateman's point, outlined above, is that the use of the image of contract employed by the contractarians to evoke the ideal of free and equal persons is tainted by its association with the image of the possessive individual, owner of property in the person. However, Pateman recognises that for Hampton the work is not being done by the image of contract,

> [Hampton] lets the cat out of the bag by admitting that in Rawlsian moral reasoning the contract metaphor does no real work. References to contract, she states, is not "in any sense foundational, or even necessary" (Hampton 2001: 357). Moral reasoning can be conducted without it – and I would add, so can political analysis, criticism and recommendations (Pateman and Mills 2007, 22).

Given that Hampton could rely solely upon her "Kantian view" of the equal worth of persons for her analysis then the positions do appear compatible. However, as a result of focusing at an individual level, Hampton points to the way in which being exploited (by having an unfair deal in the home, for example) leads to individuals perceiving themselves as subordinate. Whilst the psychological analysis linked with morality does express ways in which such subordination is perpetuated, this is only part of the story. In contrast, Pateman demonstrates that exploitation occurs as a result of relationships of subordination that have been created by marriage contracts and employment contracts. Hence, subordination opens the door to exploitation.

All the feminist philosophers whose work is examined provide much more than a critique. All of them have positive political or moral projects. For example, Pateman's dismissal of the use of contractarianism is based upon a positive vision of a participative society in which there is democracy in the workplace and home. In promoting this, she not only criticises the fiction of property in the person but also considers pragmatic ways in which subordination can be reduced, such as the guarantee of a basic income for all (Pateman 2004). Her arguments will be teased out, along with those of Hampton, Cornell and Okin, who employ Kantian contractarianism in support of feminism as a mechanism for thinking about equal moral worth and the implications of the law (Cornell, Hampton), political equality (Okin) and personal relationships (Hampton).

Feminist Philosophy within both Analytic and Continental Traditions

A major strength of feminist theory is that, unlike some other areas of political or legal theory, it cannot ignore practical issues of subordination, even whilst employing abstract analysis. As a result of this practical imperative, feminist philosophy draws from diverse sources, including both analytic and continental philosophical traditions. This can be illustrated in the readings of the social contractarians by Hampton (of the analytic tradition) and Cornell (whose work is situated with the continental tradition). Both theorists employ the Kantian move of asking what free and equal persons would agree to, if they were given a choice. Cornell, as a legal theorist, asks this question in order to propose a test for legitimacy with regard to legislation and judge-made case law within the common law, whereas Hampton employs the test as a heuristic means of ascertaining whether there is justice within a particular relationship, such as that between husband and wife, as well as relationships between strangers. Both employ a similar Kantian test and do so in a manner that is committed to feminist concerns about the freedom and equality of women.

The fact that these theoretical frameworks converge serves to undermine a clear divide between analytic and continental philosophy. This is stark in disciplines outside of philosophy, such as law, which could be described as being unrepentant "burglars in the house of philosophy" in that they often develop applications of prevailing philosophical concepts, whilst also altering them. Contemporary continental theory has been very influential in law, for example. This has often been expressed by an interest in epistemology – which is not my project. Instead of focusing upon the politics of truth, I am concerned with ontology and psychology: the ways in which we view what it is to be a self and how we envisage – in different ways – our relations with others. This is informed by diverse strands of feminist philosophy.

Chapter 2
Hobbes

Introduction

There are two major areas that I want to consider when reading Hobbes through the lens of contemporary feminist theory: firstly, Hobbes' concept of the individual; and, secondly, his ideas on equality, examining both political equality and the concept of equal moral worth. These two areas are closely linked. Hobbes' rigorous and consistent individualism (his view of isolated competing individuals as constituting the basis for analysis) leads him to what in 1651 was the radical view that women and men are naturally equal. Despite the fact that there are places in his writings in which he appears to have more traditional attitudes to women,[1] in *Leviathan* he argues that there is no natural subordination in a world without laws because all individuals are able to kill each other. Whilst sometimes the word "man" is used ambiguously, Hobbes' logic and specific comments about women imply that women are included in this argument. In other words, when Hobbes considers equality he makes the point that there cannot be natural domination. Generally, he argues that even though some individuals may be stronger or more intelligent, the difference in their abilities is not so great that the weak cannot kill the strong "either through secret machination or by conspiracy with others who are in the same danger with himself" (Hobbes 1994, 74. XIII [1]). It is consistent with his materialism that he does not address the question by arguing, with Locke, that an external power, God, made us equal but considers whether domination could be practically imposed. This is an approach that was to be developed by Spinoza, to be discussed in the next chapter.

When talking specifically about the sexes and who should have dominion over a child, given that no-one can have two masters, he says,

> And whereas some have attributed the dominion to the man only, as being of the more excellent sex, they misreckon in it. For there is not always that difference of strength or prudence between the man and the woman as that the right can be determined without war (Hobbes 1994, 128. XX [4]).

Hobbes also recognises that in a state of nature only a woman would (potentially) know the identity of the father and, if she brought up the child alone, would have "dominion" over the child (Hobbes 1994, 129. XX [4]).

1 See for example Hobbes 1994, 126 [XIX] 22; 132 [XX] 15; 153 [XXII] 26; 167 [XXV] 9; 224 [XXX] 11.

I will start by exploring Hobbes' image of separate "atomistic" individuals, whose characteristics within the state of nature famously render such life "solitary, poor, nasty, brutish and short" (Hobbes 1994, 76. XIII [9]) but whose rationality allows them to escape it by agreeing amongst each other to give up their freedom to a sovereign, who is then authorised to enforce the law. As Pateman points out, this enforcement of the law includes all contracts, including marriage contracts through which women's subordination is regulated within modernity. In particular, I want to highlight the way in which the relationship between oneself and other individuals is envisaged by Hobbes. The term "atomistic individuals", which stresses individuals' separation from each other (as isolated atoms) and from society generally is a phrase which, as Charles Taylor points out, tends only to be employed by its opponents (Taylor 1992). Obviously, Hobbes is not arguing that anyone could survive alone as a child. The position of mothers highlights particular tensions around such individualism – given that women's traditional role has emphasised not only a sentimental ideal of family connectedness but also the plain fact that at different stages in life isolated individuals could not survive alone.

After discussing the Hobbesian individual, the issue of equality will be considered in two different ways. First, I will look at Hobbes' work in the context of political equality, drawing on Pateman's ground-breaking arguments regarding the legal fiction involved in the social contract. Whereas contract comes to be viewed as representing an exchange between equals, I will show how Hobbes is useful, given the clarity with which he spells out his position that contact can form the basis of subordination. He is clear that agreements made under duress are still valid and can include an agreement to obey. The same argument is therefore applied to justify slavery, in that a slave who has been allowed to live should obey his/her master. In these circumstances, the slave is then classified as a servant in Hobbes' nomenclature. From this perspective, a child who is cared for and who would otherwise die, is in the position of the slave, save that the child does not have the capacity to give consent and therefore must be deemed to have agreed to obey his or her carer.

Hobbes' answer to the question of why anyone would agree to obey others, given his assumption of natural equality, is that it is a way of avoiding an early death; to promote peace. In his answer to the fool, who questions the rationality of keeping a contract, Hobbes' (1994, 90. XV [4]) argument is based upon self-interest, i.e. that it is prudent not to gain a reputation as a contract breaker, for example. Hampton (1988, 56) therefore argues that, by connecting virtuous action with peace, Hobbes produces an instrumental justification for the "moral" behaviour of contract keeping. I will return to his point in the next chapter on Spinoza.

After examining Hobbes' political equality, I will turn to the idea of equal moral worth. As introduced in the last chapter, Hobbes argues that someone's worth is simply defined as his or her price, i.e. how others value his or her services. However, Hobbes' individualism means that he argues that there is no obligation to make oneself the "prey to others" (Hobbes 1994, 99 XV [36]). It is this aspect of Hobbes that Hampton employs in support of her criticism of the ethos of women's "self-sacrifice", for example the housewife who views it as her duty to act as servant for her family to the extent of neglecting her own interests or even making herself ill.

It is a curious fact about Hobbesian individualism that Hampton is able to rely upon Hobbes as part of her attack upon the effects of being beholden to the arbitrary will of others – which is the position of women who are economically dependent upon men and who are taught that their role depends upon pleasing them. Given that Hobbes makes the historical shift from a republican view of freedom, as not being subject to the arbitrary will of another, to a negative view of freedom, defined simply as the absence of external impediments (Skinner 2008), Hobbes would seem an inauspicious author to employ to highlight the psychological effects of subordination within the home.

One answer to this problem is to consider ways in which the republican view of freedom should not be defined simply in terms of non-domination. It was also defined in terms of natural status, that those persons not subject to the domination of others were free men in comparison to wives and slaves. I will examine this point and discuss Hampton through a criticism of this element of her work by Sorell (2007, 151). This leads to the final section on the problem of judgement and the conflict in Hobbes' work between obedience and the ideals of rational thought. The fact that we do not reason well in isolation, i.e. that thought requires others, is a theme that is taken up in later chapters, particular in those focused upon Spinoza and Kant.

Hobbes' Individualism

Hobbes starts his political argument in support of (almost) absolute sovereign power by detailing his understanding of human nature, in keeping with a reductionist approach in which individuals are viewed as the parts which make up the political structure. Hobbes' reductionism could have started by viewing the patriarchal family as a natural building block but instead recognises all relationships of domination as socially constructed rather than natural. Famously, Hobbes argues that, as a result of individuals' natural psychological characteristics, the state of nature is a state of war and social co-operation is only possible as a result of an agreement between such individuals to give up their natural freedom. The (hypothetical)[2] social contract between these individuals is to obey a sovereign,

2 "It may peradventure be thought there was never such a time nor condition of war as this, and I believe it was never generally so, over all the world" (Hobbes 1994, 77. XIII, [11]). He then references Cain and Abel in the 1668 Latin version of *Leviathan* along with some areas of America but his argument does not rely upon the veracity of these alleged possible examples.

who benefits from, but is not a party to, the contract. She[3] or he will then enforce the law, ensuring that contracts will be kept and resolving disputes. The only case in which it is permissible to disobey the sovereign is if a subject's life is threatened and it is for the subject to decide if this is the case. This is consistent with the fact that Hobbes' argument is based upon the central assumption that individuals want to survive. If they judge that the sovereign intends to kill them then they would be better off taking their chances in the state of nature:

> A covenant not to defend myself from force is always void (Hobbes 1994, 87. XIV [29]).

Otherwise, given the horrors of the English civil war which Hobbes witnessed, subordination to an almost absolute sovereign who would keep the peace was, he argued, preferable.

To consider Hobbesian psychology in detail it is useful to ask why he felt that humans could not live together peacefully without such a sovereign. Hobbes describes the causes of war in the state of nature as arising as a result of human beings' natural equality. No one is so easily dominated that he or she will not fight over scarce resources. This means that they will also be reluctant to work, knowing that the fruits of their labour may be stolen. So, equality results in distrust. Some individuals may also enjoy the idea of conquest, which may cause those who would not otherwise want to fight (and who would be happy with the resources they have without expanding them) to feel the need to do so as a matter of self-defence (Hobbes 1994, 75. XIII [3]). So, Hobbes summarises that the causes of war are: competition, diffidence (i.e. distrust) and concern with reputation (Hobbes 1994, 76. XIII [6]).

The importance of reputation is also central to Hobbes' analysis. Prior to his discussion of human behaviour in the state of nature, he outlines different virtues and vices, along with the meaning of power and value. It is clear that, whilst it may be prudent to have a reputation as strong so as to deter enemies from attacking, some men are viewed as fighting because of their need for "glory". Hobbes states that men are naturally concerned with evaluating themselves with respect to others:

> For every man looketh that his companions should value him at the same rate he sets upon himself, and upon all signs of contempt, or undervaluing, naturally endeavours, as far as he dares (which amongst them that have no common power to keep them in quiet, is far enough to make them destroy each other), to extort a greater value from his contemners, by damage, and from others, by example (Hobbes 1994, 76. XIII [5]).

3 Hobbes was born during the reign of Elizabeth I. He accepted that there could be female sovereigns and refers to male and female monarchs (Hobbes 1994, 130. XX [7]).

Given the ambiguous use of the term "men" in this passage, it is difficult to know whether this is meant to include women. His view that women are equal within the state of nature would suggest that this is the case. However, Hobbes does go on to say that,

> The first [those who fight for gain] use violence to make themselves masters of other men's person, wives, children and cattle (Hobbes 1994, 76. XIII [7]).

Chapman (1975) cites this example, along with others, in which Hobbes appears to refer to a traditional family structure in which women are viewed as naturally subordinate but he nevertheless concludes, like Pateman, that Hobbes subverts the traditional view of the patriarchal family. Chapman characterises Hobbes' image of the family as "Leviathan writ small", i.e. that Hobbes views the family as a projection of his view of the state. This is the opposite of Filmer's (1991) view of the state, which was based (and supposedly grew out of) the patriarchal family in which domination is based upon the father's generation of children. Chapman argues that, for Hobbes, any group, whether a family or larger body of individuals, including states, has the same problem of security and is defined in such terms. For Hobbes, it is therefore the preservation of life – and not reproduction *per se* – that results in the child being deemed to have contracted not to attack whoever has looked after him/her, whether the mother, father or anyone else. I will consider Hobbes' conception of the family in more detail below.

Whilst Hobbes is clear that men and women are equal, the examples he uses to illustrate "vainglory", which involves overconfidence in one's ability, and "dejection", which arises as a result of an absence of power, are drawn from his experience, in which young men are subject to vainglory and women and children to dejection. Taylor argues that Hobbes' criticism of vain-glory is part of Hobbes' reaction against the ancient honour ethic (Taylor 1992, 214), which, I would add, also supports such a gender stereotype:

> The vain-glory which consisteth in the feigning or supposing of abilities in our selves (which we know are not) is most incident to young men, and nourished by the histories, or fictions of gallant persons; and is corrected oftentimes by age and employment (Hobbes 1994, 32. VI [41]).

In contrast, "*grief* from want of power, is called DEJECTION of mind" (Hobbes 1994, 32. VI [44]) and

> *[S]udden dejection*, is the passion that causeth WEEPING; and is caused by such accidents as suddenly take away some vehement hope, or some prop of their power; AND they are most subject to it that rely principally on helps external, such as women and children (Hobbes 1994, 32. VI [43]).

For Hobbes, when one's level of self-esteem is either too low or too high it could act as a "perturbation" that affects one's reason (see James 1997, 126–136). It is arguable that individuals who undervalue themselves are more likely to be modest and tractable and hence the prey of others, which Hobbes warns against when explaining the problem of performing a contract first in the state of nature:

> For he that should be modest and tractable, and perform all he promises, in such time and place where no man else should do so, should but make himself a prey to others, and procure his own certain ruin, contrary to the ground of all laws of nature, which tend to nature's preservation (Hobbes 1994, 99. XV [36]).

Whereas Hobbes starts with a presumption that adults are unproblematically (naturally) to be viewed as ontologically separate individuals, who are the source of any explanation of their behaviour, this is currently viewed as problematic within the human sciences and within much feminist thought. For example, Foucault (1977; 1990; 1998; 2002), whose work is not feminist but has been very influential within contemporary feminist theory, can be viewed, in this context, as having the opposite approach to Hobbes. Hobbes starts with the individual and then asks how we can come together to form a body. In contrast, Foucault starts by asking how we come to view ourselves as individuals. He illustrates some of the ways in which we become "individuated", not only through our daily habits but also by comparing ourselves with others through both educational and medical examinations and the employment of statistical analysis such that everyone can be viewed as a case file. Whilst Hobbes does not view "the individual" as a problematic starting point for an explanation for human action, he nevertheless relies heavily upon a psychological analysis that gives a central role to comparison with others. This can be illustrated by the way he defines natural power in comparative terms as "the eminence of the faculties of the body or mind" (Hobbes 1994, 50. X [1]).

Nevertheless, anti-humanist moves, that reject the idea that a description of the individual could be a valid starting point for political analysis, could be viewed as taking Macpherson's critique of Hobbes an additional step further. Macpherson (1962) argues that the way in which Hobbes defines power in comparative terms, along with his description of individuals' behaviour in the state of nature is not natural but reflected the selfish, competitive, acquisitive behaviour produced in Hobbes' own market society. Anti-humanism raises questions as to whether the ontological image of the individual (for example, conceived of as "atomistic" or bounded and separate from others, to be discussed in the final chapter) and not simply the individual's psychological characteristics are socially constructed.

Components of the Social Contract: Hobbes' View of the Will and Duress in Contract

The fact that Hobbes lays such an emphasis upon contract stems from the idea that free and equal individuals should only be bound by agreement. This is a central idea employed by the contractarian tradition and yet Hobbes changes the way in which "the will" is understood to argue, in favour of the sovereign and against the democrats of his time, that valid contracts can be made under duress (Skinner 2008). This derives from his image of the individual in materialist terms. His arguments on the will are therefore important to illustrate how contract creates relationships of obedience. This is in contrast to the way in which contract is often portrayed as symbolic of equality between the parties. This supports the way in which Pateman draws together evidence of actual contracts to show how this view of contract as symbolic of equality is historically incorrect.

At the time Hobbes was writing, in the seventeenth century, the legal contract was based upon the doctrine of contract at will (Atiyah 1985). In other words, to qualify as legally valid, a contract had to represent the will of the contracting parties. However, Hobbes redefines the meaning of the will in a way that then alters how contracts can be understood. This then justifies his support for the validity of contracts that are made under duress (and that perpetuate subordination). I want to trace the steps in Hobbes' argument more slowly. Prior to Hobbes, the popular view of the will was as a God given faculty, linked with the Christian idea of free will (Skinner 2008). In contrast, Hobbes describes the will, in materialist terms, as the final appetite or aversion before action:

> In deliberation, the last appetite or aversion immediately adhering to the action, or the omission thereof, is that we call the WILL, the act (not the faculty) of *Willing* (Hobbes 1994, 33. VI [53]).

Therefore actions taken under duress, such as the example Hobbes gives of throwing out cargo from a sinking boat, are "willed actions":

> Fear and liberty are consistent, as when a man throweth his goods into the sea for *fear* the ship should sink, he doth it nevertheless very willingly, and may refuse to do it if he will; it is therefore the action of one that was *free;* so a man sometimes pays his debt only for *fear* of imprisonment, which (because nobody hindered him from detaining) was the action of a man at *liberty.* And generally all actions which men do in commonwealths for *fear* of the law are actions which the doers had *liberty* to omit (Hobbes 1994, 136–137. XXI [3]).

Hobbes' framework therefore has no place for the common law doctrine of duress, let alone the equitable doctrine of undue influence that mitigates the common law of contract. The common law of duress, under which a contract is invalid if someone entered into it because he/she was threatened with violence such that "a man of ordinary firmness would succumb to it", has been part of the common law since the time of Bracton in the thirteenth century. The court of equity, which mitigated the harshness of the common law, developed the law of undue influence when duress was viewed as too narrow. The doctrine of undue influence refers to the overwhelming of the will, the aim being "to protect the weakened who were not in fact incapacitated nor subject to duress" (Teeven 1990, 134). This image of the will that is no longer properly expressed in the contract because it has been overpowered by a stronger force is precisely the move that Hobbes avoids by his redefinition of the will.

This issue is still debated. For example, when discussing matrimonial property law, feminists have considered whether the law should view wives as subject to the undue influence of their husbands or whether it is no longer appropriate (Auchmuty 2005). The image still evoked is whether the "will" has been overwhelmed but the legal position does not need to rely upon an ontological view of the will, merely that contract law should be tempered in certain circumstances. Hobbes' redefinition of the will (as simply the last appetite/aversion before an action is taken) does not appear to have affected the law in relation to undue influence nor, of course, duress – even though it may now be a more accepted materialist view of the will.

Skinner (2008) contextualises the political implications of Hobbes' argument that individuals are still liable for their consent to contracts entered into by duress by looking at the democratic arguments of Hobbes' contemporaries, whom he is attacking by this reformulation of the will. Hobbes supports his argument for almost absolute obedience to the sovereign, based upon the claim that individuals who (in his hypothetical tale) enter into the social contract should be bound by it, despite the fact that it is entered into out of fear of an untimely death in the state of nature. The idea of being bound by contracts that are made under duress also has broader implications, outside of this aim, in that it produces a general theory of obedience through contract. As I will examine in the next section, Pateman discusses the ambivalent treatment of women that arises from Hobbes' position. As introduced in chapter 1, in civil society women were viewed as capable of consenting to the traditional marriage contract, which then took away their rights to enter into other contracts as they were no longer to be treated as persons in law.

Pateman: Hobbes and Political Equality

As outlined in the last chapter, Pateman uses what she later describes as a deconstructive technique to rewrite Hobbes' story of the social contract (Pateman and Mills 2007, 219). She argues that, in contrast with Hobbes' usual rigour, he is inconsistent with regard to women. Pateman highlights this by asking the question: why would free and equal women in the state of nature agree to be part of a social contract that resulted in their subordination? It is inconsistent for Hobbes to envisage that women in this fiction would agree to enter into a social contract that produces a sovereign who would enforce marriage contracts, under which they would become subordinate to men. Pateman argues that Hobbes' story makes more sense if it is assumed that women had all been enslaved within the state of nature, possibly because they had been weakened by pregnancy or child care and hence captured, and do not enter into the social contract. The social contract then allows men to access women's sexual and domestic services, organised through the marriage contract.

There have been a number of objections to this retelling of a story. In an annotation to *Leviathan*, Curley (Hobbes 1994, 129 fn. 6) points out that Hobbes' recognition of women as potential sovereigns is difficult to reconcile with this aspect of Pateman's argument. However, from the text and from Pateman's later work, it seems clear that rewriting the story of the state of nature is irrelevant to, what I view as, Pateman's central aim: to trace the historical role of contract in organising and inculcating subordination, which in turn allows exploitation within the workplace and traditionally within the home, that undermines the possibility of a genuinely participative democracy. Whilst there can be some discussion about whether women were envisaged as already enslaved within the state of nature, this reworking of a fiction is merely meant to illustrate Pateman's analysis of the role of contract.

For Pateman, Hobbes represents a turning point away from classical patriarchy, in which rule was viewed as stemming from the rights of fathers, to modern patriarchy, based upon contract. The use of contract appears to take place between equals but in fact, as Hobbes makes very plain, involves the obedience of one party. Linked with this point, Pateman discusses a curiosity evident in Hobbes' description of the family, which he defines in terms of father, sons, servants but omits to mention wives. This is illustrated by the following quotation:

> ... whether that family consists of a man and his children, or of a man and his servants, or of a man and his children and his servants together (Hobbes 1994, 132. XX [15]).

Similarly in *De Cive* (Hobbes 1991, 121, IX.), he refers to "a father with his sons and servants". Only in *Elements of Law* does he refer to the mother (Hobbes 1999, 158. IV).

Against Hinton's (1968) claim that Hobbes was a patriarchalist, supported by passages in which Hobbes refers to the traditional view of the family as a small kingdom (Hobbes 1994, 107. XVII [2]), Pateman (1988, 46) draws a similar conclusion to Chapman: that the family is "Leviathan writ small", with its parties bound together through contract, which includes contracts formed under duress. In a state of nature if one male conquers another, who then agrees to obey him to avoid death, they form a "family" or master and servant, governed by contract. If a man defeated a woman in such circumstances then again it would be a "family" in Hobbes' odd use of the term and again she would be a servant. (This could also occur the other way round, in the state of nature, though Hobbes' main reference is to fathers.) There are no wives in the state of nature as there is no sovereign to enforce the marriage contract. In civil society there is no need for women to be "captured" as civil law upholds matrimonial law.

Chapman (1975, 83) accounts for Hobbes' odd definition of the family, which excludes wives, by claiming that Hobbes draws his description of the family in the state of nature from the laws relating to Roman marriage, in which wives were to be treated as belonging to either their father or – after a ceremony of *manus* in addition to the marriage ceremony – belonging to their husbands. So, for Chapman, wives are not mentioned because they are to be treated as akin to children. There is little to distinguish between his position and Pateman's view that the Hobbesian "family" in the state of nature occurs through capture, given that the power of the paterfamilias was absolute, which – unlike the common law – allowed the father to kill or sell his children.

The distinction Hobbes draws between servant and slave is that a servant has contracted to obey and therefore should not try to escape, whereas a slave is held by force and has every right to escape (Hobbes 1994, 131. XX [11]). As I will discuss in the next chapter, Spinoza agrees with Hobbes' materialist view of the will (in contrast with the Will as a God given faculty) but, makes a more materialist claim, that there are no rights that exist as separate from what a body can do. This leads Spinoza to argue simply that there is no reason that anyone should comply with a contract made under duress when he or she is free to escape.

As mentioned above, Pateman's analysis of contract and modern subordination is the important part of her work, so that speculation and retelling of Hobbes' story is merely illustrative. In this context, Hobbes' clarity that coerced "contracts to obey" are valid is useful. Whereas the contractarian tradition is associated with the idea that obligations are valid because the parties entered into them of their own free will, Hobbes is clear that contracts can be made under duress. Similarly, the position of the child (as akin to the slave turned servant by virtue of contract, because both are kept alive) highlights the politics of the way in which dominion over children is also a political, not a natural, issue. Hobbes (1994, 224. XXX [11]) argues that, in civil society, fathers should inculcate obedience (and hence obedience to the sovereign) in children by reminding them that in a state of nature the father would have the right of life over the child. (Whilst this section refers to fathers, elsewhere in *Leviathan* Hobbes (1994, 128. XX [4]) is clear that whoever raises a child in the state of nature has dominion over that child. This can include mothers, especially as there is no marriage contract within a state of nature so it is only the mother who may know the identity of the father.) Again, this subordinate relationship is not viewed as natural but as something which is to be taught, the main reason being the need for subjects to obey the sovereign and not any natural right of fathers.

Pateman illustrates the distinction between workers (who were viewed as being juridically equal, worked for a set wage for fixed hours and who have the potential to alter their status through competition) and traditional wives who initially were not jurisdictionally equal and do not have fixed hours and for whom the idea of success through competition does not apply. In terms of Macpherson's model of status-based and competitive market societies, women's traditional position sounds more like a status-based feudal serf. (This is illustrated by the judicial reference to a husband's right to *consortium* of his wife as akin to a feudal right in twentieth century common law,[4] to be discussed in the final chapter.) In contrast, Pateman is original and important in highlighting the role of contract in the historical organisation of subordination of wives as well as workers in modernity.

Hampton: Hobbesian Morality

Hampton describes Hobbes as having a common sense idea of morality because he does not appeal to God. We simply need to appear moral because it is in our self-interest to enlist the co-operation of others. Hobbes' analysis also benefits from the fact that there is no need for him to attempt to justify (as Hampton needs to do) an objective view of equal worth. Hobbes adds a further step: that we learn to decide if we are being deceived and therefore the most certain way of gaining co-operation, that is vital for survival, is actually to tell the truth and keep promises, even when it would be possible to gain in the short term by deception. This is close to contemporary evolutionary explanations of moral behaviour that also avoid the need for objective transcendent morality (see, for example Axelrod 1990; Dennett 2004).

It is useful to examine one particular criticism of Hampton in detail because it raises interesting theoretical problems beyond a disagreement about the meaning of Hobbes' text. I will then go on to discuss the apparent tension between Hampton's (albeit limited) employment of Hobbes to discuss issues of subordination within the household and Skinner's argument that Hobbes marks a turning point away from liberty viewed as non-domination to a negative view of liberty as merely the absence of an external impediment, a move which would appear antithetical to Hampton's criticisms of everyday domination.

Sorell's (2007) criticism is straightforward: that Hampton interprets Hobbes incorrectly when she employs the term "prey". She argues that the Hobbesian idea that we should not be under any obligation to make ourselves the prey of others is useful for moral theory as a credo. This is explained in an interview (Pyle and Hampton 1999, 235) in which Hampton is asked,

> You suggest that if you do not factor self-interest into an analysis of morality, in some way, then morality will become inherently exploitative, an idea that I find appealing.

In reply, Hampton cites "a Hobbesian remark" stating:

4 For example, *Best v Samuel Fox and Co. Ltd.* [1952] AC 731–732.

> He says in chapter fifteen of *Leviathan* that we are not under any obligation to make ourselves prey to others. In the Hobbesian context that makes sense; it would violate rationality for you to do that. But if you extract that remark and think about it from a slightly different moral perspective it seems that it should be every person's credo, that you do not have to make yourself prey. Surely, that is politically very important (Pyle and Hampton 1999, 235).

She then discusses literary illustrations of women who are raised to believe that they have little self-worth and judge themselves only in terms of their usefulness for others, making them ripe for exploitation. Whilst Hampton usually appears to prioritise exploitation to show how unfair treatment can lead to a view of oneself as subordinate (as discussed in the last chapter), here, in common with Pateman, Hampton recognises subordination as primary, drawing upon a wider social analysis than Rawlsian methodology. She continues to highlight the psychology of the way in which these feedback upon each other. This is illustrated by the stereotyped discussions of the morality of Jake and Amy, discussed in the last chapter (Hampton 2002).

Sorell argues that when Hobbes says that we are under no obligation to make ourselves the prey of others he means this to refer to physical injury or death and not to "hurt feelings". This, he argues, is consistent with Hobbes' view that the sovereign owes subjects protection against death and physical injury (Hobbes 1994, 191. XXVII). Sorell's point could also be supported by the fact that it is also in keeping with the common law, which continues to refuse compensation for feelings save for exceptional circumstances. In tort, mere injury to feelings is distinguished from "psychiatric damage" by medical evidence and is not subject to compensation. However, I do not think that the reference to "hurt feelings" (Sorell 2007, 151) captures the idea that Hampton wants to convey, of individuals who are diminished by their relationships in a way that restricts their self-development or their ability to follow any sort of life plan because they are beholden to others. (This is not to assume a telos of development, merely that such a situation has undesirable effects, such as the creation of servility.) This has more in common with – and draws from – Rawls' (1999, 440–445) idea that shame and lack of self-respect is crippling and prevents someone from having the confidence to undertake projects.

When discussing her use of the Hobbesian "credo" that we are under no obligation to make ourselves the prey of others, Hampton talks about "extracting the remark" from Hobbes in order to look at it from a slightly different moral perspective and so the issue is not one of textual interpretation. The more important question that can be drawn from Sorell's criticism is whether the image of the individual, who is not under an obligation to be prey to others, is problematic. Basically, it is Hampton's argument that women (and men) who consistently put others' interests before their own do so as a result of lack of self-respect and not as a result of their respect for others. Returning to consider Hobbesian individualism (which is lost with the rise of the "sentimental family") opens up a line of argument that does not readily dismiss "the wisdom of the egoist", which has historically appeared particularly inappropriate for women. In making this move, Hampton draws upon one aspect of Gauthier's argument about Hobbes in which he employs the image of the rational individual in game theory:

> Thus the contractarian insists that a society could not command the willing allegiance of a rational person if, without appealing to her feelings for others, it afforded her no expectation of net benefit (Gauthier 1987, 151).

As outlined in chapter 1, Hampton applies this argument by employing the following test for unfairness within personal relationships:

> Given the fact that we are in this relationship, could both of us reasonably accept the distribution of costs and benefits (that is, the costs and benefits that are not themselves side effects of any affective or duty based tie between us) if we were the subject of an informed, unforced agreement in which we think of ourselves as motivated by self-interest (Hampton 2002, 351).

Sorell argues that Hobbes' morality precludes allowing others to kill you but not to subordinate you (Sorell 2007, 151). As discussed above, this is right and would be accepted by Hampton, who is not drawing from Hobbes in detail – given that she states that our not being under an obligation to make ourselves "prey to others" is the only true phrase he uses (Pyle and Hampton 1999, 235). She is employing, what she takes to be, Hobbes' description of the self-interested rational individual. This move emphasises the ideal of consent, as Hampton asks whether women who were free and equal would enter into particular arrangements if it were not for their emotional involvement. It is also clear from the way in which Hampton (1988, 208–284) employs game theory to analyse Hobbes that she ascribes to him an image of the individual as rationally self-interested that she finds useful. This is a move that she shares with Gauthier and which Sorell describes as "not wild" (Sorell 2007, 147). It may be that this criticism highlights a difference of approach. Sorell's point is useful if your emphasis is upon an analysis of Hobbes' meaning, within its historical context. It fails to recognise the way Hampton is trying to use an idea – to make it do some work – in an analytical context.

I now turn to the curious fact that Hampton draws upon (one aspect of) Hobbes in order to argue against the subordination of women. This appears odd because Hobbes successfully replaces the republican view of freedom (as not being subject to the arbitrary will of another) with his definition of freedom (as the absence of external impediments). The republican definition of freedom appears more promising as a way of highlighting women's subordination in the home, yet Hampton finds resources in Hobbes rather than republicanism to focus specifically upon this issue. As discussed, Skinner (2008) traces the development of Hobbes' redefinition of freedom, away from the then accepted idea of not being subject to domination, to the final version simply as the absence of external impediments, in *Leviathan*. Skinner is compelling in illustrating that republican freedom is concerned with the negative impact of living in a way which is dependent upon the arbitrary will of another. The traditional republican concern was with the servility that arises when courtiers dealt on a daily basis with a powerful monarch. It clearly fits with feminist concerns about the traditional position of women in the family, when they are economically dependent upon men; as well as to the position of employees, when they are desperate for work; see for example Phillips (2000) and Pettit (1996). However, whilst republican freedom is concerned with non-domination, it is also defined in terms of status: the free man holds this status in comparison to slaves and women. Benjamin Constant (1988) describes this freedom as being dependent upon status, which was viewed as natural, and the shift to a view of freedom in Hobbesian terms, as the absence of external impediments, that becomes associated with liberal rights rather than the right to participate in decision-making. It was the political shift from status to individualism in contract, albeit dependent, in part, upon the image of economic man, that opened up space for women to argue against the idea of their natural subordination.

Hobbes on Judgement

An area of tension appears in Hobbes' work where there is a clash between his ideals of rational thought of the self-interested individual and his concern not to undermine sovereign power. He deals directly with the question of when an individual should continue to judge for his/her self or defer judgement to another. Ultimately, it is for the individual to judge if his/her life is at stake and to disobey the sovereign at that point. When the family is viewed as "Leviathan writ small" in Hobbes' analysis, this question can be seen as akin to those feminist concerns about the cost to a woman (or anyone in a similar position) who defers judgement to another. This is still an important issue, which is raised by feminists. This is based upon the contingent form of women's oppression, which has involved women having been encouraged to defer to others' beliefs, both moral and epistemological.

Bartky (1990), for example, graphically describes the problem of women who support their partners in a manner that involves suspending their own judgement about both morality and also the truth of an issue on which judgement is required. Bartky discusses its most extreme example, expressed in Jill Tweedie's damning comments about Teresa Stangl, the anti-Nazi and catholic wife of Fritz Stangl, Kommandant of Treblinka:

> Behind every great man is a great woman, we say, but behind every monster there is a woman too, behind each of the countless men who stood astride their narrow worlds and crushed other human beings, causing them hideous suffering and pain. There she is in the shadows wiping blood from their hands (Tweedie 1979, 49; cited by Bartky 1990, 113).

Bartky comments,

> Few of us would take female tenderness to these lengths, but many of us, I suspect, have been morally silenced or morally compromised in small ways because we thought it more important to provide emotional support than to keep faith with our own principles (Bartky 1990, 113).

Just as Pateman argues that an ability to participate in democracy is undermined by daily subordination when workers and wives fail to learn the confidence, necessary skills or the expectation to have their voices heard in their everyday lives, so it is clear that the ability to make ethical judgements can be similarly undermined. This can arise from a similar lack of confidence as well as an abdication of ethical beliefs. It can also be undermined by an inability to have faith in one's judgement of the causes of events. This can arise in societies in which one is part of a class whose views are treated with less credibility than other groups, as illustrated by the way in which women have been treated as less reliable witnesses in court (Fricker 2007; Kennedy 1992). This is obviously worse for isolated individuals who do not have the opportunity to think about their position in concert with others. This is a point that both Spinoza and Kant recognise with regard to cognition generally and provides a concern for free speech. In this context, Hobbes' position is problematic because of the conflict between his enlightenment ideals of thinking rationally compared with his view of obedience, opposing him to free speech.

There is a tension in Hobbes' work regarding what Ryan (1988, 84) calls "epistemological individualism", the ability to believe something for good reason irrespective of external demands, such as peer pressure for example.[5] Hobbes wishes to encourage such a rational response but becomes inconsistent on this issue when it conflicts with sovereign power. Hobbes (1994, 23. V [1]) argues for the sort of moral derogation that worries feminists like Bartky. He claims that the sovereign should be the judge of moral issues, including religion, so as to avoid conflict. Hobbes only allows subjects to retain the right to judge whether their lives are threatened and to protect themselves accordingly. This is based upon the central Hobbesian concern that the social contract will deteriorate unless the sovereign has (almost) absolute power.

This tension in Hobbes' work can lead him to be inconsistent in his materialism (Montag 1999, 52). For example, when answering the question of what a subject should do if the sovereign demands that s/he should worship a God other than the Christian God, Hobbes argues that it is possible to separate one's action, in entering a non Christian church, from one's own beliefs. This sets up a separation between the realm of ideas and material practices. The claim that God will recognise such beliefs sits uncomfortably with Hobbes' materialist claim that there

5 This should not be confused with Steven Lukes' (2006, 92–93) alternative definition of "epistemological individualism": that the source of knowledge lies within the individual.

is only matter and so if God exists then God is matter. This move plays down the role of the body and the idea from Pascal summarised by the quotation, "Kneel down, move your lips in prayer, and you will believe" (Althusser 2008, 42). The role of such behaviour upon belief has influenced recent continental readers of Spinoza from Althusser onwards, who wish to emphasise the importance of bodily habits and movements in shaping "who we are". As I will discuss in the next chapter, Spinoza's rereading of Hobbes is more consistently materialist. Montag's (1999) reading of Spinoza follows Deleuze (1988) in emphasising the importance of "what a body can do" (Spinoza 2000a, 2, P2, S, 167). Spinoza, against the grain of the social contract tradition, does not ask about what can validate rights but redefines rights simply in terms of what a body is able to do.

Chapter 3
Spinoza

Introduction

There are good reasons for taking the unusual step of including Spinoza in a book on the social contractarians. He employs a Hobbesian vocabulary – including the social contract – and radically changes the meaning of the central terms and concepts. In doing so, Spinoza produces a different image of what it is to be an individual or part of any social body. Spinoza can be used to think about how "developing into an individual" is achieved in a way that takes seriously the fact that it is impossible to be isolated from our environment and that, even as adults, we would not easily survive apart from others. In addition, he provides a conception of the imagination that feminists have found useful for thinking about social responsibility (Gatens and Lloyd 1999). This can also be mobilised to consider the effect of images such as the social contract and the fiction of property in the person. Whilst there has been much useful discussion about the imagination, I argue that Spinoza's emphasis is upon reason and that he also provides a different (and useful) conception of reason from the other social contractarians.

Commentators usually make the point that Spinoza's work has been neglected. There are a number of explanations offered, one of which is that he is difficult to classify. Den Uyl (1987, 371) points out that it is common to divide the early modern period of philosophy into two schools of thought: rationalist and empiricist, with continental thinkers including Spinoza being placed in the rationalist camp and compared with the British empiricists. However, Spinoza shares more with the British tradition of social theory than would be expected from this classification. Just as in chapter 1, I commented that there is some convergence between different areas of contemporary feminist theory, irrespective of the division between the continental and analytic traditions, here again there is an instance of traditional divisions in philosophy being unhelpful in that this division occludes some of the nuances of Spinoza's politics. As an alternative explanation for the marginalisation of Spinoza's work, Althusser goes further in arguing that Spinoza's thought has been repressed within the history of philosophy (Althusser and Balibar 1977, 102; discussed in Montag 1999, xvi). There are also attempts to account for the neglect of Spinoza in specific areas of Spinoza's thought. James points to Isaiah Berlin's claim that Spinoza produces a positive theory of freedom as a possible reason for its marginalisation in this particular area (James 1996, 208).

There have been a number of debates as to whether Spinoza should be classified as a social contractarian, for example Den Uyl (1983, 20–37). This question may come down to an assessment of what is at stake and what is useful in the move.

At one extreme, if the qualification of being a contractarian is the assumption that parties employ the "faculty" of volition to enter an actual contract, then Hobbes, with his redefinition of the will as the last appetite or aversion before action, and his view that the contract is hypothetical, as discussed in the last chapter, would not even be included. However, at the other extreme, if Hampton's view – that the contractarian tradition is an umbrella term for a number of diverse perspectives whose common features derive from their reliance upon an image or mental picture of the "contract" – is accepted then Spinoza's analysis of the transition from state of nature to civil society satisfies this criteria. It does so in a way that potentially disrupts the boundaries and meaning of the tradition and I am including Spinoza's position in order to do so. I want to support this approach by considering Deleuze and Guattari's reading of Spinoza, which they use to inform their answer to the question: "what is a philosophical concept?", to be discussed in more detail in the next section.

This next section therefore serves two purposes. It affords a brief discussion of how to view the question: "what is a philosophical concept?" in order to think about the meaning of the concept of the social contract. It allows me to support my position that it is productive to juxtapose Spinoza to classic social contractarian thought because of the ways in which he changes the central terms of the concept, opening up new ways of thinking. Secondly, the explanation itself draws upon a Spinozan framework and hence serves as an introduction to Spinoza's metaphysics. After this discussion, I will then outline Spinoza's social contract and examine the role of Spinoza's analysis of the imagination in relation to reason that informs his understanding of the relationship of individuals to each other, along with the formation of civil society. I will address the role of women in Spinoza's work as the issue arises at each stage.

Spinoza does not really discuss women and so introducing this issue does involve reading current concerns into his work – in particular that democracy should involve all of the population. However, at the end of his final unfinished *Political Treatise*, Spinoza mentions women specifically in order to deny them citizenship (Spinoza 2000b, 137. [XI, 4]). I will illustrate how this brief denial of citizenship to women contradicts Spinoza's overall conceptual framework.

The Concept of the Social Contract: Applying Spinozan Thought to the meaning of "Concept"

Paul Patton (2006, 12) has used the example of the social contract to illustrate the way in which Deleuze and Guattari (1994) describe a philosophical concept. I will give a simplified version which does not do justice to the full complexity of this analysis (see also Smith 2003). Deleuze and Guattari describe a concept as always being comprised of many parts, which can also be considered as concepts. In this example, supplied by Patton, the different "component concepts" of Hobbes' concept of the social contract include,

> the state of nature, the restless desire for power, natural laws of human reason and the artificial person or Leviathan which results from the compact (Patton 2006, 12).

The concept of the social contract comes into being once these component concepts are joined in a particular way. If one of these parts, or the characteristic relationship it has to other parts, is changed then the concept changes. Patton gives a couple of examples of the way changes in one "component concept" affects the overall concept of the social contract. One example is the question of who is a party to the contract (who, in Locke, is no longer envisaged as Hobbes' atomistic individuals but as property owners). A further example is the extent to which the overall concept of the social contract changes when the subjects/citizens are viewed as relinquishing less power to the sovereign than envisaged in Hobbes' social contract. Patton concludes that, as a result of these variations in component parts (by the way in which they are added to or subtracted from and the relationship between them), the concept of the social contract changes. In each case, the outcome is a singular concept of a social contract where the nature of this "singularity" is determined by its component concepts and the complex relations between them.

This way of looking at concepts (as comprised of other concepts) opens up a way of thinking about the history of these concepts. Sometimes the concepts themselves appear only as components of other concepts. In addition, they alter depending upon the specific problems to which they are addressed. Hence the social contract is transformed by the different ways in which it is employed, from the legitimation of law to issues of morality, for example, as discussed in the introduction. Deleuze and Guattari are interested in the way in which concepts are defined and the "bridges" between them, along which they can be transformed into other concepts by alterations to one or more of their component concepts. Whilst Patton illustrates this by looking at the way the meaning of "power" in Hobbes and Nietzsche differs and the pathways that could lead to an alignment between them, I want to use a different example, relevant to my concerns.

As I will discuss further in this chapter and in chapter 6 on Kant, Spinoza has been contrasted to Kant as the producer of a materialist philosophy, which rejects the faculty of the will and is viewed to be potentially more politically progressive (Montag 1999). However, despite the fact that Kant and Spinoza have very different conceptual frameworks, there is an interesting strand in contemporary feminist philosophy (Gatens and Lloyd (1999; 2000) and Cornell (1995)) that focuses upon the way in which one "component concept" (the imagination) is envisaged in order to think about social change. There is also some convergence between the reference to the use of an exemplar linked with the imagination. In political philosophy this includes both a reference to the use of an exemplar as a model of a free life or an ideal democracy in Spinoza (James 1996, 138) and in Kantian aesthetics (Arendt 1989; Ferrara 2008). This may reflect a broader interest in the politics relating to the imagination in different forms. Dan Smith (2003,

318) places the Spinozan analysis of Gatens and Lloyd (1999) within the current interest on the imagination as also exemplified by Anderson (2006), Castoriadis (1998), and Le Dœuff (2002). This convergence could be viewed as forming an unexpected "bridge" between the work of Spinoza and Kant – illustrating Deleuze and Guattari's way of looking at concepts.

Lefebvre (2008, 201–207) has argued that Spinoza is the unacknowledged source of Deleuze and Guattari's description of a concept. Spinoza describes all bodies and minds as made up of component parts which share a relation of motion and rest, for example, the human body's organs, heart beat, and blood flow. There are no simple parts because each part, for example an organ, is made up of other parts, which need to relate to each other in a particular way in order to enable the body to live. Importantly, all things take parts from other things and join with them, as we do for example when we eat food. We can also join with others to form associations, such as friendships, organisations, families and the state. From this description, Spinoza appears to be evoking the long standing analogy that treats the state as if it were a human body, illustrated by the image of Hobbes' Leviathan, which is depicted as holding a sword and comprised of many smaller citizens who make up his body.[1] This analogy is historically employed as part of a conservative argument against rebellion – which is viewed as self-defeating if we are all parts of the same body – and is also depicted in contrast to female bodies (Cavarero 2002). In contrast, Spinoza is not making a normative claim against citizens' right to rebel or even prioritising human bodies. On the contrary, as I will outline below, Spinoza's metaphysics is employed to argue that natural right is co-extensive with power. The question of whether he literally views individuals as coming together to create bodies greater than themselves or whether this is a metaphor, along with the implications for his politics, is contentious and will also be discussed further below.

Lefebvre draws a parallel between the way in which Deleuze and Guattari describe a concept – which is made up of component concepts, all of which have a history, and can change or be destroyed by their encounters with other concepts – and Spinoza's description of a body, as comprised of parts. He is arguing that Spinoza provides the "precise and technical model" for Deleuze and Guattari's explanation of what is meant by concepts (2008, 201). This interesting argument only needs to rely upon an analogy with Spinoza's understanding of bodies. However, Lefebvre strengthens this argument by reference to Spinoza's "parallelism". I will outline this because it is also useful to understand Spinoza's view of freedom, to be discussed further.

For Spinoza, there is only one substance (described as God *or* Nature) and nothing outside of this substance. It is fully expressed under different attributes: thought (i.e. all ideas) and extension (i.e. all bodies). Spinoza also posits that there are an infinite number of attributes of which we are unaware. For a human being

1 Skinner (2008, 185) states that Hobbes may have had a hand in the design of this image himself and that he undoubtedly approved it.

(who is a particular mode – or part – of this one substance) his/her mind and body are therefore modifications of the same substance expressed in different ways. There is no dualism between the mind and body, i.e. they are not separate substances, as for Descartes (1996). In addition, a human mind is an idea which has as its object that human being's particular body. In other words, we are initially informed about the world by forming images of our bodies and the ways in which other bodies impinge upon us. When a body thrives so does the mind and vice versa because they are the same mode expressed through different attributes. We are not "an empire within an empire" (Spinoza 2000a, III, Preface) set apart from nature. On the contrary, we depend upon our interactions with many other bodies in order to endeavour to survive and thrive. Spinoza terms this endeavour as our "*conatus*". In contrast with the definition of an individual thing's "essence" as relating to some fixed underlying property, for Spinoza, its essence is its *conatus*. To return to Lefebvre's claim, for Spinoza, just as the body is made up of parts so is the mind. Indeed, as we strive to increase our *conatus* we expose ourselves to greater richness and complexity and that is reflected by both body and mind. Hence, Spinoza also thinks of the mind as composed of ideas, which increase in complexity as our understanding of the world improves and we thereby increase our *conatus*. Lefebvre's point is that this is the mechanism developed by Deleuze and Guattari to describe concepts.[2] The way in which Spinoza's description of the interaction of bodies and minds with others is relevant to his politics is to be discussed below.

The State of Nature and Social Contract

Reasons For the Contract: Security and Freedom

Spinoza shares Hobbes' starting position: Hobbes' claim that political theory should be concerned with how individuals behave in practice and not in some ideal world. Spinoza's different analysis of the passions and reason starts from this presumption, as illustrated by the start of the *Political Treatise*:

> The fact is that [philosophers] conceive men, not as they are but as they would like them to be. As a result it is not ethics that they have written but satire; and

2 This may remain merely an analogy, however, because the meaning of "idea" in Spinoza may not map directly onto the meaning of "philosophical concept" in Deleuze and Guattari, despite the fact that both are viewed as comprised of component parts. So, for example, for Spinoza the mind is the idea of the body. This is not to say that the mind has a concept of the body but that it apprehends the body intellectually (for more detail on this point (Mark 1979)). My view is that "philosophical concepts" would be a sub set of ideas – some adequate and some inadequate. Nothing rests on this point with regard to this chapter and neither does it undermine Lefebvre's position.

> they have never worked out a political theory that can have practical application (Spinoza 2000b, 33. [I, 1]).

Like Rousseau, Spinoza produces a radical rereading of Hobbes that employs the image of a transition from the state of nature to civil society and addresses the question of how such a transition could be understood and what is transferred (lost or gained) when a civil society is formed.

Spinoza's contractarianism in the *Theological Political Treatise* initially follows Hobbes in pointing out that it is "much more to their advantage" (2001, 175) for men (and women?) to live by their own laws and dictates of reason. Following Hobbes, he argues that there is nobody who does not wish to live in safety, free from fear, and that this is impossible if individuals can do as they please (2001, 175). Similarly, he argues that life without mutual assistance would necessarily be wretched and "lack the cultivation of reason" (2001, 175), a position that repeats Hobbes' famous description of life in a state of nature, which would have "no place for industry … no arts, no letters, no society" (Hobbes 1994, 76. XIII [9]). Spinoza recognises that, given the extent to which humans can offer each other "mutual aid" it is unlikely that we ever lived as isolated individuals. Individuals' security and freedom is increased if "men should unite in one body" (2001, 175). Similarly, in *Political Treatise* he envisages individuals coming together because of passion rather than reason:

> Since men, as we have said, are led more by passion than by reason, it naturally follows that a people will unite and consent to be guided as if by one mind not at reason's prompting but through some common emotion, such as ... a common hope, or common fear (Spinoza 2000b, 64. [VI, 1]).

Spinoza adds that men (humans) fear isolation because alone they do not have the ability to defend themselves or acquire what they need and so always strive for civil order.

Whilst this line of argument emphasises the need for security as the main reason for the formation of civil society, Spinoza is clear that individuals join with others to increase their freedom:

> It is not ... the purpose of the state to transform men from rational beings into beasts or puppets, but rather to enable them to develop their mental and physical faculties in safety, to use their reason without restraint and to refrain from the strife and the vicious mutual abuse that are prompted by hatred, anger or deceit. Thus the purpose of the state is, in reality, freedom (Spinoza 2001, 223. [XX]).

There is no contradiction between the need for security and that of freedom because the two concepts are linked as a result of Spinoza's redefinition of the term "freedom". Here again, whilst he appears to be working within a Hobbesian framework, Spinoza's redefinitions of the central terms (or "component concepts") shifts the concept of the social contract in a different direction. Whereas, Hobbes views freedom as the absence of external impediments and envisages a loss of freedom in exchange for security upon entering into civil society, Spinoza argues that individuals enter into civil society in order to increase their freedom. It is therefore important to examine the reason why he views this to be the case.

In the *Ethics,* Spinoza describes a free man as one who increases his *conatus*, his power of acting (and hence freedom) through the use of reason. As reason does not demand anything that is contrary to nature, it demands that,

> each person should love himself, and look for what is useful to him ... that everyone, in so far as he is in himself, should endeavour to preserve his being (Spinoza 2000a, IV P18, S).

Human beings are able to increase their freedom by developing an understanding of the passions that they experience passively as a result of encounters with other bodies that either increase or decrease their *conatus*. These passions are passive but by working out the reason why some encounters are joyful (i.e. the reason why certain encounters increase their *conatus* and are hence associated with joyful passions) individuals can become active in seeking out such encounters. This reasoning takes place more effectively with others (and, indeed is difficult to perform in isolation). Spinoza therefore argues that,

> Nothing, therefore, is more useful to man than man. I mean by this that men can ask for nothing that is more efficacious for the preservation of their being than that all men should agree in everything in such a way that the minds and bodies of all should simultaneously endeavour, as far as they can, to preserve their own being, and that all should simultaneously look for the common advantage of all (Spinoza 2000a, IV P18, S).

Spinoza and The Stepford Wife Problem

Given that Spinoza refers to only men in this passage – which in the past has been ambiguously applied as both gender neutral and male – raises the question of whether Spinoza actually includes women in this analysis or whether he views women as being so different in nature to men that they are less useful to men than men are to each other. Further, given that Spinoza argues that men are more useful to each other when they are rational, it also raises the question of whether Spinoza views women as less rational than men and hence less useful. This is worth asking because his final lines of the *Political Treatise* exclude women from citizenship (Spinoza 2000b, 136–137 [XI, 4]). In addition, there is little reference to women in his work, save in the context of women as objects of men's sexual desire (for example Spinoza 2000a, III, P35, Sch) and to "effeminate pity" which is contrasted negatively to reason (Spinoza 2000a, IV, P37, Sch1). However, in favour of the view that women are to be included in the above quotation, there is evidence elsewhere in the *Ethics* that Spinoza does view women as capable of reasoning. Spinoza refers to Adam in the following terms,

> Then, when the man had discovered a wife, *who agreed very much with his own nature, he knew that that there could be nothing in Nature that could be more useful to him*; but after [eating from the tree of knowledge] he believed the beasts to be like himself he began at once to imitate their emotions ... and to lose his liberty (Spinoza 2000a, IV, P68, Sch; emphasis added).

In order to agree with Adam's nature and to be useful to him, Eve would have to be rational. So, at least in this "state of nature"[3] women are envisaged as rational. The idea that this may pertain in civil society is supported elsewhere by Spinoza's comments on marriage. He initially criticises lust that arises from beauty and all love that "recognises some cause other than freedom of mind" (Spinoza 2000a, IV, App. 19) which he says easily passes into hatred or, worse, a form of madness. In a move that looks forward to his final comments in the *Political Treatise*, in which one of the reasons for excluding women from citizenship is the sad passion (jealousy) and discord that lust for women can engender between men (Spinoza 2000b, 137. [XI, 4]), he point out that such "love" can foster discord. However, he then says,

> As to what concerns marriage, it is certain that this agrees with reason, if the desire of sexual intercourse is not engendered by beauty alone, but also by the love of begetting children and educating them wisely; and also if the love of each person, namely of the man and the woman, has as its cause, not beauty alone, but above all the freedom of the mind (Spinoza 2000a, IV, App. 20).

From this reference to women as being capable of "freedom of the mind", it does appear that Spinoza recognises women in civil society as rational (because this is what freedom entails for Spinoza). It is therefore inconsistent of him to provide (brief) arguments against women's citizenship at the end of the unfinished *Political Treatise.*

To support this comment and explain why Spinoza could not consistently agree with a view that it could be in men's interests to curtail women's opportunities and to subordinate and exploit them (which I will refer to as the Stepford Wife problem)[4] it is necessary to emphasise the importance of reason in Spinoza's framework. For Spinoza, it is a contradiction both to employ reason and to be in "servitude". A woman who is employing reason thereby increases her *conatus*

3 For the argument that Hobbes' state of nature was a reworking of the Christian story of the fall see (Strauss 1963).

4 The Stepford wives were subservient stereotypes (and it transpires that the Stepford husbands replaced their independent wives with robots – although this last point is irrelevant for my purposes) in Levin and Strab (2004), made famous in a film in 1975.

and hence her freedom. This implies, not only that she will work out why some encounters with other bodies are joyful, but also that she will act upon this higher form of knowledge, thereby increasing her powers of acting by forming more joyful associations with other bodies and further adequate ideas in the mind. As discussed, when we strive to persist on the basis of merely inadequate ideas – linked with our passions – we are passive and more prone to sad encounters then when we understand how other bodies affect our bodies (or other ideas affect our minds) and actively seek out encounters which increase our *conatus*. Importantly, the ability to reason is *in itself* associated with intense joy because the ability to reason, in itself, increases our freedom. Spinoza points out that men will not fight over ownership of the joy that comes from conceiving of adequate ideas because the ability to reason is not akin to a scarce resource (Spinoza 2000a, IV, P37, Sch). On the contrary, an individual increases his or her understanding of the world through association with others who are also rational. In common with Kant's critical project, Spinoza recognises that we do not reason well in isolation (see chapter 6). Therefore, returning to the Stepford Wife problem, for Spinoza, it would be rational for men (i.e. in their interests) to try to ensure that others with whom they associate in any way (whether women or men) have the opportunities to develop their rationality. This would include taking part in the activities of being a citizen.

To illustrate Spinoza's framework further, the "Spinozan" arguments I have employed can be compared to the position of Hobbes and Kant when applied to this problem. The question arises as to whether this "Spinozan position" can be viewed as offering a different approach from that of either Hobbes or Kant. Is it possible to supplement Hampton's (1991a) "Two Faces of Contractarian Thought" with a third approach to ethics? As discussed in the last chapter, Hobbes' egoistic individuals, as understood by game theory for example, would happily exploit anyone if they calculated that it was in their interests to do so. (There are situations when it is sensible to reciprocate, of course, especially as real women will react differently from the robotic Stepford wives, but this is irrelevant to the point that Hobbesian individuals are motivated by self-interest.) In contrast, Hampton finds resources in Kant (despite Kant's actual position on women and on race) to argue that all persons should be respected and treated as ends in themselves. It is therefore objectively wrong to fail to treat women as persons. This sets an objective level of treatment of others derived from Kant's view of reason that should operate irrespective of existing social norms, which will be discussed further in chapter 6.

In contrast, my "Spinozan approach" relies upon Spinoza's analysis of reason (as an understanding of why encounters increase or decrease our *conatus*) which differs from both Hobbes' and Kant's definitions of reason in order to argue that it is not in men's best interests to subordinate and exploit women. This argument combines some elements of both Kant and Hobbes. In common with Kant, Spinoza's emphasis upon the use of reason (albeit a re-conception of the term) produces an argument against the subordination and exploitation of other humans. However, this is only because other human beings have the potential to be useful to us and not out of respect for personhood. From a Kantian perspective, this element is crucial and Spinoza therefore can be subsumed within Hobbes' individualism. Does this "third" Spinozan approach actually collapse into a version of Hobbesian egoistic individualism that simply entails a more sophisticated judgement of what is in the husband's long term interests? A straightforward reading of Spinoza can (rightly) describe him as an advocate of individual self-interest. However, to make this move without further examination may be to proceed too quickly because the meaning of both "the individual" and of "self-interest" changes with Spinoza's analysis, along with the way in which Spinoza produces a conception of reason that is neither instrumental rationality nor a faculty.

Before developing this argument further it is useful to bear in mind Taylor's warning that it is necessary to avoid confusing *ontological* issues of atomistic – holistic views of society (in which the debate concerns the right level of explanation for social structures and whether this lies with the individual) with *advocacy* issues that concern moral and political policies and oppose individual rights to a concern with the community life (Taylor 1997). Much of the debate around Spinoza has been focused upon whether he can be classified as atomistic or holistic. Rice (1990), for example, describes this split by categorising readings of Spinoza as either "literalist", i.e. that Spinoza understands the state as literally an individual (a holistic model in Taylor's terms) or "metaphoric", i.e. that Spinoza's reference to the state as if it were an individual is purely a metaphor (an atomistic model). My claim, so far, is that Spinoza's denial of rights to women in the *Political Treatise* is inconsistent with his view of reason and of how individuals relate, described in the *Ethics*. Hence this criticism does not depend upon a particular view of whether or not Spinoza's reference to the state as a body is metaphorical, *per se*. However, the way in which Spinoza envisages the relationship between bodies is relevant to both issues and will be discussed further and then applied to the Stepford Wife problem.

Matheron (1969, 266; cited in Balibar 1997, 7) describes Spinoza as producing: "ego-altruism". Balibar argues that this expression still appears to maintain an inappropriate duality and that Spinoza's work is better described as a "relational ontology". Balibar stresses the fact that, for Spinoza, our self-interest (i.e. our endeavour to increase our *conatus*, which is the same as increasing our freedom) necessarily draws upon an argument that can be opposed to both individualism (atomism, in Taylor's terms) and to holism. Balibar's analysis is clearly not classifiable as a metaphoric approach (to return to Rice's vocabulary, derived from whether Spinoza's reference to the body of the state is a metaphor). However, it is necessary to be cautious in classifying it with the literalist approach, as described by Rice, because this would be to miss the way in which Spinoza changes the meaning of "the individual". In other words, Spinoza does not keep the Hobbesian image of the individual and then view the state as just another individual, which is often the way in which states have been envisaged (as competing egoistic individuals) within international relations. For a discussion of this practice, see example Hutchings (2001).

Balibar (1997) employs the term "transindividual" to stress that, for Spinoza, an individual cannot exist or flourish in isolation; that his, her or its powers of acting only increases or decreases as a result of encounters with other bodies. As discussed, the bodies that are of particular importance for that individual are those which agree with its nature, in our case, other humans. So, the pursuit of self-interest, which involves increasing our understanding and our freedom, is not in competition with others. On the contrary, their attempts to understand the world help us. So our essence, i.e. our *conatus* (what we do to survive and thrive) is therefore necessarily related to that of other individuals. This can be distinguished from psychoanalytic models, for example, in which one is defined in terms of a split from the Other or by what is rejected in order to think of oneself as whole. On the contrary, Spinoza produces a model of desire that is not based upon lack (or on being "cut off" from anything) but upon making different connections in order to flourish. Balibar does not start with the individual but is interested in how Spinoza accounts for "individuation" – the process of becoming an individual. Balibar therefore points out that, for Spinoza,

> (against "individualism") ... the autonomy or power of the individual is not reduced, but enlarged, by the constitution of a State or Civil Society, and (against "holism") … the sovereignty or power of the State is not reduced, but enlarged, by the growing autonomy of the citizens (especially their freedom of thought and expression) (Balibar 1997, 10).

Spinoza's "self-interested individual" is therefore very different from that of Hobbes' competitive atomistic individuals. This form of "self-interest", which involves reasoned understanding is always in the interests of both the collective and the individual. Balibar (1997, 28) contrasts this social aim of increasing knowledge with that of reciprocal dependency, stating that – with the exception of discussions concerning primitive conditions – Spinoza is not interested in questions about the division of labour or exchange of goods. However, there is a curious footnote, in which Balibar claims that,

> By borrowing Levi-Strauss' famous tripartition, it could be said that (in the *Ethics*) Spinoza is not really concerned with the exchange of Goods (see however E4App 27 to 29), but rather with the exchange of Women (or better said, objects of sexual love) and the exchange of Words or, more generally, signs (but of course a developed analysis of linguistic communication can be found only in *Theological Political Treatise*) (Balibar 1997, 28. fn. 32).

The Stepford wife problem – whether it is in men's interests to subordinate and oppress women – includes the situation of women being treated as a form of commerce between men. (Examples of this can include the selling of women to be wives but also the Western image of "trophy wives", i.e. women serving as the symbols of success, presumably to other men.) Balibar's footnote is curious because – whilst Spinoza is concerned that women may produce jealousy and discord amongst men – he is clear that the aim of civil society is the increase of freedom. Given that Spinoza has accepted that women are capable of reason, as discussed above, it would not be in men's interests to treat them as objects viewed as circulating between men for two reasons. Firstly, it constrains women in their ability to increase their *conatus*. Secondly, as a way of relating between men, this does not have the aim of increasing freedom. On the contrary, it increases the (passive) passions, for example jealousy. So, whereas a "Kantian approach" would stress that such a way of men relating to each other through a commerce of women would be wrong because it treats women as objects rather than persons, from a "Spinozan perspective" it is wrong because it fails to increase the *conatus* of both individuals and the collective. To misquote Balibar, quoted earlier:

> the power of any collectivities, including "the family", is not reduced but is enlarged, by the growing autonomy of women (especially their freedom of thought and expression) (Original quotation at Balibar 1997, 10).

Note that as component parts of the family change by an increased understanding, the *conatus* of the group may be increased but this will produce a different form of association that may or may not be termed a "family". It would certainly differ from Rousseau's image of the sentimental family into which women are constrained, to be discussed in chapter 5.

Natural Right and the Retention of Individual Judgement in Civil Society

Following Hobbes, Spinoza argues that, given human nature, individuals will not keep their promises unless they fear a greater evil arising as a result of breaking their word. However, against Hobbes, Spinoza is clear that if a robber makes me promise to give him my goods – given that "my natural right is determined by power alone" (Spinoza 2001, 176. [XVI]) – then I am within my rights to try to deceive him. If I am able to do so then it follows, for Spinoza, that it is my natural/sovereign right to do so. In other words, Spinoza has no problem with the right to break promises that are made under duress, including the social contract, if a threat is no longer present.

Like Hobbes, he argues that when it comes to the constitution of the state, men cannot be relied upon to keep their word because they are not purely motivated by reason but by their own pleasure. Sovereign power must therefore be backed by force, making it more difficult for men to go back on their promise – such power lasting only as long as it can be enforced. He concludes:

> Therefore, without any infringement of natural right, a community can be formed and a contract be always preserved in its entirety in absolute good faith on these terms, that everyone transfers all the power that he possesses to the community, which will therefore alone retain the sovereign natural right over

> everything, that is, the supreme rule which everyone will have to obey either of free choice or through fear of the ultimate penalty. Such a community's right is called a democracy, which can therefore be defined as a united body of men which corporeally possesses sovereign right over everything within its power (Spinoza 2001, 177. [XVI]).

To recognise the radical way in which Spinoza reworks Hobbes' argument, it is important to understand the way in which Spinoza also changes the meaning of the concept of power, as well as that of freedom, discussed above. For him, power is no longer to be viewed as something exercised from above, such as God's Will or sovereign power, by one who stands outside of nature or the society. For Spinoza, power is reconceived as a body's *conatus*, its endeavour to survive and thrive. Contemporary continental philosophy, drawing in part upon Marx, has emphasised that this is a materialist position in that it focuses upon bodies and what bodies are able to do (Deleuze 1988; Negri 1991; Balibar 1997; 1998; Montag 1995; 1999). For example, Montag (1995) links Spinoza with Althusser and Foucault to argue that Spinoza's emphasis upon bodies offers an approach to political theory that brings to light issues of subordination, which are otherwise obscured by reference to the will and consciousness. As part of such an approach, he cites feminist work on Spinoza that shifts the analysis from thinking about unequally distributed rights and property to an examination of "corporeal forms of subjugation not only independent of all legality but even opposed to it" (Montag 1999, xxi).[5] Den Uyl (1983, 9–10) contrasts Spinoza's position with that of Hobbes for whom natural right is normative. Hobbes links natural right to reason but, because Spinoza talks about the natural right of non-human things, there is no such association for him. Right is associated simply with the power that a body has to act, which therefore cannot be given up in civil society, a point which is explicitly discussed in *Theological Political Treatise* (Spinoza 2001, 222. [XVII]). I will look in more detail at how Spinoza arrives at this position and then discuss its implications. Spinoza starts by stating that "the right and established order of Nature" simply refers to the rules governing the nature of every living thing. All natural things have the "sovereign" right to do all they can do. The reason given for this derives from the way in which Spinoza alters how God is conceptualised. As mentioned above, God is no longer viewed as a legislator who stands outside of nature. Instead God is immanent with nature, which is one substance that is all fully expressed in different forms, such as extension (in bodies) and thought (in minds). This allows Spinoza to argue that nature's power is the same as the power

---

5 Whilst this work is of great interest, it is not new to feminism to look at corporeal forms of oppression rather than legal rights, of course, given the diversity of feminist thought. For example, the anarchist Emma Goldman criticised an emphasis on the vote compared to the need to attack the conditions in factories. She was also concerned about the need for contraception (Goldman 2006).

of God, which is classed as "sovereign". Since all individual things taken together make up the whole of nature then, Spinoza argues that:

> each individual thing has the right to do all that it can do; i.e. the right of the individual is co-extensive with its determinate power (Spinoza 2001, 173. [XVI]).

Each individual thing (not only humans) tries to persist in being, therefore each has the right to do so.

Given that this description of right clearly includes women because it includes any entity (as all such "modes" or individual bodies are part of the one substance), this move is relevant to one strand of argument employed by Spinoza to exclude women from citizenship. Spinoza argues that whenever women have lived with men they have been dominated by them and hence concludes that "women do not naturally possess equal right with men" (Spinoza 2000b, 137. [XI, 4]). This cannot amount to more than a (supposedly) empirical observation. Within Spinoza's framework, this statement cannot be understood as an argument for denying women rights because, once women have rights, then it is in their power to have them and therefore they are entitled to have them (given that power is co-extensive with right).

Lloyd makes a different point on this issue. She argues that Spinoza's view – that irrespective of women's capacities in the state of nature, they do not share men's capacities in civil society – is a reflection of the stress that he lays upon the,

> interconnections between the life of reason and the forms of social organisations that enhance freedom. If our natural powers are enriched by the operation of good forms of social organisation, which foster the collective pursuit of reason, it is only to be expected that groups excluded from full participation in that shared pursuit of reason will miss out on the full flourishing of their natural powers and pleasures, leading distorted and mutated lives (Lloyd 1994, 163).

Whilst Lloyd makes a good point (and is actually focused upon an elegant distinction between Descartes and Spinoza with regard to sexual difference) this comment is too generous to Spinoza when applied to his final comment in *Political Treatise* because he is claiming that women are subordinate to men in all cultures to date and therefore concludes that this is natural, irrespective of any type of social organisation. Again, it should be noted that this conclusion is inconsistent with Spinoza's other work, in which he defines an individual's essence as its *conatus*, its endeavour to survive, in contrast to any fixed underlying essence. In addition, he states that we do not know what a body can do – leaving open the question of what all individuals (including women) can become (Spinoza 2000a, II, P2, Sch).

Spinoza's view that power is coextensive with right is critical to the way in which he envisages the transition from state of nature to civil society. He views it as an absurdity that citizens could suspend their own judgement (Spinoza 2001, 179. [XVI]; Spinoza 2000b, 49. [III, 3]). As discussed in the last chapter, Hobbes argues that individuals retain the right to disobey the sovereign if they judge that they are in danger. Given that they would have to assess any given situation to make such a judgement, it follows that Hobbes does not assume that citizens can stop themselves from judging, simply that they should not oppose the sovereign's judgement unless they view their lives to be in danger. Hobbes' example of the situation in which a sovereign demands that someone follow a different religion from Christianity illustrates the way that his materialism is strained at this point, as discussed in the last chapter. Hobbes' solution is that it is possible to obey physically whilst continuing to believe in the Christian God. For Montag (1999, 52), this illustrates an important difference in that Spinoza's emphasis upon the body allows him to highlight subordination. The actions of the body cannot be dissociated from the understanding of the mind, in Spinoza, because they are both expressions of the same substance as a particular mode. In addition, Spinoza's emphasis upon surviving goes beyond Hobbes in that it involves increasing one's power of acting and freedom by using reason to increase the number of joyful encounters. This involves the pursuit of knowledge, along with others, and therefore provides arguments in support of free speech and against the idea that it would be meaningful to appear to obey but think differently in isolation.

Spinoza makes it clear that he is talking about a democratic state, which is the "most natural form of state, approaching most closely to that freedom which nature grants to every man" (2001, 179. [XVI]). He supports a democratic position, arguing that it is preferable to have as many individuals as possible involved in making a decision because they are less likely to be overcome by passions (2001, 178. [XVI]). This argument is dependent upon Spinoza's understanding of the relationship between different forms of knowledge and the associated importance of reason compared with emotions, to be outlined below. Civil rights are defined following the argument:

> By a citizen's civil right we can only mean the freedom of every man to preserve himself in his present condition (Spinoza 2001, 179. [XVI]).

Spinoza describes a state of nature in which there is no issue of justice or injustice and, in common with Hobbes but unlike the later Locke, there is no property. Justice is therefore defined as "a set disposition to render every man what is his by civil right" (2001, 180. [XVI]). Spinoza deals with the argument that it is against God's law that we should harm each other and that this would also pertain in a state of nature. However, he argues against the existence of religion in the state of nature because "nobody knows by nature that he has any duty to obey God" (2001, 181. [XVI]). The state of nature is therefore not only before law but before the "revelation of religion".

Spinoza's position on the meaning of good and bad and his argument against the existence of evil is illustrated by his example of God telling Adam not to eat the apple, in Letter 19 to Blyenbergh (Spinoza 2002, 807–811; see also Deleuze 1988). Spinoza explains that, to view God as commanding Adam not to eat the apple thereby dictating what is good and evil is to misunderstand what is happening. The "command" not to eat the apple should be understood as advice that an apple would poison Adam. There is no external realm outside of the material existence of bodies that is able to define "evil". Spinoza replaces the idea of evil with the idea of something which is "bad" for a particular body. This is the case when its encounter with another body (such as Adam's body being poisoned by the apple) reduces its body's *conatus*. This is always understood from the particular perspective of that body. For example, if Adam eats an animal then it is clearly bad from the position of that animal (because it reduces its body's *conatus* – in this case drastically) but it is a joyful encounter for Adam in that his *conatus* is increased; his body continues to flourish. If from this joyful encounter he then works out why this occurs rather than just thinking "meat is good" his freedom is increased.

Spinoza and the Imagination

I will now examine Spinoza's view of the imagination for three reasons. Firstly, there has been recent feminist work that employs the imagination in Spinoza to consider current problems. Secondly, an analysis of the imagination is necessary in order to consider in more detail Spinoza's concept of knowledge and the role that reason plays in increasing our *conatus*. Thirdly, whilst Spinoza does not appeal to the imagination in this way, the social contract itself can be viewed as depending upon an act of imagination: applying to an "image" or "picture" of free and equal persons, for example (Hampton 2002, 382–383). This is a theme that I will develop in chapter 6.

Spinoza describes the imagination as the "first type of knowledge", occurring prior to the employment of reason. It is to be superseded because it is inadequate in explaining what is really happening, nevertheless it continues to have an effect upon us:

> An imagination is an idea which indicates the present constitution of the human body rather than the nature of an external body – not distinctly indeed but confusedly – from which it comes about that the mind is said to err. For example, when we see the sun, we imagine it to be about 200 feet distant from us. In this we are deceived, as long as we are ignorant of its true distance. But when the sun's true distance is known, the error is removed, but not the imagination, that is an idea of the sun which explains the sun's nature only in so far as the body is affected by it. So, although we know its true distance we nevertheless imagine it to be close to us (Spinoza 2000a, IV, P1, Sch).

In Spinozan terms, the transition from the first to the second type of knowledge increases our ability to act because we move from a position in which we employ only confused images of the world – created by our passive interactions, which may make us joyful or sad – to a state caused by our finding the explanation of these passions. Our imagination is not faulty, it merely lacks knowledge. The information it yields regarding the state of our bodies and the impact of our encounters with other bodies stays with us even when we have greater knowledge of the actual reason for the effects of other bodies upon us.

Gatens (1995, 136–141) employs this Spinozan analysis to discuss the imagination employed by judges in the West. She argues that when (male, white) judges encounter women in everyday life, women usually play a subordinate role. It is therefore difficult for judges to free themselves of this imaginary bodily perception of women, with its link to emotions, when it comes to judging legal cases involving women. Spinoza therefore provides her with a model to think about the tenacity of stereotypes. Using Spinoza, Gatens provides an explanation as to why this transition may be difficult for judges and may require more than a few training days on diversity issues. (Obviously, there is also a question as to the way in which the judiciary are selected, which fails to reflect diversity.)

Gatens extends this analysis of the imagination to do the work of what has previously been termed "ideology" (James, Lloyd, and Gatens 2000, 56). For Gatens, this is informed by the way in which Spinoza views knowledge, thereby adding a richness to the idea of a collective imaginary. Gatens cites Yovel to make this point,

> [For Spinoza] knowledge is more a mode of being than of having, not something we possess but something we *are* or *become*. As Monique Schneider notes, in attaining knowledge we do not gain an acquisition, as if something new were added to an inventory of our possessions, but rather we exist differently (Yovel 1992, 159; cited by Gatens 1995, 127).

Whilst this analysis of the imagination has so far been negative, in the sense that it is only the first type of knowledge produced as a result of confused images of our bodily state, James, Gatens and Lloyd have provided more positive examples of the use of imagination, bearing in mind that we never have complete understanding of the world and therefore are always informed by this first type of knowledge. I will discuss James' employment of the imagination which she uses to think about Spinoza's view of civil society and then consider how Gatens and Lloyd extend the way in which imagination in Spinoza is conceptualised.

James (2008) highlights the importance of the imagination to the way Spinoza describes the role of the sovereign, which is to recognise the need for co-operation and to persuade the community of this need. Given that it is important that citizens develop their powers of acting and freedom, it would not be in a sovereign's self-interest to threaten them in order to enlist their co-operation. This would produce an unstable society but, as an approach to sovereignty, the use of fear is also problematic because the aim of entering into civil society is to increase freedom, which necessarily involves everyone becoming as rational as possible and to increase joyful encounters. This aim is undermined if sad passions, such as fear are encouraged.

In her reading of *Theological Political Treatise*, James points out that, Spinoza views prophets as rulers with exceptional imaginations. The imaginative ability of prophets allowed them to recognise the need for co-operation and to persuade a particular community of this need. Those citizens who are absorbed by their own passions will be appealed to by a prophet who draws upon images and stories that convey this message, tailored to the imaginations of specific groups of people. Spinoza says that there are no longer prophets to whom "divine law" is revealed; that it is civil law that individuals must obey in order to co-operate. Therefore, prophets and sovereigns have in common the fact that they must be effective in getting people to believe in the law – divine law in the case of the prophet and civil law in the case of sovereigns. Failure to do so would mean that they ceased to have this role.

James expands upon Spinoza's comments that the wise must recognise and be sensitive to the imaginations and passions of others, that they should think through the impact of their actions, whilst resisting the urge to respond in passionate terms (Spinoza 2000a, IV, App 13). So, Spinoza does not envisage the wise as rigidly sticking to virtuous so-called "rational actions" irrespective of their consequences but of trying to find a solution that furthers co-operation. James (2008, 135) expands upon the example of a "free man" (employing Spinoza's term) who is given a favour by a merchant. He knows that this will incite envy in others and wishes that he had not accepted the favour. However, he also knows that if he fails to reciprocate then the merchant will be resentful and co-operation with him later will be difficult. He therefore finds a solution that involves a legal way of reciprocating and tries to avoid such situations in future.[6] James concludes that,

> Freedom, as Spinoza conceives it, is therefore always dependent on the extent to which particular individuals and communities are able to *imagine* ways of life that are able to embody the general truths revealed by reasoning, thereby bringing cooperation within reach (James 2008, 136; emphasis added).

Spinoza envisages the relationship between reason and imagination as they are employed by sovereigns, who must encourage subjects to understand the reasons behind the laws but (like the wise man in the example above) are also aware of the

6 It is of interest to note that this emphasis upon the need to maintain relationships rather than to apply fixed principles based on strict duty bears some passing resemblance to Gilligan's (1982) ethic of care. However, Spinoza's free man is motivated by self-interest alone, albeit that this is within a broadened meaning of self-interest, which is not in conflict with collective interest, as discussed above.

impact of their passions so as to tailor the message according to the imagination of their subjects.

James then argues that democracy is the form of government most suited to imaginatively representing laws in a manner that is persuasive to citizens (2008, 137). This is because they have a say in producing laws that are then recognised as "reflecting both rational and imaginative resources in the community" (James 2008, 138). In making this claim, James points out that, because our imagination reflects our different bodily states and experiences, different individuals can bring different imaginations to bear on a problem and therefore produce laws to which they will then be responsive. If the state did not include everyone's contribution then it would deprive itself of insights that can help it sustain a secure and harmonious way of life.

Whilst Spinoza argues that democracy is the most natural form of state because it is the one that retains as far as possible individuals' natural rights in the state of nature, he describes some states that find it impossible to form a democracy. Spinoza therefore claims that limited freedom is the best that can be obtained in the circumstances but is not the ideal. James (2008, 145) argues that, drawing from the *Ethics* it is possible to envisage an ideal sovereign drawn from all persons, which guarantees its own good. However, in the *Political Treatise* only a subset of the population, which excludes women and servants, make the law on behalf of the rest. She concludes that, for Spinoza, whilst democracy represents an exemplar through which we can increase our freedom, it is not an ideal that all societies can achieve because their imagination is limited. She turns this Spinozan argument against Spinoza himself to conclude that, in excluding women and others from his vision of democracy, Spinoza's own position provides an example of the lack of imagination with which he is concerned. He thereby illustrates,

> one of his central claims: that successful democracies crucially depend on the imaginative abilities of their sovereigns and subjects, and that lack of imaginative power is among the chief factors that hold them back (James 2008, 146).

This is an interesting re-valuation of the role of imagination in Spinoza. Given the importance that Spinoza places upon reason, it would be a more straightforward reading to claim that he had (like Gatens' judges) failed to move beyond the images of women in his imagination (linked with the passions) and to employ reason. Had Spinoza understood why he views women as bad (as a potential source of discord between men), he would then have been able to recognise the components of them (i.e. their rationality) that accord with men's nature. Such an understanding would therefore have increased his *conatus* by allowing him to recognise how women could be useful in further increasing his understanding of the world.

Instead, James' move of describing Spinoza as having a failure of the imagination, rather than reason, re-values the meaning of imagination, in a manner that underscores the way in which it is re-valued in her paper. Imagination, she argues, is important politically, in the production of exemplars of what it is to live freely. Imagination provides a way of portraying laws that convince those who cannot work out their own interests to follow them. Whilst James' paper employs different subject matter, her re-valuation of the imagination has much in common with that of Gatens and Lloyd's argument to be discussed below.

James' approach to Spinozan imagination can be understood further by considering the way in which she has employed it elsewhere. James (2006) criticises cognitivist theories of emotion, i.e. theories that link emotion with strong belief and hence claim that individuals are able to modify their emotions by virtue of a change in their beliefs. In contrast, James offers a different view of emotion, drawing upon the work of Teresa Brennan (2004), to argue that emotion is not purely internal to the particular individual who feels the emotion; that it can be transmitted by others, for example by a reaction to the smell of fear (see also James 2007). James highlights the fact that our emotions are manifestations of the way we experience our relationship with both our environment and self, drawing from Spinoza (James 2006, 243). This is interesting for two reasons. Firstly, it informs discussions about the way in which the self is understood because, in this example, the self cannot be viewed as separated from others by clear boundaries. It therefore resonates with the feminist criticisms of the "bounded self" and different approaches to autonomy, which I discuss in the final chapter. Secondly, James draws out the political implications of the cognitivist theory of emotions to argue that it fits within liberalism in that it draws upon an image of the autonomous subject that is able to change emotions through a change in beliefs. This analysis fits within her re-valuation of imagination in Spinoza as a way to think about social change.

In an interview conducted by James of Lloyd and Gatens (James, Lloyd, and Gatens 2000) they discuss the imagination in Spinoza. Gatens refers to the problem of the way in which judges imagine women, particularly in rape cases and states that,

> In the way we live at present everyone is seen as free and equal, but at the same time people have imaginaries and ideas about the relations between the sexes that place some people in subordinate positions. These imaginaries have become embodied in our ways of life and our institutions and are a great support to sexist and racist practices (Gatens in James, Lloyd, and Gatens 2000, 52–53).

They do not suggest that the solution to this problem would come from an appeal to reason to understand these images and their associated passions. Instead, they argue that there is a need for an intervention at the level of the imagination; for "better and more constructive fictions" (Lloyd in James, Lloyd, and Gatens 2000, 53). To expand upon this development of Spinoza's imagination I will turn to Gatens and Lloyd (1999).

Gatens and Lloyd point out that, for Spinoza, the imagination is necessary for human flourishing but is also associated with "debilitating illusions" (Gatens and Lloyd 1999, 34). They divide Spinoza's concept of the imagination into three types. Firstly, he describes the way that the human body is disposed to make particular mistakes (for example, the sun appears to be close by). This continues to be the case even after the truth is known. This illusionary imagining can co-exist with our knowledge of the truth because of the materiality of the imagination. It tells us the state of our body and the bodies that impinge upon us – such as the sun. Hence, as mentioned above, there is not a positive error in the imagination, which reflects the state of our body of which it is the idea. Error occurs as a result of lack of knowledge, which can be supplied by reason, i.e. by working out why our body is affected in particular ways. The illusion of free will is another example. Spinoza argues that people assume that the reason they take a course of action is because they will it. This demonstrates ignorance of the actual cause of the action.

Secondly, there are more pernicious mistakes, the "illusions of the multitude" (Gatens and Lloyd 1999, 37), which may be encouraged by those in authority in order to exploit others. This category appears to be what Gatens has in mind when she describes the imagination in Spinoza as doing the work of the concept of "ideology", save that her reading of him provides a richer analysis of the imagination as constituting bodily knowledge that remains after an understanding of the situation is known (James, Lloyd, and Gatens 2000, 56). The belief in divine will is another example of such an "organising fiction" for Spinoza because it is associated with attempts to dominate through the manipulation of hope and fear.

Thirdly, Gatens and Lloyd describe Spinoza as employing the term imagination to replace these fictions with,

> new fictions which better serve the effort to persist in being, individually and collectively, as thriving unities of mind and body (Gatens and Lloyd 1999, 38).

In common with James, Gatens and Lloyd's reading of Spinoza is productive. They stress the imagination (and the hope of producing better fictions) rather than Spinoza's concern that we move to a greater understanding, from inadequate to adequate forms of knowledge, which, I think, is a more obvious reading. Gatens and Lloyd also support their position with their analysis of the final section of the *Ethics* to argue that the imagination can be used to help us to understand something complex and that it is employed in this way by Spinoza. I understand an example of this to be the way in which August Kekulé claimed to discover the structure of the benzene ring after having a dream in which the carbon atoms became a snake swallowing its own tail. The image prompted the leap of understanding. Similarly, the way in which Hampton describes philosophers as employing images or pictures could be viewed as such an example. The image of "property in the person" illustrates Gatens and Lloyd's point that some fictions may be debilitating fictions rather than ones that prompts actual understanding.

This useful analysis of imagination need not play down the role of reason through which we decide which are debilitating fictions and which are not. As well as altering the way in which the imagination is considered it is also possible to employ Spinoza to think differently about the use of reason or understanding in a way that draws it closer to the imagination, as being employed by embodied individuals to understand their encounters in the world. This intersects with some work carried out by contemporary philosophers of cognition. For a discussion of the way in which cognition should be viewed as "not simply in the head" but as bodily see, for example, Clark and Chalmers (1998). As discussed in the second section, our concepts can be viewed as being composed of different "component concepts" that have a history and are employed to address different problems. In addition, as Gatens and Lloyd rightly point out, reason in this model is "an immanent achievement of human collective endeavour" (Gatens and Lloyd 1999, 127).[7]

Interestingly, in contrast to James' (1996) argument that, for Spinoza, the pursuit of freedom, and hence the use of rationality, in civil society would be related to a move towards individuals becoming similar, Gatens and Lloyd argue that reason as a collective endeavour of understanding can prompt a different reading. Such collective attempts at understanding can produce,

> collective transformations of previous identities rather than the exclusion of or overcoming of difference (Gatens and Lloyd 1999, 127).

Spinoza's Concept of the Individual, Civil Society and Other Bodies

Rice (1990) argues that supporters of the literalist view of the state as one body (with its own *conatus*) would have to show a scientific theory that would explain it at the level of "laws of society / politics". Further, he claims that Spinoza did not believe in this view and was correct. He therefore agrees with Den Uyl's methodological individualism. The failure of any "laws of politics" is clearly argued and so it is useful to address this question by exploring instances when such an analysis at a level greater than the individual seems warranted. We know in nature that there are organisms, such as slime-moulds, that are able to exist as individuals and then, when triggered by scarcity of food, come together to form one different organism. If Rice's question is whether this sort of analysis literally holds for humans then he is right but this seems to set the bar too high. It may be that there is a continuum of degrees to collectivity or that at different points in history there is greater individualism (in the sense in which it is meant here, i.e. that in understanding social phenomena the individual is the right level of analysis, in contrast with mere selfishness). It should be noted that as a libertarian, Rice's concern may be a support for "advocacy individualism" but this is irrelevant because the issue under discussion is the separate issue of atomism-holism (to employ Taylor's terms, outlined above).

7 There is a "bridge" between this important move and shifts in the way in which Kant is being reread to think about collective reason by, for example, O'Neill (1989).

The ways in which individualism gives way to an analysis of a collectivity appears within psychology and sociology literature, as well as being heavily debated in political theory. Some possible contenders as examples of when an analysis of the individual seems to be inadequate are: institutional racism in the police, the results of the Milgram and the Zimbardo experiments, in which individuals react in a particular way as a result of authority, group think, and hysteria in crowds. There are also self-conscious attempts to team build within military or other institutions, trust games or hazing. It may be that at different times in history people have had stronger, less transient, bonds with others. Taylor (1997) for example, gives examples of shared republican values that he views as of continued validity. Similarly, the work of Durkheim focuses upon tracing aspects of collective identity and "social facts" that he argues cannot be analysed at an individual level, such as collective views of "the sacred" as opposed to the profane (Durkheim 2008). For a short general discussion of methodological individualism, see also (Lukes 2006, 94–101).

Blocking any analysis that goes beyond the individual rules out some important questions: how to increase support for individual judgement in the face of group think, crowd hysteria or a family determined to dictate to women how they live their lives, whose aim is to discourage epistemological and moral individualism, which can be systematically undermined. This scenario traditionally evokes an image of free will – associated with a Kantian "hero" who can employ reason and hence duty in the face of external pressure (see chapter 6). This model is denied in Spinoza's use of reason. Before explaining this point, it is clear that it is easier for such women to stand up against oppression with the help of others who are similarly positioned. Hence, in this situation autonomy can be viewed not as the ability of an individual to isolate herself but as something that can be facilitated in concert with others, to be discussed in chapter 7. This is clearer in the Spinozan model in which there is no image of isolation against an outside.

There are times when it is useful for us, as individuals, to recognise a level of analysis that is greater than the individual when trying to attribute cause to particular interactions. For example, women who are subject to sexual harassment are faced with situations which make them uncomfortable. In Spinozan terms, this is a sad encounter and the aim of reason is to work out why it has occurred. Women in such a situation commonly question whether they are to blame. Therefore, it comes as some relief to know that their reactions are common (and that they do have a legal cause of action). This knowledge that others have been in the same situation and reacted similarly goes beyond viewing the situation from the position of two individuals. It is not enough to blame an individual because this act only has meaning within a particular culture at a particular time. To blame the individual man alone would demonstrate a failure to understand the historical and cultural meaning of sexual harassment and the way in which the term itself was brought into existence as a way of fighting against women's subordination. When a woman understands the reason for her sadness or anger at being harassed, the rational explanation goes beyond that of the individual harasser to a cultural and historical analysis.

Gatens employs the literalist interpretation of Spinoza: that the body of the state is understood like any other body, including the human body, to be made up of parts, which are held in a characteristic relationship to each other. If this characteristic relationship is destroyed then so is the body. It is possible to think of other bodies from this perspective to ask how they are made up of parts that react in harmony or disharmony with the world of which they are a part. This includes not only the individual and the state but also the family and different family forms. For example, Gatens (1995, 143) asks what impact it would have on the family if one of its members is thwarted in her ambitions because of sexism. As discussed above, Spinoza opens the way to questioning how some associations of bodies, such as family and state, change as a result of change in their component parts in a way that does not assume that freedom for some decreases freedom for others.

The social contract is itself a creation of the imagination – a way of thinking about how we should envisage the individual and social life. As discussed in previous chapters, Pateman has argued that the fiction is linked with that of property in the person as a way of justifying subordination. An alternative conception is therefore required. This can be viewed as an act of collective imagination, but I would also point out that, for Spinoza, this also involves an act of collective reasoning, not in the sense of employing a faculty or a context-transcendent view of reason but as an attempt to understand why certain encounters are sad and joyful so as to move from passivity to activity. Whilst there is much exciting work that involves rethinking the imagination, an associated move is to think about the meaning of what it is to use reason. Spinoza's view of reason offers an approach that is not simply "instrumental rationality". The way in which rationality is rethought in Spinoza is incompatible with the way in which Hobbes starts with an account of the individual rather than with a way in which the process of becoming an individual occurs.

A corollary of this is that, for women, whose interests are so often subsumed within the family, to be treated as "an individual" may be a positive move. However, it is important to recognise the ambiguity of this term "individual" and to untangle the many different ways in which it is employed, as illustrated by, for example, Steven Lukes' useful analysis (Lukes 2006). As I will explore in other chapters, the abstraction of the individual who has "free will" and certain fictions, including the "property in the person" have been employed to justify subordination. The term is also linked with economic liberalism in ways that make it a problematic term, given that freedom of the working class is decreased by the effects of "freedom of contract" (Cohen 1995). It is necessary to recognise these arguments can become entwined with (and can trade upon) more positive views of the individual, as having legal rights as a person and as independence of judgement, termed "epistemological/moral individualism" above. It should also be recognised that such autonomy can be helped by social movements such as feminism. References to "the individual" appear to carry with them the (wrong) idea that the alternative of being under undue influence is to judge in isolation. This also draws upon an image of the self as maintaining autonomy by maintaining its boundaries, by standing apart from others. This is a common view of the self employed by Hobbes, Locke and Kant to be discussed in the final chapter. The next chapter will look in more detail at the fiction of property in the person and its political impact.

Chapter 4
Locke

Introduction

In contrast to Hobbes' strictly individualist image of humanity in the state of nature, Locke envisages a state in which property rights and commerce can develop and in which humans live in families with a male head of household. Locke read anthropological reports extensively and Laslett, in his introduction to the *Two Treatises of Government* (Locke 1999, 99) concludes that Locke was therefore aware that the evidence did not support his description of the state of nature. Nevertheless, he argues that Locke's position was that, whilst there was no evidence that humans lived peacefully in a state of nature, nevertheless such an assumption was not impossible. Further, what was known of life outside of states with laws did not support the Hobbesian assumption that they lived in a state of war (Laslett 1999, 99).

Locke's description of the state of nature, whilst not being a state of war, has the disadvantage that all individuals are able to judge if they have been wronged and to take action accordingly. This means that without an independent judge, it is difficult for them not to be biased and to extract too much compensation from the offending party (Locke 1999, 275). Importantly, for Locke, laws were required for the preservation of property, defined broadly as "lives, liberties and estates"[1] (Locke 1999, 350). As in Hobbes' account of the state of nature, humans (or possibly only propertied men, in the case of Locke, to be discussed below) are rational and therefore able to enter into a social contract. The way in which one family form is treated as natural, along with the way power within the family came to be defined against "the political", thereby removing issues of women's oppression from political analysis, will be discussed. I will start by examining Locke through the lens of Macpherson. Macpherson's interpretation of Locke has been described as providing the unwritten engagement of Marx with Locke (Mansfield 1979). Whilst it has been subject to much criticism (Miller 1982; for an assessment, see for example Tully 1993, 71–95), it is considered in detail here because of the importance of Macpherson's analysis of Lockean "property in the person" in relation to aspects of Pateman's analysis. I will draw out this element of Macpherson's work in order to situate Pateman's arguments.

---

1 Property is defined in its narrow sense of material possessions in the chapter "Of Property" (Locke 1999, 285–302). For Macpherson's understanding of this inconsistency, see below.

Tully (1993) argues that the conceptual basis for a "market society" had not emerged by the time Locke was writing because work was allocated by government rather than by the market. However, Pateman (2002, 30) indicates that her theoretical position does not rest upon this point. What is important is that,

> the existence of a "capitalist" economy becomes a widely accepted "fact", and the institution of employment is central to this economy (Pateman 2002, 30).

Similarly, I want to focus upon Macpherson's arguments regarding Locke's limitations on property and upon the associated conception of self rather than discussing arguments regarding the "Macpherson thesis" and its historical appropriateness more generally. Tully argues that Macpherson wrongly claims that Locke's "property in the person" (or as Macpherson describes this: "possessive individualism") is an economic issue. Here, I agree with (and want to illustrate and develop) Pateman's argument that the fiction of property in the person is a political issue. Locke refers to property to make a political claim about the rights of owners, an idea which is required to justify subordination in the workplace (Pateman 2002, 30).

Pateman (2002) continues this analysis of Locke when she points to the contradiction between the ideals of democratic citizenship and the absence of workplace democracy based upon a conception of the individual as self-owner, holder of "property in the person". The fact that most people do not have a say in the decisions which affect their working lives appears normal and inevitable when it is assumed that someone's labour power is sold for a wage. They can then be given "reasonable orders" (as implied into current common law employment contracts) for a duration specified in the contract (now limited also by legislation in the EU, for example) rather than being viewed as a participant in decision-making. Importantly, in *The Sexual Contract* Pateman illustrates how such a (broadly) Marxist analysis of the employment contract is only part of the story, which she supplements with the history of the marriage contract. The marriage contract develops alongside the employment contract, both of which presume each other, with the idea of the family wage paid to a man who has authority over a housewife. These contractual relations were presumed by the welfare state.

There are also similarities in the actual method of analysis employed by Macpherson and by Pateman. Both recognise points of tension in Locke when viewed from the position of working class and women, respectively, and both highlight these by rereading Locke's story of the social contract, focusing upon where points of tension arise. This involves making suggestions as to how Locke's social contract can be reread when the weak points of class and gender are brought to light. Both recognise that the story of the social contract is a fiction, of course. This rereading is carried out to illuminate the otherwise hidden presumptions about class and gender and not to take seriously Locke's social contract as a historical fact. However, both also analyse the meaning of actual contracts that produce subordination: employment contracts in the case of Macpherson, with Pateman adding in the historically important missing marriage contract and relating both employment and marriage contracts to each other and to citizenship.

After outlining the readings of Locke offered by Macpherson and then Pateman, I will extend her analysis of property in the person by outlining Okin's reading of Nozick on slavery. I will then assess criticisms of Pateman's arguments, particularly with regard to the way in which the self or individual is envisaged and apply her work to consider the way in which workmanship plays a role in Locke's thought.

Locke's Social Contract: Macpherson's Critique

Macpherson's argument on Locke is summarised in his comment that,

> Locke's astonishing achievement was to base the property right on natural right and natural law, and then to remove all the natural law limits from the property right (Macpherson 1962, 199).

In other words, it is Macpherson's argument that Locke starts with the idea that, in the state of nature, men (males)[2] are reasonable and, with some exceptions to be discussed below, able to obey natural law. This meant that there were limitations upon the acquisition of land based upon rules that came from God's will and the ability to reason that he implanted into men. Locke starts by examining these natural laws and, whilst he does not argue against them, he ends up circumventing them, thereby providing arguments for the removal of medieval constrains upon the emerging market of his own day.

There are two natural limitations in the use of land and resources in Locke's analysis of property in the *Second Treatise*: the spoilage limitation and the sufficiency limitation. In addition, Macpherson discusses the "supposed" labour limitation, to argue that this turns out not to be a genuine limitation at all. I will take these in turn. Firstly, Locke argues that there is a natural law that God given resources should not go to waste. It is against natural law to hoard food that will spoil, thereby depriving others of it. This argument was used in the eighteenth century to argue that the poor had rights to subsistence (Ashcraft 1995). Locke also argues, for example, that there is a claim on the spoils of war by women and children who would otherwise starve (Locke 1999, sec. 183).

---

2 The use of the term "men" renders the text unclear as to whether women are included in the analysis and the issue will detract from Macpherson's arguments about class, which ignore women. I will use the term men meaning only males and discuss women's potential inclusion in the section on Pateman's analysis onwards. There has been some academic debate about the question of whether Locke viewed women as rational, to be discussed below.

However, Locke manages to narrow the application of this limitation. He points out that money does not rot. So, once money is introduced into society, its accumulation does not present the same problem. Locke is concerned about the waste of resources, particularly when others are in need, and not with accumulation, *per se*. Macpherson (1962, 208) provides textual support to maintain that Locke is sympathetic to this accumulation of money, not for the sake of hoarding or the purchase of more gratifying commodities, but to be used as capital. He points out that Locke's abstraction, of the way men behaved in his own civil society that is applied to his story of the state of nature, includes the idea that both money and commerce could occur before the transition into civil society, as illustrated by the passage:

> This partage of things, in an inequality of private possessions, men have made practicable, *out of the bonds of Societie and without compact*, only by putting a value on gold and silver and tacitly agreeing in the use of Money (Macpherson 1962, 209 citing Locke's Second Treatise, s50; italics added by Macpherson).

So, for Locke, in a state of nature, men are viewed as free, equal and rational. Unlike Hobbes' image of all individuals, these men are able to consent to the use of money and to adhere to commercial contracts. This makes possible the accumulation of money in a state of nature, without breaching the spoilage limitation.

Secondly, Locke supports (but then renders irrelevant) the natural limitation that land should only be appropriated if it is possible to leave "enough and as good" for others. He claims that, in his time, this was still the case, given the existence of uncultivated land in America. However, this is not his main argument, which is detailed at section 47:[3]

> To which let me add, that he who appropriates land to himself by his labour, does not lessen but increase the common stock of mankind. For the provisions serving to the support of humane life, produced by one acre of inclosed and cultivated land, are (to speak much within compasse) ten times more, than those, which are yielded by an acre of Land, of an equal richnesse, lying waste in common (Locke 1999, 294).

This is a reference to the *Enclosure Acts* of the time in England, which deprived anyone of feudal rights below that of copyhold (a type of tenure), thereby criminalising many of those without property who continued to use their feudal rights over the land (Thompson 1977). In other words, Locke argues that the

3 Macpherson (1962, 211) complains that this section, representing an amendment by Locke in the fourth edition of the *Two Treatise* (1713) was excluded from recent editions when he was writing. Given the importance of Macpherson's arguments it is unsurprising that this appears in later editions (Locke 1999, 211).

natural limitation – that land can only be appropriated if "enough and as good" is left for others – no longer applies as soon as the greater cultivation of land makes up for this loss. The proviso does not apply where cultivation of land allows for higher standards of living for those without land, than would otherwise have been the case. In amending this limitation, Locke assumes that the products of this cultivation will be distributed. This is clear when he argues that English labourers, living at subsistence levels, are better off than in areas where there is no such extra cultivation (Locke 1999, 297; discussed by Macpherson 1962, 212). In addition, Macpherson (1962, 215) argues that Locke assumes tacit agreement for the overriding of this proviso as a consequence of the tacit agreement as to the introduction of money.

The final "supposed" labour limitation discussed by Macpherson is particularly relevant to Pateman's analysis, in that it concerns the wage relationship. In contrast with Filmer (1991) who argued that God had given the earth to Adam and that its ownership was then inherited, Locke argues that, in the state of nature, men (males) were equal and land was held in common. He then examined what could justify the removal of land without the consent of others. He relies upon a theologically-based argument that God would not have wanted humans to starve. Food must be eaten before it can support his life and whoever has eaten it can be viewed as owning it. It is at this point that he views the relationship of ownership as one of a relationship between subject (the individual) and object (the food) rather than a way of ordering social relations. Reasoning backwards from the point at which the food has been consumed and, in his view, is therefore owned in a state of nature, Locke asks at which point this food actually starts to belong to that individual. Famously, he concludes that,

> Though the Earth, and all inferior Creatures be common to all Men, yet every man has a *Property* in his own *Person*. This nobody has any Right to but himself. The *Labour* of his Body, and the *Work* of his hands, we may say, are properly his. Whatsoever he removes out of the State that Nature hath provided, and left some in, he hath mixed his Labour with, and joined to it something that is his own, and thereby makes it his Property (Locke 1999, 288).

This initially appears to appeal to a third natural limitation on the appropriation of property: that someone owns what he alone has worked upon. However, Locke then states,

> this Labour being the unquestionable Property of the labourer, no Man but he can have a right to what that is once joyned to (Locke 1999, 288).

As Macpherson (1962, 214–215) points out, this reference to labour as "property of the labourer" is consistent with waged labour because it treats labour as a type of property and hence something that can be alienated. Therefore, Locke is not setting up a limitation that property ownership depends upon the property owner actually doing the work him/her self. Property owners merely have to *own* the labour of another, such as their servant or slave. This is clear in the following paragraph in which Locke assumes that the product of someone's labour belongs to the person who owns that labour (either fully as in the case of a horse – which would be akin to a slave – or for a limited time as governed by contract in the case of a servant):

> Thus the Grass my Horse has bit; the Turfs my servant has cut; and the Ore I have digg'd in any place where I have a right to them in common with others, become my Property, without the assignment or consent of any body (Locke 1999, 289).

Macpherson (1962, 220) compares the position of the worker (the servant) and that of a slave. He points out that Locke differentiates between labour, which can be alienated (and hence, the products of "my servant's" work "become my property"), and someone's life, which is owned by God and therefore cannot be alienated. Macpherson attributes this view of slavery to Locke's continued adherence to medieval values, which Locke abandons (or rather reworks) with regard to the property limitations discussed above. In "Of Slavery" in the *Second Treatise*, Locke (1999, 283–285) argues that workers cannot sell themselves into slavery, which involves giving away the right of life and death over themselves, because they cannot enter into a contractual exchange of what they do not own. Their life is owned by God whose "workmanship" they are (i.e. whose labour went into making them) and therefore can only be ended "at his pleasure". However, Locke did justify slavery on the basis of a just war and was instrumental in drafting the "Instructions to Governor Nicholson of Virginia" in 1689, which justifies US slavery on the basis of a just war by the Royal African Company (Locke 1999, 284).

Laslett (1999, 101) refers to the "almost contradictory" move made by Locke in that men are viewed as owning their own attributes and yet, men (presumably including their attributes) can also be viewed as being owned by God.[4] Whilst Macpherson does not discuss this specific point regarding ownership of attributes, he does say that it is odd that Locke should assert a natural right to alienate labour but not life (Macpherson 1962, 219). Applying Macpherson's general approach, it is possible to speculate that what lies behind this point of tension in the text reflects an unresolved conflict in Locke's position, as he shifts away from medieval limitations with regard to labour (allowing men to own and alienate the fictional

4 This analogy between the workmanship of God and of man, linked with ownership is also subject to critique by (Murphy 1992), which I will discuss further below. As the term "men" is used it is difficult to unpick which aspects apply to women, which will detract from the argument. Presumably God also owns women but there is a question regarding whether married women could be viewed as owning their "property in the person". Laslett's use of the term "men" indicates that he was not focused upon the issue.

"property in the person") but not with regard to slavery (in which God owns men as a result of his workmanship).

Locke's argument appeals to the idea that individuals should be allowed to keep what they have worked for, providing others are not worse off, which is to be guaranteed by the other limitations. However, the assumption regarding the ownership of "my servant's work", forces us to evaluate the social assumptions that lie in the background of Locke's argument, including the way in which the fiction of "property in the person" is used to then justify wage labour. The workmanship analogy between individuals and God does not really fit, given that the Christian image of God envisages him producing the universe *ab initio*, rather than by shaping existing materials. Murphy (1992) argues that, with regard to God's workmanship, Locke's model owes more to Plato than to Christianity. Plato describes the universe as having been created by incorporating eternally given forms into eternally given matter (For an exploration of the way in which the form/matter distinction is gendered in Plato see Cavarero 1995.) Murphy (1992, 321) comments that the closest thing there is to such creation occurs within reproduction because parents do not simply inform matter but create it anew. This adds a twist to Okin's arguments regarding the impact of adding women into the analysis of Nozick's reading of Locke, to be discussed in the next section.

Nozick (1974, 175) asks why mixing something you own with something you do not own necessarily confers ownership. He gives the example that mixing tomato juice with the sea does not result in ownership of the sea but merely wastes the tomato juice. Irrespective of Nozick's further arguments, the example brings out the point that Locke's claim appears to describe something metaphysical (i.e. the relationship between a subject acting upon an object in some way that expresses their rights in concrete form). Instead, it should be recognised that property ownership is a legal fiction; a form of regulating social relations.

There is another example, this time from contemporary US legal case law, (*John Moore v. The Regents of the University of California*[5]) that illustrates this point because it entails a separation between: (1) an ownership claim derived from something being part of the body (Locke's starting position); against (2) an alternative claim that ownership should depend upon labour (Locke's final position). Moore had hairy cell leukaemia and his doctors removed body parts, which they worked upon to produce a (medically beneficial and lucrative) scientific discovery. To protect this they patented his cell line. The courts' view was that he did not have ownership rights in the cells after they had been removed from the body.[6] This had the effect of ruling that it was the labour of those who had worked

5 *John Moore v. The Regents of the University of California* (51 Cal. 3d 120; 271 Cal. Rptr. 146; 793 P.2d 479) – Supreme Court of California case settled on July 9, 1990.

6 A further issue in the case, which is not relevant to the way in which this case is employed as an example of the separation between ownership of parts of the body and of work, is that Moore's informed consent should have been sought for the removal of his

on the discovery and not the supposed "ownership" of the body part that should be rewarded.

Macpherson argues that Locke's description of the state of nature starts with natural equality between men (males) but then divides men into those with property and those without, thereby reading back into the state of nature, the assumptions of Locke's own society. In a move that is familiar in feminist theory, Macpherson points to the tensions and outright contradictions in Locke's work, as it strains to deal with different images of men that are dependent upon class. For example, Locke is inconsistent about the extent to which the state of nature is initially defined as peaceful. He describes the vast majority as rational and able to obey natural law (Locke 1999, sec. 6). However, Macpherson (1962, 240) argues that, in other passages, Locke describes a state of nature that is more akin to a Hobbesian state of war precipitating the need for the social contract (Locke 1999, sec 123).

Macpherson explains this ambiguity by arguing that Locke had in mind two different images of the state of nature, which occurred in succession: one in which all men are undifferentiated, and the other as containing two classes of men, differentiated by their levels of rationality. This rationality is based upon whether or not they are "industrious and rational" property owners. Macpherson argues that this rereading of Locke's story makes sense of Locke's discrepancy. The existence of the two classes of men can be viewed as occurring in a later stage in the state of nature when all the land in an area has been appropriated and some (the less rational) are without land. Pateman refers to this view of different rationalities depending upon class as perhaps Macpherson's most contentious claim (Pateman 1979, 75). She points out that all men are viewed as rational enough to govern their families.[7]

So, Macpherson's reading of Locke's story – which can be viewed as employing a similar method to Pateman's later rereading – illustrates Locke's political presumptions by tracing a weak point in the framework and using it to explain ambiguities within the text. In this example, he traces how Locke envisages differences in rationality as appearing in the state of nature, resulting from different economic positions that develop as a result of the appropriation of land. This in turn is transferred into civil society (Macpherson 1962, 246). He supports this interpretation with textual analysis including Locke's comments

spleen, which should have included an explanation of the doctors' interest in removing it for the purpose of research.

7 Locke does not state that women are not rational. Nevertheless, married women could not be "industrious and rational" property owners under the common law doctrine of coverture. There has been some debate around Locke's "ambiguity" on this issue (Hirschmann and McClure 2007, 165–174). Butler (1978) concludes that he views women as capable of reason and entitled to an (almost) equal education. For a summary see (Hirschmann 2007, 165–174) who concludes that, for Locke, women and the poor were less rational as a result of culture but had the capacity for reason.

about those individuals without property, which clearly do not envisage them as rational political actors within civil society.

Leaving aside the question of rationality, which has been used to justify subordination generally, there is a further interesting analogy between the treatment of the non-property holders and women in Macpherson's reading of Locke. Macpherson (1962, 249) points to an ambiguity in Locke's view of which members of society are parties to the hypothetical social contract. This explains the fact that Locke sometimes uses the term "property" to include "life, liberty and estate" and sometimes he means only land and goods. Locke employs this ambiguity in his arguments that non-property owners should be bound by the social contract but that only men with property were viewed as incorporating themselves through express agreement as full members of society in order to protect property. As a result of his reading of Locke, Macpherson is able to conclude that,

> The greatness of seventeenth century liberalism was its assertion of the free rational individual as the criterion of the good society; its tragedy was that this very assertion was necessarily a denial of individualism to half the nation (1962, 262).

The "half the nation" to whom he refers are those men without property, not women, an analysis that is corrected by Pateman, along with further feminist critique of the meaning of the "free rational individual". I will start by illustrating the implications of Pateman's work by looking at her description of the potential ways in which the fiction of property in the person could be employed and then turn to her broader approach to Locke.

Pateman: Undemocratic Implications of Locke's "Property in the Person"

Pateman argues that, when it came to women, Locke closes the door to feminists that was left open by Hobbes' rigorous individualism (see also Okin 1989). As discussed above, when Locke treats male domination within the family as natural rather than constructed, he divides "political power" from "power within the family", thereby allowing both political theorists and popular culture to marginalise women's subordination as non-political. This move was also associated with a conception of power that views it as an operation of the sovereign through laws and ignores everyday subordination in the workplace and home. Given that Locke's arguments mark such a separation between the public political power of government and the private natural hierarchy in the home, it may appear that he has no need of any reliance upon a marriage contract. If marriage simply represents women's natural status why should women's agreement be necessary? However, his position is more progressive than this. An analogy can be drawn between: 1) feudal status and forced marriage, in which there is no choice; and 2) between employment in which there is a choice of employer (but working for someone in a hierarchical relationship is necessarily) and a hierarchical marriage in which there is a choice over the husband. As Pateman recognises, to see Locke in such terms as (1) would be to miss the importance of contract for him and hence of women's consent to marriage. As she illustrates, this consent is paradoxical because women's consent to marriage is necessary and yet, under the doctrine of coverture, it took away further rights. Locke clearly does not advocate forced marriage and is also progressive in arguing for the right of women to divorce. Locke states that,

> Conjugal society is made by a voluntary Compact between Man and Woman; and tho it consist chiefly in such a Communion and Right in one anothers Bodies, as is necessary to its chief End, Procreation; yet it draws with it mutual Support, Assistance, and a Common Interest too, as necessary not only to unite their Care and Affection, but also necessary to their common offspring, who have a Right to be nourished and maintained by them, till they are able to provide for themselves (Locke 1999, 319).

Locke then goes on to argue that this bond lasts longer than in other animals, which allows the couple through "their Industry" to "lay up Goods for their common Issue" (Locke 1999, 320). However, once the inheritance is secure, Locke argues that the marriage should last whilst it is needed to support children but then allows the possibly of divorce, instigated by either party. This argument for the right of women to divorce "where Natural right or their Contract allows it" (Locke 1999, sec. 82) is pro-feminist but Locke also makes clear that men, "the abler and the stronger" (Locke 1999, sec. 82), have the right to make decisions about joint property. In addition, the contract, rather than natural right, can be used to decide whether the children fall to the father or "mother's lot" (Locke 1999, 321). Pateman recognises this liberatory potential in contractarians' insistence on the consent of weaker parties, whilst showing the ways in which consent is treated as problematic. For example, women's "no" is too often understood as "yes" within rape cases and individuals are deemed to consent to an undemocratic arrangement when they enter into employment contract. (For an overview of all her work in this area, see Pateman 2008.)

As well as showing the limits of husband's control over their wives, Locke then goes on to discuss the limits of the father's power with regard to other family members who include children, servants and slaves. Pateman (1988) differentiates between these subordinate positions and the way in which they change historically. Whilst Locke talks about the exchange of "Communion and Right in one anothers bodies", the traditional wife can be viewed as exchanging continuous labour within the home for "protection" or financial support. This labour is unlimited and historically she did not have the same status as a citizen. In contrast, a male servant/employee gained civil recognition earlier and had the number of hours labour limited by contract but – as a result of the Lockean fiction of property in the person – did not have any say in decision-making processes in the workplace.

One of the questions that Mills raises with Pateman is that,

> It seems to me that you are working with a hybrid concept that is drawing on two different and conflicting strains of contract theory: property in the person as foundational, which is Lockean, and morally unconstrained freedom to make all kinds of property transactions, which is more Hobbesian. That's why I am unsure that property in the person necessarily has all the pernicious consequences you are attributing to it (Pateman and Mills 2007, 19).[8]

Mills is relying upon the natural law limitations that Locke provides, but which, as just discussed, he is able to overcome. The exception to this is the example of slavery but the reason that Locke gives for arguing against someone's ability to sell him/herself into slavery does not derive from the internal logic of the fiction of property in the person. As discussed above, it derives from Locke's view of God. Pateman (2007, 20) refers to her earlier paper, Pateman (2002), in response to Mills' question and I will look at this in detail. She is criticising libertarians, particularly Nozick, who follows Locke's conceptual framework, because she is attacking the employment of property in the person which is used to justify subordination. In this framework, coerced slavery is wrong but any contractual exchange of the fiction of property in the person is acceptable, including civil slavery (i.e. by contract).

Pateman (2002) demonstrates that there is potential for different degrees of acceptance of the fiction of property in the person, only one of which assumes a society in which there is "contract all the way down". Pateman (2002, 31) in an engagement with Tully (1993), considers three possible scenarios that could develop in societies, depending upon the way in which laws regulated the use of the Lockean conception of "property in the person", the fiction that one's abilities, such as labour power, could be treated as a commodity that can be separated from the body. If a society were to treat all aspects of humanity as capable of alienation then all human rights and abilities could be subject to contract. It would be legal to sell oneself into slavery or to sell the right to vote for example. Against Tully (1993), this example makes it clear that the fiction of property in the person impacts upon political rights and cannot be separated off into an area described as merely "economic".[9] Tully (1993, 81) describes this as "absolutism" and Pateman (2002, 31) points out that "the outcome is not democratic but is voluntarily created" and that "libertarianism follows this direction".

The second possibility describes the current situation, which Pateman (2002, 31) describes as "constitutionalism", in which some aspects of property in the person (and hence some rights) are treated as alienable and some are not. Hence employment contracts are legal but not slavery contracts. Pateman returns to her central concern with freedom (and subordination) when she points out that

---

8 For the same point that is not pursued see Mills (2008, 54).

9 There is an analogy between the separation of public and private, which marginalises women's oppression as "non-political", and the separation between economic and political, which can serve to marginalise working class interests and workplace subordination.

this leads to the existence of democracy in the polity but not in the economy. The employment contract like the marriage contract, that she analyses elsewhere (Pateman 1988), becomes a distinctly modern form of managing subordination.

Pateman is not arguing that the subtleties of human interaction are dictated by the contract but that the "roles" themselves, that are formed by contract, position employees and housewives in such a way that they are exposed to the arbitrary decisions of others. As explained in the introduction, I write "role" in quotation marks to highlight the fact that the term "role" is an inadequate description of the way in which "who someone is" becomes defined by the term. Foucault captures this sense of "what it is to be a self" when he asks what it costs us to tell the truth about ourselves (for example Foucault 1977; 1990). In doing so, Foucault envisages a shift from the view of power as symbolised by the sovereign's sword to the way in which operations of power are intimately related to the creation of "who we are". This can be illustrated by the way that he describes the confessional, which allowed priests to ask for minute details of their congregation's sex lives, information which then allowed them to classify and hence reify particular "perversions". These terms could then be used to label and then produce ways of life. Individuals are not passive and can challenge the meaning of the terms in which we are defined, as illustrated by the way in which the term "queer" has been adopted as part of "queer politics" (Butler 1999). This challenge includes, amongst other tactics, tracing the genealogy and hence historical contingency of particular terms to show that their meaning is not fixed. For example, the implication of Pateman's analysis is that there would be greater equality if we were to get rid of both traditional housewives, to the extent to which they still exist since their peak from 1840–1970, and also, employees. By this I mean that these "roles" would be changed so that marriage or its equivalent would be equal (and she recognises the important shift that has already occurred in that husbands in the West have lost their legal rights over wives) and that workplaces would involve greater democracy. She is too pragmatic to argue that there should be a legal prohibition against contracts involving "property in the person", arguing that "blanket legal prohibitions on alienability are virtually guaranteed to be ineffective" (Pateman 2008, 240). Instead, she has argued for the more practical step of introducing a basic guaranteed income (Pateman 2003).

So, whilst Tully only envisages the two types of society that are detailed above, Pateman posits a third possibility: that of a society in which the fiction of property in the person that can be alienated is not allowed at all, the corollary being that all rights are viewed as inalienable. Employment relationships (and traditional marriage relationships) would be radically altered because this would impact upon any subordination – the aim being to produce a substantive participative democracy. The details may potentially be gleaned from Pateman's very early work *Participation and Democratic Theory* (Pateman 1970) in which she considers practical examples of attempts to engender workplace participation, which involve allowing workers to develop the skills and confidence to participate in decision-making. Further, this allows workers, not only to gain social skills, but also to understand the workings of social institutions, necessarily to participate in decision-making within a broader political arena. This analysis also accounts for Pateman's rejection of any pragmatic use of contract or contractual thought-experiments as tainted by the fiction of property in the person. I now want to draw out the implications of Pateman's potential society in which there is no restraint upon contract by looking at Okin's argument against this society.

Okin's Critique of Nozick on Locke

Nozick provides a very different reading of the implications of Locke's property in the person than that of Pateman, linked with the way in which freedom is central to both their work but is envisaged very differently. For Pateman, her positive view of freedom entails having the ability to be involved in decisions that affect your life, including the way in which you work. Her attack upon Lockean property in the person highlights areas in which subordination has occurred. In sharp contrast, Nozick's reading of Locke enables him to conclude that,

> The comparable question about an individual is whether a free system would allow him to sell himself into slavery. I believe that it would (Nozick 1974, 331).

Pateman makes plain that the reason that Nozick is able to view civil slavery as acceptable stems from his adoption of the framework of property in the person. As discussed, for libertarians, such as Nozick, to be coerced into slavery by violence would be wrong. However, if one is viewed as owning the rights to oneself (standing in relation to oneself as a master to a slave in a slave owning society) then one of these rights is the ability to sell oneself into slavery through contract (Cohen 1995, 68). As I pointed out above, there is nothing within the framework of "property in the person" that prevents this move, given that Locke relies upon concerns about slavery being tantamount to suicide (which is inconsistent with God's ownership of humans) and does not derive this from property in the person.

In an analysis that is consistent with that of Pateman, Okin (1989) illustrates the way in which Nozick's reading of Locke depends upon a blindness to the position of women. When she looks at his definition of ownership and includes women in the picture his position is "reduced to absurdity" (Okin 1989, 75). Nozick starts with Locke's fiction of property in the person (and ownership of their abilities) to argue that individuals should be able to keep the products of their labour. He argues that things are not simply brought into the world without ties of ownership; they are the products of someone's labour. He then argues that, provided the "set of holdings is properly generated" then the state does not have the right to reallocate this in taxation, even to help someone in much greater need (Nozick 1974, 230). Government's minimal role is only to protect people from each other and from invasion.

Okin cites the following comment from Nozick as the clearest summary of his position:

> Whoever makes something, having bought or contracted for all other held resources used in the process (transferring some of his holdings for these cooperating factors), is entitled to it. The situation is *not* one of something's being made and there being an open question of who is to get it. Things come into the world already attached to people having entitlements over them (Nozick 1974, 160; discussed in Okin 1989, 78).

Nozick is clear that, whatever people's natural assets are, they are entitled to them and to what flows from them (Nozick 1974, 225–226). Okin therefore argues that, applying Nozick's definitions, mothers can be viewed as owning their children. They produce them from their own abilities, legitimately transferring the sperm that is required, usually by gift. Unlike Locke's concerns about the suicidal nature of the slave contract, Nozick is clear that slave contracts are valid. There are no other definitions that make Okin's move inconsistent with Nozick's argument. He is clear that it is not necessary to understand fully and control the production of something in order to be able to claim ownership of it because this would preclude ownership of other products, such as trees. Nozick also raises the question as to why children are not viewed as being owned by their parents, who made them. In other words, he deals with Okin's argument but instead of recognising sperm as legitimately obtained and the child as the product of the mother's workmanship, he considers the parents as equally situated with regard to children.

Okin is not making a claim for matriarchal slavery, of course, but illustrating the way in which Nozick's argument, which follows the logic of Locke's property in the person to its logical conclusion, depends for its coherence upon the exclusion of the position of mothers. In an argument that is consistent with the Lockean view of workmanship and property in the person, Okin shows that there is a contradiction in assuming that individuals start by owning property in their person because, under Nozick's Lockean analysis, they start life by being owned by their mothers. It is an analysis that is consistent with both Macpherson and Pateman's critique of Locke's characterisation of the individual as owner of property in the person and of Murphy's attack upon the implications of Locke's workmanship model, to be discussed below.

Locke on Workmanship: An Application of Pateman's Approach to Locke

Pateman's analysis detailed above can be contrasted with the problems that ensue when Laslett grapples with Locke's meaning of "property in the person", within Locke's own terms. In his introduction to *Two Treatise of Government* Laslett footnotes a comment that,

> The conventional judgment of Locke's view of property, that it described a natural inalienable right, seems ... to be exactly wrong. Property is precisely that part of our attributes (or perhaps to be pedantic, that attribute of our attributes) which we can alienate, but only of course by our own consent (Laslett 1999, 103).

The first part is unproblematic in that Locke does view property as something that can be alienated (by being sold for example). In the rest of the discussion Laslett describes our attributes as "freedom, equality and the ability to execute the law of nature" (Laslett 1999, 103), which cannot actually be alienated, i.e. they cannot be separated from our bodies. They are treated as if they were alienable as a result of the Lockean fiction of property in the person. Whereas, as a result of medical intervention, parts of our bodies can be separated from us and sold, the idea of selling "freedom" is a fictional way of organising certain social relations.

This highlights a problem with the way in which Locke defines property inconsistently, sometimes including life, liberty and estate and at other times more narrowly as lands and goods. Laslett is discussing property in its broader sense. However, as outlined above, Locke does not view "life" as something that can be alienated (as it belongs to God) so his definition of property must be split because he only allows the alienation of other attributes, such as labour power for a time limited by the labour contract (unless someone has been enslaved in a just war, which is Locke's justification for slavery). Again, this ambiguity is consistent with Macpherson's argument that certain tensions in Locke's text arise because Locke maintained a medieval limitation with regard to slavery but is modern with regard to wage labour and the two conceptual frameworks do not fit easily together.

It is worth quoting Laslett in full to consider his position. Laslett says of Locke's view of property,

> Property moreover seems to give the political quality to personality. A slave lacks all political rights because he is incapable of property ...
>
> For property to Locke seems to symbolize rights in their concrete form, or perhaps rather to provide the tangible subject of an individual's powers and attitudes (sic).[10] *It is because they can be symbolized as property, something a man can conceive of as distinguishable from himself though a part of himself, that a man's attributes, such as his freedom, his equality, his power to execute the law of nature, can become the subject of his consent, the subject of any negotiation with his fellows.* We cannot alienate any part of our personalities, but

10 It is odd to claim that your attitudes – i.e. your perspective or beliefs – can really be changed by consent rather than persuasion in this context. For example, I cannot be employed to actually *believe* X is innocent even if I am paid to represent X in court. This makes more sense if it is a reference to "attributes" given that there is no supporting discussion of the claim or evidence that this was Locke's position.

> we can alienate that with which we have chosen to mix our personalities (Laslett 1999, 103). Italics added.

Laslett then footnotes to the comment cited above:

> The conventional judgment of Locke's view of property, that it described a natural, inalienable right, seems ... to be exactly wrong. Property is precisely that part of our attributes (or, perhaps to be pedantic, that attribute of our attributes) which we can alienate, but only of course by our own consent (Laslett 1999, 103).

Laslett is examining Locke's claims by thinking within Locke's own terms about "property in the person". So, one's freedom and equality can be viewed as something "distinguishable from himself although a part of himself". This goes further than the sentence in which Laslett registers the fictional nature of property in the person (that we cannot actually alienate our personalities). He says that we can alienate that with which we have mixed our personalities, which presumably would refer to the material products of work. However, in the sentence I have italicised, "freedom" is given as an example of an attribute that can be distinguished from a person, whilst also being part of him and which can be the subject of negotiation with others. In making this claim, Laslett goes further than Locke in opening the way to civil (i.e. contractual) slave contracts, still barred by Locke (who maintains natural limitation on the grounds of God's ownership of humans, discussed above).

Laslett, in his speculation within Locke's own position reifies the way in which attributes are described. Whilst it is true that we are able to use language in such a way that our attributes can be symbolised as property – or the idea that everything has its price – it is misleading to describe this as a specific "attribute of attributes", that allows them to be commodified. It depends upon language but also upon the existence of a social system in which this makes any sense. By analogy land becomes viewed as a commodity only at a certain point in time. This does not reflect a special property of land. Whilst it is possible to organise a society in which the fiction of property in the person is accepted this does not provide a sufficient argument that this should happen based upon a metaphysical assumption about the self.

Another way of expressing this point is to draw on Marx's argument that private property reflects social relations – my right to keep you out of my house, for example – and not the relationship between a subject and object. Part of Locke's discussion, in particular his discussion on workmanship, invites Laslett's analysis of the relationship between subject and object and the view of the self that classifies both its parts and attributes as commodities. This move is explored in Murphy's (1992) exchange with Shapiro (1992) in a manner which is consistent with, and complements, Pateman's approach.

Murphy examines the Lockean concept of workmanship by considering Locke's analogy between humans (being a product of God's workmanship and therefore owned by him) and property (which is the product of a "workman", whose labour power is owned by someone, such that its owner becomes the owner of the product). He draws upon the Arendtian distinction (Arendt 1958) of the separation between work (which involves the production of an artefact, such as a pot) and labour (which is the repetitive toil necessary for life to continue, such as washing up, that does not produce any physical object that exists in the world). However, Murphy amends this definition so that labour covers all activity that is performed to fulfil a social need and this includes work, in which an artefact is produced. He argues that the ideal of workmanship distorts social and economic activity for two reasons:

> First because work (that is fabrication) is but one species of labour (that is, social service), and second because workmanship takes as its end (the production of an artefact) what is really only a means to meeting a human need (Murphy 1992, 322).

Murphy complains that the production of artefacts as the paradigm of workmanship has been problematic because it marginalises the production of services and renders labour, such as housework, as non-productive. Relevant to Laslett's discussion of Locke, it also encourages the view that it is the relationship between the subject (the "workman") and the object (the artefact produced) that gives meaning to the activity. The aim of workmanship then appears to be the creation of an object. The important relationship seems to be between the subject ("workman") and the object produced. This obscures the fact that this is not really the end of the process; that in fact the aim is to meet socially defined human needs. He therefore argues that,

> The reification of social relations that Marx attributed to capitalism is actually embodied in the workmanship ideal shared by Marxists and liberals alike (Murphy 1992, 323).

Murphy's analysis is useful, partly because of the way in which it deals with the marginalisation of housework and the provision of services, but mainly because it complements Pateman's position. It highlights the problems with the way in which Laslett, following Locke's logic, thinks in terms of the relationship between subject and object rather than recognising that property ownership concerns a way of regulating social relations.

Pateman's Critics

Criticisms of Pateman's position on Locke, have tended to accept some of her arguments whilst wanting to be kinder to Locke. Gordon Schochet (2007) accepts that Locke ignores women in his conception of the nature and origin of the state and that this silence is curious, given that Filmer (1991) was using the possibility of women's equality as an argument against contractarianism. Locke argues for women's right to divorce and power over children but not citizenship. However, Schochet concludes with a broad brush that,

> through a shift in the focus of politics from the patriarchal *father* to the rational rights bearing *individual* – who remained an adult male – Locke created the theoretical possibility of full political membership for women (Schochet 2007, 136).

Similarly, whilst not discussing Pateman specifically, Butler (2007, 128) concludes that Locke did not champion women's equality and that the public/private divide is problematic but also that Lockean ideas of equality, freedom and individualism carried a logic of their own that ultimately benefited women. Pateman recognises that contractarianism had the potential to challenge all natural hierarchies, once those relating to white men were challenged. The problem she highlights, as Butler recognises, is that Locke's public/private divide made this claim for some men in the public sphere but defined subordination in the home in non-political terms.

Schochet concludes that,

> Pateman's argument rests on an unspecified and unwarrantedly essentialist conception of historical development that makes it impossible to alter institutions and practices without first rooting out their historical foundations (Schochet 2007, 241).

On the contrary, Pateman is only relying upon the fact that such contracts developed and is exposing their logic to move beyond them. There is a similar criticism of *The Sexual Contract*, in which its rewriting of a fictional state of nature is taken to position women as fixed in an oppressive position through an originating act: the fictional creation of the sexual contract (Dean 1992). This raises broader issues than simply Pateman's reading of Locke but is relevant to it. It is my view that, in contrast to the criticism that Pateman's work draws upon a fixed essentialist view of women, Pateman's work is consistent with that of (a rather partial) reading of Foucault, mentioned above. In order to illustrate the point further I will examine the main feminist arguments against Pateman and then explain my constructive reading of Pateman.

I will argue that Pateman's analysis of contract adds to some of Foucault's arguments on power, further situating them historically. Pateman illustrates that, following from Locke, political power is viewed as operating in a distinct realm. When politics is defined narrowly as being concerned with the state it is easier to view power as something that operates in a top-down manner from the Sovereign command to the populous, through laws. When Locke views male dominance within the family as natural and as occurring in a distinct, private non-political realm, the operations of power within the home falls from sight within political theory. Similarly, in his influential middle period, particularly in *Discipline and Punish* and *History of Sexuality: An Introduction*, Foucault (1977; 1990) describes the way in which power has been understood, by shifting from the view of power as a thing that was held by the sovereign body to an analysis of micro-processes of power. He is attentive to the way power operates, through different techniques and discourses, as *productive* of different ways of viewing "who we are" and of different ways of living, in contrast with the image of power as something that can be held by those in authority. These simple "techniques of power" operate in order to inculcate discipline upon "docile bodies", for example the factory bell, indicating where someone was to be at any given time – which operated in the same way as the prison bell and the school bell. Similarly, Foucault refers to the panopticon, Bentham's model of a prison in which the guard at the centre may not be seen but prisoners know that they may be watched at any time, a technique that becomes employed in the factories and schools.

My linking of Pateman's work with that of Foucault is a controversial claim because Pateman has been accused of working in the opposite direction, with an opposed set of premises. In Foucauldian terms, she is accused of having "baggy trousers" (Foucault 1991) i.e. producing an overall theory – in terms of the role of contract in subordination – that tries to cover too much but is insufficiently detailed, explaining everything in its own terms, without fully understanding the subtleties of a situation, particularly from the position of those who are oppressed. I think this is to misunderstand the role of Pateman's analysis of contract and the claims that are being made. To explain this I will discuss two of the strongest criticisms of this type, by Wendy Brown (whose work could be broadly characterised as influenced by poststructualism) and by Nancy Fraser (from within critical theory).

Wendy Brown (1995, 135–165) argues that, whilst in the past women's oppression may have been linked with the marriage contract, this is no longer necessary. Further that the state can be the "man in the life" of women who are recipients of welfare benefits. Nancy Fraser (1996, 225–235) argues that women's oppression is based upon more subtle issues than analysed by Pateman. In both marriage and co-habitation, the ability to have an equal voice in the decisions made in a relationship reflects a number of factors, such as the exit costs to each party, i.e. how difficult it would be to leave. This in turn may be based upon a number of factors, for example, the ability to support oneself, which relates to earning power and the approach of the welfare state.

As mentioned in the introduction, Pateman (1996, 204) is clear that the heyday of the traditional marriage contract with housewife and breadwinner was broadly from 1840–1970. Nevertheless, the way in which this model of housewife/

breadwinner influenced the development of the welfare state and the employment contract, with their notions of the family wage, informs current debates and court decisions, as discussed in chapter 7. These represent different levels of analysis. The history and development of the marriage contract affects the exit costs of each party in a marriage, for example. Pateman is therefore telling part of the story: the way in which the meaning of what it is to be a housewife and employee comes into existence, which in turn produced particular ways of living. What it means to *be* or live as a "housewife" and "employee" were socially constructed, just as the meaning of "criminal" has been constructed. Pateman is tracing how this occurred (its genealogy) in order to consider relationships today. Her focus is upon institutions but that does not rule out an analysis of what it means to be a housewife or employee. Pateman does not discuss this issue at length but in a brief discussion of Foucault states,

> [T]he actual contracts entered into in everyday life form a specifically modern method of creating local power relations within sexuality, marriage and employment (Pateman 1988, 16).

To return to my claim that Pateman's work is compatible with a certain reading of Foucault, consider an argument by Ian Hacking. In *Historical Ontologies*, Ian Hacking (2002) demonstrates Foucault's position by a thought experiment. He compares what would happen if there were to be a collective forgetting of what it meant to be a criminal compared with the forgetting of how a voltage battery worked. Batteries would still work even if we forgot the theory and history behind them. In contrast, what it means to be a criminal (or, to use Pateman's concerns, a housewife or employee) is a way of living – something that defines "who you are" in ways that depend upon humans knowing its "meaning". Its history informs its contested and developing social meanings. Pateman's analysis of marriage contracts and employment contracts (or the meaning of housewife and employee) is compatible with a further understanding of the psychological implications of the daily negotiations and compromises within this way of life.

If Pateman's analysis of contract is viewed as concerned with tracing the emergence of the employee and the housewife in the same way as Foucault traces the emergence of the criminal, it can be seen that this is not an argument for quietism in the face of something that has already occurred. This reading is supported by the way in which Pateman describes her work in terms of a genealogy, asking "what form of life has been supported ... by a particular narrative about the origins of a body politic" (Pateman and Mills 2007, 202). This is a form of life that she is taking positive steps to alter by both arguing for practical reforms and tracing the contingent way in which readings of Locke's thought in particular continues to affect the way in which we view ourselves.

Chapter 5
Rousseau

Introduction

In his *A Discourse on the Origin of Inequality*, Rousseau (2004, 31–126) speculates on the state of nature and on the subsequent development of humanity. Here, the story of the social contract works as a thought experiment to challenge the conclusions of Hobbes and Locke on human nature and individuals' political organisation. As each use of the social contract involves an abstraction from society in order to then import human characteristics that are viewed as essential, this approach could be viewed as a way of framing the nature/nurture debate, backed only by speculation. It raises questions that are tackled within later disciplines, such as linguistics and anthropology and can be seen as a tool for drawing out some of the questions addressed by these disciplines. Neuhouser (2007) has considered Rousseau's genealogy in the context of a broader analysis of the role of genealogy in the history of philosophy. He argues that, as inequality is not natural in Rousseau's account, the aim of Rousseau's genealogy is to trace the point at which the inequality arose. It should be noted that, for Rousseau, gender inequality arises at an early stage, whilst individuals are still envisaged as within the state of nature. What is curious, Neuhouser argues, is that this genealogy is of a conjectural history, employed to elucidate the nature of things, in particular the development of the human mind. For example, I will discuss the way Rousseau outlines the development of *amour propre*, such that the meaning of human worth develops into an assessment of human value to others, which is variable over time.

I will situate this analysis by outlining Rousseau's story of the state of nature, drawing mainly from *A Discourse on Inequality* and then illustrate how women are positioned with regard to *amour propre* and to morality. I will then outline central moves in *The Social Contract,* drawing upon Althusser's close reading of it. In some ways this serves an analogous function to that of Macpherson's work in the previous chapter. Althusser raises useful arguments about Rousseau's conceptual framework and the problems that emerge when considering class inequality. However, for Rousseau, poor men are in a very different position to women, who are viewed as naturally subordinate (i.e. their subordination arises in a second stage in the state of nature). I will then return to the position of women, who are precluded from being either citizens or natural persons – roles which are themselves in conflict within Rousseau's thought. Althusser points to class interests as undermining of Rousseau's general will at a practical level that produces discrepancies in his thought that cannot be "ironed out" theoretically. Whilst I am sympathetic to Althusser's argument, he ignores the position of women. Class interests do produce problems for the general will but this issue of the particular will is also recognised by Rousseau. In contrast, Rousseau's view of women undermines the coherence of his thought more clearly because his basic institutions (the patriarchal family and the republican state) can be seen as likely to conflict in practice. This cannot be easily amended by simply adding women into the role of citizen because of the way they are positioned in the sentimental family. Instead of recognising this, Rousseau views women themselves as naturally "disordered" (Rousseau 1968, 109).

Rousseau's State of Nature

Rousseau traces the development of inequality in stages. In the first stage, in nature, he views both men and women as solitary animals, who come together only to reproduce. There is an initial "bond" between women and their children, although this is slight, as illustrated by the fact that the woman breast feeds to relieve her swollen breasts and only later develops a sympathy for the child (Rousseau 2004, 65). In this state, both men and women are viewed as more healthy and robust and able to look after themselves than in the later civil society. Children mature quickly and then leave their mother. He even speculates that if a mother and child were to run into each other again, they may not recognise each other (Rousseau 2004, 65). In this early state of nature there is equality, including equality between the sexes. Rousseau (2004, 81) discusses the idea that if someone tried to make another individual into his slave then it would be easy to escape and hide. Whilst this is discussed in general terms – given the solitary nature of humans in this state – it is reasonable to assume that the same argument can be applied to both men and women. There is no property and hence no discussion of the possibility of women or children being treated as owned by a man.

It is in the second stage in the state of nature that Rousseau envisages the start of a gendered division of labour, which is prior to any other such division. Individuals are viewed as starting to live together. This allows the development of the family unit, which Rousseau (2004, 88) projects back into his state of nature, complete with an image of women spending more time tending to huts rather than hunting. Given Rousseau's criticisms of later division of labour, he is sanguine regarding this division. It is nevertheless viewed as part of a historical development, not present in his initial state of nature. However, in contrast to other areas of historical development, Rousseau provides no argument that this should be ameliorated. On the contrary (and against some of his contemporaries who were enlightenment thinkers, optimistic regarding human progress), Rousseau famously views this as the most perfect stage of humanity. Little work needed to be carried out and people could come together to socialise.

Unfortunately, this socialisation leads to people comparing each other's worth, deciding who is better at singing or dancing for example, and this leads to the development of *amour propre*, or self love (Rousseau 2004, 90). *Amour propre* is a perversion of *amour de soi*, which is merely concern for survival. It refers to the pride and vanity that emerge when individuals live together. There is a link between the Hobbesian view of "vainglory" as pernicious within the state of nature, which plays a role as one of the causes of war, and the importance that Rousseau places upon the role of *amour propre*. Rousseau points to Hobbes' failure to recognise that such competitive behaviour could not occur in early humanity because both view this as pre-social. Comparison with others that gives rise to vanity and pride are clearly social passions. As I discuss in the next section, Rousseau blames women, in particular, for such passions and views them as susceptible to vanity.

At the final stage in the state of nature there is the development of agriculture and metallurgy. As some areas are more fertile and some individuals have greater aptitude and willingness to work, this results in inequality. This is more insidious because of the psychology of *amour propre*. It is at this point that Rousseau's description of the state of nature starts to resemble that of Hobbes. In a critique of Hobbes and Locke, Rousseau makes it clear that a fraudulent social contract is then initiated by the rich in order to protect their property from others. Here, Rousseau reworks the idea of the social contract to make an egalitarian point: that it is the rich alone who benefit from the laws. In contrast to this "fraudulent" social contract discussed in the *Discourse on the Origin of Inequality*, Rousseau describes his own version in the later *The Social Contract*.

Women, Morality and *Amour Propre*

Rousseau associates women with the problem of *amour propre* in two ways. He views women themselves as vain but also blames them for their affect upon men's *amour propre*, given Rousseau's assumption that men compete for women's approval. In a letter to D'Alembert, he is critical of the way in which he views men pandering to the opinion of women in the salons – a "public sphere" in which women were influential (Rousseau 1968). Curiously, Rousseau views women as having less power over men in the state of nature than in civil society because, he claims that, they later attend to their appearance with,

> cleverness and care, to establish their empire, and put in power the sex which ought to obey (Rousseau 2004, 77).

This is appreciated by men in civil society who have learned greater aesthetic judgement than in a state of nature. Women are viewed as having greater vanity (than pride) which Rousseau argues is a more anti-social passion in that pride can be harnessed and transferred into pride in one's republic.

Given the central role of *amour propre* in Rousseau's analysis of the relationship between self and other, it is worth considering this in detail. Gauthier (2006, 10) discusses the way that Rousseau's understanding of the "sentiment of existence" and freedom is linked with this move. Initially, as solitary animals in Rousseau's story, both men and women were free, in that each individual was able to provide for his or her own needs. If anyone stole another's food it would have the same impact as a wild animal doing the same thing. It would not affect the individual's pride. So, an individual's feeling about himself or herself, his or her "sentiment of existence" is focused upon himself or herself alone. It is only at the next stage, with socialisation that "sentiment of existence" is based, not upon oneself alone, but from the estimation of value by others. So, we start to be hurt by the lack of respect accorded to us by the theft of food rather than viewing it as we would if an animal had stolen it.

This element of the argument is similar to a point made by Hampton (1992) drawing upon Kant's analysis of retribution, to argue that a crime is more painful than the same loss or physical harm caused by accident because we are stung by the way that the criminal holds him/herself above us. (The role of the state is to make it plain that all are of equal worth. I will return to this in chapters 6 and 7.) Whereas Rousseau emphasises a problem with *amour propre*, Hampton deals with this in more detail. She distinguishes between cases in which we are treated as of less than equal worth (when the hurt is warranted) and cases in which individuals suffer hurt to their pride because they (wrongly) expected to be shown deference by others whom they view as subordinate, on the grounds of gender or race, for example. Only this latter case would be viewed in terms of unwarranted pride (Hampton 1991b; 1992).

In contrast with Hampton's Kantian approach which is predicated upon an idea of fixed worth, Rousseau describes different historical stages in the meaning of human worth. He describes a shift from the view that we are unaware of this issue (hence would treat theft by others as simply the same as a theft by a wild animal) to a view of human worth as reflecting our usefulness to others, a comparative estimation that can alter over time, as described by Hobbes. This shift cannot be undone but its development and its pernicious effects can be minimised. This is the project of education, described in *Emile*, in which Rousseau argues that boys' environments should be manipulated by the tutor in order to avoid experiencing opposition by others (as opposed to natural objects). The aim of this is to prevent the child pitting his will against others and learning about domination by others. For a typical strategy of the tutor see (Rousseau 1993, 144). In contrast, girls,

> should early be accustomed to restraint. This misfortune, if such it be, is inherent in their sex. They must be trained to bear the yoke from the first, so that they do not feel it, to master their own caprices and to submit themselves to the will of others (Rousseau 1993, 332).

At this early stage in the state of nature, Rousseau describes *amour propre* as applied to the family rather than the individual. Therefore, the sentimental family could offer a conception or image of the individual that differs from that of the liberal possessive individual, who competes in the market. However, Rousseau avoids such a positive evaluation of women's traditional role (as providing an alternative model of human relations than one based upon competition) because he sees women as more dependent than men on others' approval and hence to comparisons of worth, competition and *amour propre* itself. He comments that,

> "What will people think" is the grave of a man's virtue and the throne of a woman's (Rousseau 1993, 328).

The way in which this move is linked with morality, for Rousseau, means that the position taken by Gilligan is blocked. Gilligan (1982) argues that the role of women in the family provides the moral example of an "ethic of care". In contrast, Rousseau's women are positioned very awkwardly with regard to morality. For them, public opinion is the most important judge of their virtue and this is also linked with the aim of ensuring that they are monogamous. This is problematic because Rousseau's conception of morality is based upon the exact opposite: the enlightenment view of being one's own judge and of rejecting *amour propre* to think for oneself. This puts women in a double bind as they cannot behave morally by both courting public opinion – and hence being open to *amour propre* – or by rejecting public opinion and thinking for themselves. As the quotation above shows, Rousseau argues that their education should be different from that given to boys. Girls are to be trained to "submit themselves to the will of others" whereas boys are to be prevented from becoming dependent upon the evaluation of others. Therefore, the best women can attain is a second rate morality of being viewed as modest in the eyes of the public. This theoretical position reflects the practice that women were dependent upon men for financial support, where other opportunities were denied them. Curiously, for a philosopher who is so worried about liberty in other contexts, Rousseau makes a virtue of women's lack of liberty. Women are viewed as having to put up with injustice within the family, a view that sits uneasily with Rousseau's concern for education and the idea that it is a forum for teaching future citizens, to be discussed further below.

Joan Tronto (1993) traces how the emergence of gender roles in moral development are historical, showing the similarity between so-called "women's" morality of care and the eighteenth century theory of "moral sentiments" and tracing a movement away from morality rooted in feelings to one based upon reason and abstraction. Similarly, Battersby (1989, 113) illustrates how the value placed upon different qualities has changed over time. Rousseau values passion and it is passion that women are viewed as lacking. In contrast, as discussed in the next chapter, Kant values reason and women are then viewed as lacking reason. Drawing upon Tronto's work, Butler (2002) argues that Rousseau was contemporaneous with the historical shift in the eighteenth century, within philosophy, from the concern with "moral sentiments" (feeling and context) to moral decisions based upon reason and abstraction. Like Gauthier (2006), Butler links the role that Rousseau gives to Emile's tutor (in *Emile*) with that of the legislator in *The Social Contract*, as someone with superhuman powers. For Butler, writing within a perspective of an ethic of care, this role is linked in that both are male figures who have the ability to show sensitivity to context, required by a care perspective, whilst also establishing rules for a social order, "characterised by their personal immunity from human passions" (Butler 2002, 222).

Gauthier makes a complementary move by pointing out that both the tutor and legislator provide a *deus ex machina* to Rousseau's system. If Emile requires his education in order to allow him to be his own man, then how was his tutor educated to avoid such pitfalls? This is similar to the legislator who must be,

> a superior intelligence beholding all the passions of men without experiencing any of them (Rousseau 2004, 213).

These figures could be viewed as providing the conditions of possibility of Rousseau's account of the world. No explanation of them is given but they are nevertheless necessary for the emergence of the "natural man" though education and of the citizen though the operation of the general will, respectively. Whilst these images of men are in conflict in Rousseau's work, they are positively evaluated. Women are denied the possibility of attaining either status.

Althusser's 'Discrepancies'

I want to consider Althusser's reading of what he calls "discrepancies" in Rousseau's social contract to draw out the way in which Rousseau thinks about what it means to be an individual and the relationship between ourselves and others. Whilst Althusser traces theoretical discrepancies to a practical cause based upon class, I want to examine this in the light of a "discrepancy" in Althusser's own account: the way in which gender is completely omitted. This raises an old question about the disruptiveness of women to the social order. The focus is upon women and class but this also raises questions about the other ways in which different "others", who are denied citizenship, are conceptualised within Rousseau's work.

Althusser views the social contract as a "philosophical object", which he explains in the following introductory paragraph:

> In interrogating the philosophy we have inherited, we can start from one simple observation: each great doctrine itself thinks itself in a specifically *philosophical* object and its theoretical effects. For example: the Platonic Idea, Aristotelian Action, the Cartesian Cogito, the Kantian Transcendental Subject etc. (Althusser 2007, 113 italics in the original).

So, by examining this "philosophical object" it is possible to clarify the theory, detailing which problems it highlights and which it obscures. Althusser argues that each discrepancy (or inconsistency in Rousseau's text, focusing upon *The Social Contract*) is able to function by being transformed into a further discrepancy, producing a chain – each "solution" making the next one theoretically possible

– until he traces this chain to what he describes as a practical problem: that of class differences in a capitalist society.

First Discrepancy: The Parties to the Contract

In a legal contract there are usually two or more parties who exist prior to the contract and come together to make an agreement. However, Rousseau's social contract envisages the agreement as taking place between:

1. the first party – all individuals as individuals, described by Althusser as Recipient Party 1 (RP1) – and
2. the second party, consisting of the same individuals in their capacity as the community (PR2).

The discrepancy consists in the fact that the second party to the contract only comes into being as a result of the contract itself. As Rousseau puts it,

> This formula shows us that the act of association comprises a mutual understanding between the public and the individuals, and that *each individual, in making a contract, so to speak, with himself*, is bound in a double capacity; as a member of the Sovereign he is bound to the individuals, and as a member of the State to the Sovereign (SC I, VII p13–14 cited in Althusser 2007, 130 italics added by Althusser).

As sovereign, he (and it is he not she, for Rousseau) is part of the citizenry whose general will is given expression in the law and – as a member of the state – he is bound to obey it. Rousseau's social contract evokes a change in status that encourages individuals to think of themselves as citizens, to consider general interests and general will of the whole community. There is an image of the creation of a new body that is greater than the individual. This image has some parallels with the way in which individuals can subordinate their interests to a partnership or social group – a move that can be potentially progressive or open to exploitation.

Althusser argues that Rousseau's use of the phrase "so to speak" in the above quotation signals a recognition of the discrepancy: that the two parties to a legal contract usually pre-exist the contract, whereas this "peculiar contract" brings the second party (individuals as citizens) into being. It could be objected that the contract itself is merely a legal/philosophical fiction and so Althusser should not be concerned about a further fiction; that an alternative reading of Rousseau would be of individuals contracting amongst each other to change their status from a particular date (or change their status when they act in concert to produce the general will at any given time). This would make it analogous to a marriage as a *performance* that produced a change of status (save that the social contract is a philosophical fiction and marriage takes place within an already-established legal system). It could be argued that the so-called "change in status" simply manufactures the consent of the weaker party, while the focus upon 'contract' abstracts the individual from the context in which her/his weaker bargaining position was produced – as Rousseau complains is the position of the earlier social contractarians, Hobbes and Locke. This is an argument adopted and developed by Marx and by feminists. As Althusser highlights, this is not the way in which Rousseau discusses his fictional contract, which is described in terms of an exchange between individuals in two different capacities. A number of points flow from this conceptual framework. Althusser's reading opens up two arguments. First, it allows him to indicate how Rousseau's work can be pushed in the direction of Kant (but also distinguished from it) and second, it opens up the possibility of Althusser's second "discrepancy". I will look at each in turn.

In the above quotation, Rousseau refers to RP2 (individual *qua* citizen) as RP1 (individual *qua* individual) by referring to the individual "making a contract with himself". Here, he refers to an individual (as RP1, i.e. individual not citizen) who makes and obeys his own law. If the stress is placed upon the individual *qua* individual rather than citizen, a Kantian reading is evoked. As I will discuss in the next chapter, the Kantian enlightened individual is able to self-legislate, to make and obey the moral law by appealing to a universal of individuals rather than citizens. Althusser therefore provides a useful way of thinking about how Kant's categorical imperative (which involves an appeal to a universal by the individual RP1) differs from Rousseau's conception of the general will, which involves the individual making a decision as citizen (RP2). Instead of asking what any individual in his place would do, Rousseau's citizen is to ask: what is in the best interests of the community? Both the Kantian categorical imperative applied by an individual (RP1) and Rousseau's citizen (RP2) appeal to a universal but Rousseau envisages the creation of a greater body whereas Kant's categorical imperative asks what rules could be universalised by individuals as individuals.

Rousseau, like Hobbes but not Kant, argues that individuals are motivated by self-interest rather than duty in his conception of self-legislation. For Rousseau, individuals as citizens act in the best interests of the community because they learn to recognise that it is in their own best interests to do so. In other words, Rousseau's individuals want the happiness of everyone because they view themselves as part of that whole. He states,

> The undertakings which bind us to the social body are obligatory only because they are mutual; and their nature is such that in fulfilling them we cannot work for others without working for ourselves. Why is it that the general will is always upright, and that all continually will the happiness of each one, unless it is because there is not a man who does not think of "each" as meaning him, and consider himself in voting for all? (Rousseau 2004, 205).

As Rousseau recognises, this evocation of a greater whole is undermined by any strong group conflict of interest.

Before turning to consider the way in which Althusser's detailing of Rousseau's first discrepancy opens up a discussion of his second, I want to make an observation from a legal perspective. Althusser's objection hinges upon the fact that in contract law there are two pre-existing parties (at Rousseau's time these were men, not women, who are treated as legal persons, i.e. with the legal right to sue and be sued in the courts) who enter into the exchange. Under the doctrine of contract at will (which was the prevalent view of contract law at the time when Rousseau was writing in 1762)[1] for a contract to be valid, the parties to the contract had to be "*ad idem*", or of "one mind", in their shared understanding of the contractual terms. Althusser's analysis of Rousseau highlights a paradox. The two parties to his social contract really are "of one mind" because they are the same group of individuals. However, in the contractual sense, this was not the case because the temporal sequence of events raises the following question: would it be possible for individuals to know their own minds as citizens prior to the instantiation of citizenship and the general will? Rousseau's social contract can be viewed as a legal fiction that represents the transition to a situation in which individuals are to think in terms of the interests of the whole, implying that they gain an outlook or perspective that did not exist prior to the contract.

This is linked with a further question of whether to characterise Rousseau's "philosophical object" (the social contract) as that which produces a psychological change in which individuals address the interests of the community. However, this is carried out because the individual (male) views this as in his interests. Hence, this reference to "self-interest" sounds akin to the image of the social contract employed in game theory, which starts with the individual as the foundation for action and asks when it is appropriate to co-operate. However, there is also a psychological aspect of Rousseau's argument in which civil religion and education are employed to encourage the parties to view themselves as part of a greater whole. This has to be distinguished from an ontological position in which the starting point is not that of the individual but of the community as a body; in which individuation from others is something that is achieved.

Althusser's argument does not simply raise a paradox by taking a legal fiction too seriously. It highlights the importance of historical transformation and of personal education to enable democratic participation, that is considered in Rousseau's work. As discussed above, individuality and morality are understood as subject to historical change in Rousseau's conjectural history. Similarly, at the level of the individual, nobody is born with the ability to be a citizen. He must be educated to be able to produce the general will by considering the common good, rather than conflicting particular interests (between rich and poor). By extension beyond Rousseau's position, this could include the conflicting interests of men and women in a society with a gender hierarchy. Rousseau's positioning of women is more paradoxical than that of working class men because women are excluded

1 For a brief discussion of the relationship between Rousseau and the history of the law of contract see Atiyah (1985, 57–59).

from citizenship entirely. This means that their conflict of interest can only be given expression in the areas in which women have influence, which at the time included the salons of the public sphere and the family. So, again, women are awkwardly positioned in that they are allocated a role in which they are neither Rousseau's "natural individual" nor a citizen. Rousseau fails to recognise that the "general will" he describes is already only a particular will, which excludes the voice of women and anyone else denied citizenship.

As discussed, Pateman draws on productive aspects of Rousseau to argue that both the position of women and of employees represents a training in subordination that is antithetical to citizenship, which requires, not only the ability to think of the communal good, but also the self-confidence and social skills to have one's voice heard. This represents a shift from the idea of a social contract as a one-off creation of a social body (that can express the general will) to focus upon the actual exercise of the general will in democratic decision-making on a daily basis.

Second Discrepancy: Alienation of Freedom

Althusser's "first discrepancy" (that this is a contract which involves a second party not yet in existence) then leads to a second discrepancy, which Althusser highlights in order to think in more detail about the contractual exchange. He questions the possibility of an exchange in which there is complete alienation of all that the individuals have, including their freedom, but in which they then receive civil liberty and more in return. In an earlier argument against slavery, Rousseau states that total alienation is unthinkable. His reworking of Hobbes makes this thinkable but with the "safeguard" that "men give themselves totally but to themselves" (Althusser 2007, 135). So, Rousseau's response to Hobbes was to keep his idea of total alienation as an agreement between all individuals (men) but to replace the sovereign, who functions as a third party external to the contract. The structure of Hobbes' argument is maintained but the sovereign is replaced by the individuals (men) now reconstituted as a sovereign community. In common with Hobbes, Rousseau describes a sovereign power that is absolute, a "corporate body whose life is the union of its members" (Rousseau 2004, 4, 204. II). For Hobbes, the implication of this is the total alienation of freedom, which meant that – other than when the individual's life was at stake – the sovereign had the power to judge in conflicts with the subjects. For Rousseau, there is no need for an arbiter because the sovereign is no more than the people themselves. Liberals, best exemplified by the arguments of John Stuart Mill, have pointed out that this identification can serve as an excuse for tyranny, that those who act as government are not actually the same as the people themselves (Mill 2008, 7). However, Rousseau (2004, 135) does argue that government itself should be controlled so that it expresses the general will of the sovereign citizens (men).

Althusser's second discrepancy arises from his analysis of the first. He cites Rousseau:

> The peculiar fact about this alienation is that, in taking over the goods of individuals, the community, so far from despoiling them, only assures them legitimate possession, and changes usurpation into a true right and enjoyment into proprietorship. Thus the possessors ... have ... acquired, so to speak, all that they gave up (SC I, IX, p.18 cited by Althusser 2007, 140).

What a man loses by being a party to the social contract is his natural liberty and an unlimited right to everything he succeeds in getting. What is gained is civil liberty and proprietorship of his possessions. Althusser's question is therefore: how is it possible to have total alienation and also benefit from it? He discusses the paradoxical nature of such alienation that also relies upon the individual man's interest. The idea of alienation of freedom and abilities of the weaker contractual party raises parallels between the positions of the following: the subject of a state, an employee (deemed to exchange labour power for a wage which – as Marx pointed out – expresses a relationship of subordination in terms of exchange) and women in traditional marriage contracts (as Pateman analyses). Like Marx, she does so in order to challenge the legal fiction of freedom/human capacities that can be exchanged.

For Gauthier, the general will is,

> no more than the translation of the shared grounds of association into common directives for action. Human beings come together so that they may use their combined forces to defend and protect each person and his goods; the general will translates that shared intent into the actions that its fulfilment requires (Gauthier 2006, 55).

Gauthier goes on to argue that total alienation of a person means that no one holds back a portion of his forces to protect himself in opposition to others, rather than in harmony with them:

> Each is free, because the combined forces of his fellows are adequate to preserve and maintain him; the balance of needs and powers has been restored (Gauthier 2006, 55).

This makes no sense in a society that is divided by class, gender or other conflict, in which the weaker party is simply coerced. It should be noted that Gauthier is resisting any image of individuals being metaphysically part of a greater body, evoking the same argument that is discussed with regard to Spinoza in chapter 3 regarding atomism and holism. If a more holistic approach is adopted then this problem of particular wills is exacerbated. Gatens (1995, 97) for example, discusses this in terms of an imaginary creation of a male body.

Kant – who was deeply influenced by Rousseau – produces a later discussion of the legitimation of sex in marriage that appears very similar in form to this aspect of Rousseau, highlighted by Althusser's question: how is it possible to have total alienation and to benefit from it? Kant argues that, in the sexual act each party gives up himself or herself (as if he or she were a thing). However, in marriage this is acceptable because,

> the one who is acquired acquires the other in turn; for in this way each reclaims itself and restores its personality (Kant 1996, I, s.25, p. 62).

Kant's example includes the right to possession, i.e. to bring back the other party of the marriage contract if she (or, in theory, he) tries to escape. The parties that are viewed as alienating themselves are not equally positioned with regard to the rights that they give up. As will be discussed below, this is Althusser's problem with Rousseau's social contract with regard to class.

Third Discrepancy: The Role of the Particular Will

The first discrepancy: that the social contract is viewed as an agreement between two parties but actually instantiates one of the parties, is linked to the second discrepancy: that contractual exchange involves total alienation and yet is based upon self-interest. This leads to a third discrepancy, concerning the relationship between this self-interest (leading to the particular will) and the interest of the community (which gives rise to general will). Rousseau expresses concern that the general will is defeated by the existence of any particular will. However, it is the sum of all particular wills (based upon the individuals' self-interest) on which the general will depends. This last point draws upon Rousseau's reference to the self-interest that is the motivation for creating and following the general will. As Rousseau puts it,

> The undertakings which bind us to the social body are obligatory only because they are mutual; and their nature is such that in fulfilling them we cannot work for others without working for ourselves (SC II, IV p. 24 cited by Althusser 2007, 142).

Further, according to Rousseau, the general will is always in existence. So, for example, even if a voter sells his vote he is simply answering the wrong question and ignoring the general will. What is particularly problematic to the general will is if decisions are made on the basis of particular group interests. Althusser highlights the ambiguity with which Rousseau refers to the "particular will" as both individual self-interest and the dangerous sectional interest of groups or classes, which set themselves up against the general will.

This leads to the final stage of Althusser's argument that this discrepancy is no longer a theoretical problem of how to think about a legal fiction. For Althusser, the solution can no longer be theoretical but must be practical because the class interests of a capitalist society cannot be ironed out by reworking a theoretical answer to the discrepancy inherent in the relationship between particular class interests and general interests of the community. There could be no general will in a community in which there are conflicting class interests. He argues that Rousseau's social contract is shown to have the problems of the "false social contract" that Rousseau criticises in Hobbes and Locke in his earlier *A Discourse on the Origin of Inequality*, thereby reading Rousseau's reworking of Hobbes' full alienation as remaining close to Hobbes (Rousseau 2004, 31–126).

Althusser's argument at this stage can be used to highlight the different ways in which class and gender have been subsumed into Rousseau's theory. Class interests are subordinated to the general will but the male poor are still viewed as equal citizens, to be educated to participate in democracy. What Althusser's account leaves out is the way in which women – and anyone denied citizenship – are not viewed as a party to the contract at all. Having pushed Rousseau in the direction of Hobbes and Locke, Althusser then ridicules Rousseau, by pointing to a fourth discrepancy, in which Rousseau tries to reconcile this problem either by evoking the ideology of the common good through public opinion, education and civil religion or by referring back to a feudal economy. Alternatively, in the end Althusser says that Rousseau's last resort is to have recourse to literature rather than political theory – a final admission of failure.

A Feminist Response to Althusser's Reading

Ironically, given Althusser's characterisation of Rousseau's literature as non-political, it is in Rousseau's literature, in work such as *La Nouvelle Héloïse* (Rousseau 1987), for example, along with his writing on education in *Emile* (Rousseau 1993), which were both very influential in Rousseau's time, that he makes explicit the role he envisages for women. This is one that is defined as non-political but – as feminists have shown – this public/private division is itself political (Pateman 1995, 118–140).

Given that Althusser views his theoretical discrepancies as leading to a practical problem (that of class conflict) which cannot be resolved theoretically, I want to introduce the question of women by discussing practice. In the usual course of events, aside from revolutionary activity, particular interests of working class men will make themselves known through union activity, for example. Rousseau would view this as the men ignoring the general will. In contrast, acting in accordance with Rousseau's framework itself, the "particular interests" of women for their families (not their own interests *per se*) exacerbates a conflict of interest within the civic republic that has the potential to be very disruptive, both in practice and for Rousseau's theory. Okin (2002, 106) cites a number of areas where the two institutions that are central to Rousseau's framework (the patriarchal property-owning family and the republican state) are likely to conflict: the payment of taxes, the absence of the breadwinner for public duties and the regulation of private property for the public good, for example. Given that Rousseau argues that women's education should teach them to be pleasing to and even manipulative of men, women are envisaged as being capable of persuading their husbands in areas where there are direct conflicts between the family and the republic. Hence the position of women in Rousseau's framework is disruptive, even when they are acting in an "appropriate" manner. There is nothing in the education that he details as suitable for girls, nor upon their subsequent life within the home that Rousseau ascribes to women, that would allow them to develop the civic values that he advocates. As I will discuss below, this is ironic given that his work is associated with the idea of republican ideals being learned.

In her analysis of Rousseau's women in fiction, Okin (2002) draws out the tensions in Rousseau's work between "particular interests" of various sorts, paying attention to the way in which gender plays a part in these areas. It is useful to juxtapose Okin's analysis with Althusser's discussion of the particular will as opposed to the general will. Okin (2002, 97) points to three different ways in which there are conflicting claims upon the individual, which are acknowledged to varying degrees in his literature. These are: the conflict between the impulses of the "natural" individual and the requirements of the republican state; the passion of the heterosexual couple and the needs of the wider world; and, as mentioned above, the demands of the family and of the republican state. It is worth considering each in turn because they give concrete examples of different particular interests and "will" and the extent to which Rousseau acknowledges these conflicts within his work.

The first conflict Okin (2002, 97) cites is between the individual and state, drawing upon Rousseau's literature. At the start of *Emile*, Rousseau explains this tension when he says that men cannot be educated to be both a natural man and a citizen (Rousseau 1993, 5). The tutor educates Emile as a natural man, an "absolute whole" who is independent of others and does not conform to society. This is in conflict with the citizen he becomes when he marries Sophie and adopts the life of a husband and father, which requires duties above those expected of an independent "natural man" (and which he ultimately abandons). Sophie, in contrast, is not to be educated as independent (either in terms of self-sufficiency emotionally or financially) because she is to be judged by others – but nor is she a citizen. She will depend upon men for her self-respect and financial support. Since women are raised to give pre-eminence to romantic love (and this and the family are their only sources of power) they are likely to be more focused upon it than men. Rousseau brings out these conflicts in his narrative about Sophie, who despite having Rousseau's ideal education, cannot cope with having Emile become less passionate towards her and, needing men's attention, has an affair. When she becomes pregnant by another man, Emile rejects her to adopt the life of a "natural man"; having run out of options, Sophie promptly dies.

Turning to the second source of conflict, in his romantic fiction, Rousseau recognises the conflict between the exclusiveness of intense love between heterosexual couples and other forms of duty to families, state or any others. He also registers the double bind into which his ideal women are placed in that they are passionate and yet forced to deny their love through duty, as in the position of

Julie in Rousseau (1987). Okin points to a letter that illustrates the extent of the conflict in which Rousseau says:

> We are justly punished for those exclusive attachments which make us blind and unjust, and limit our universe to the persons we love. All the preferences of friendship are thefts committed against the human race and the fatherland. Men are all our brothers, they should all be our friends (Correspondence générale, vol. 4, p. 827 cited Okin 2002, 101).

As Okin points out, if Rousseau is worried about "friendship as a theft" then it should be clear that both love and loyalties to the sentimental family will come into conflict with other loyalties "to the human race and the fatherland". This second area of conflict (between heterosexual love and everything external to it) is acknowledged in his fiction.

The third area of conflict between the family and republican state has been introduced above. Okin (2002, 106) points out that Rousseau does not recognise this conflict between the two major institutions in his work. However, there are two passages where he comes close. Firstly, early in *Emile* he favourably describes the loyalty of a Spartan mother who celebrates the city's victory despite the fact that her children have died. Secondly, he wants public education and socialisation of children from an early age rather than trusting this to families. He originally wrote in draft (but then crossed out) a passage stating that fathers could not undertake education because,

> they could make [their children] into very good sons and very bad citizens (Discourse on Political Economy, p. 1400 cited by Okin 2002, 107).

These passages, one of which was omitted in the final text, are exceptions in that generally Rousseau fails to register any conflict between the patriarchal family and the republican state. For example, In *Emile* he asks,

> Can devotion to the state exist apart from the love of those near and dear to us? Can patriotism thrive except in the soil of that miniature fatherland the home? Is it not the good son, the good husband, the good father who makes the good citizen? (Rousseau 1993, 326).

In *Emile*, Rousseau (1993, 5) views the family, and particularly mothers when the child is young, as of primary importance when it comes to socialising children. In previous chapters I have mentioned that Pateman attributes an important move to Rousseau, stating that he (rightly) emphasises the argument that it is necessary to learn the skills needed to participate in democracy. Whilst this is true, the position of women undermines this claim in his own work. Rousseau's ideal women could only provide children with an example of someone whose voice could not be heard except through others and whose only power arises through manipulation

– a model of social relations that is politically problematic. Rousseau blocks the idea that they could provide a more positive model of care, arising from women's traditional role, because of the way they are uncomfortably positioned with regard to morality, discussed above.

In response to Althusser it can be pointed out that the general will is always a particular will because women are denied citizenship and so their interests are not registered. This is similar to the way in which the particular interests of working class men (and women) represent a particular interest. Clearly there is an intersection, just as there are also issues of race, sexuality and disability. However, the position of women (even when they are not representing their own interests but are acting in accordance with Rousseau's prescribed roles) exacerbates the conflict between the patriarchal family and the republican state that lies at the core of Rousseau's project. Whilst coming close to recognising this fact he fails to do so, attributing the "disruptiveness" of women, not to their position within the patriarchal family, but to their nature, which engenders all vice and can "bring the state to ruin" (Rousseau 1968, 109). The point that women's concern with the family rather than broader institutions reflects their lack of education and narrowness of experience was made in response to Rousseau in 1792 by Wollstonecraft (1996). Pateman (1995, 26) points to the limits of simply arguing for an increase in women's education (whilst not disparaging the importance of making such an argument made at the time) because it leaves intact women's role within the sentimental family.

Chapter 6
Kant

Introduction

Kant writes of the social contract in the following terms:

> [The social contract] is in fact merely an idea of reason, which nonetheless has undoubted practical reality; for it can oblige every legislator to frame his laws in such a way that they could have been produced by the united will of a whole nation and to regard each subject, in so far as he can claim citizenship, as if he had consented within the general will (Kant 1991b, 79).

Although the influence of Rousseau is clear in the reference to the general will, Kant makes no attempt to conjecture about human behaviour in the state of nature. He does have views about human behaviour, of course, given that he famously addresses the three questions: "What can I know? What ought I to do? What may I hope?" (Kant 1965, 735). When Kant describes the social contract as an "idea of reason", he is referring to a particular way in which he rethinks the meaning of "ideas" that differs from previous uses by Plato and Aristotle in particular. For Kant, an idea of reason differs from a concept of the understanding in that it does not relate to any objects of possible experience. Ideas of reason, such as freedom and God, cannot be understood (by being brought under a particular concept) but can nevertheless be thought and are central to Kantian morality.[1] Kant uses the idea of a social contract, described above, in order to argue that there are some laws, such as hereditary privilege, that the legislature should not pass because free and equal persons could not agree to such legislation. So, with Kant, the social contract no longer involves any description of a state of nature but becomes purely a thought experiment; a test of legitimacy. Despite the fact that Kant describes women as passive citizens (Kant 1999, sec. 47 [313–316]) and states, "laborious learning or painful pondering, even if a woman should greatly succeed in it, destroys the merits that are proper to her sex" (Kant 1991a, 78), there are areas of contemporary feminist philosophy that draw upon this Kantian social contract. For the feminist philosophers whose work I will examine, Kant's social contract is employed as a test, either for the legitimacy of law in keeping with Kant's original quotations cited above, although amended to include a more detailed and expanded view of harm (by Cornell) or as a basis for thinking about fairness within personal relationships (by Hampton). I will concentrate upon these two uses of Kant's contract in order to consider the benefits and problems with starting from this position.

---

1 For a discussion on the Kantian idea see Caygill (1995, 237–238).

I will start by focusing upon the work of Drucilla Cornell (1995; 1998; 2000; 2008) in particular the way in which she sets up legal arguments based upon a Kantian framework that extends to women the idea of free and equal personhood, which historically has been associated only with men. As Cornell is a legal theorist, a brief outline of legal personhood will set the background for a more detailed consideration of Cornell's employment of Kant's social contract. I will then illustrate the way in which Cornell aims to intervene in practical legal debates, including the problem of equality/difference.

Briefly, this problem is well known within feminist theory and practice and can be characterised in the following terms: that it has been pragmatic for women to claim equal treatment on the grounds that they are the same as men (for example, equally rational) but that this move has proved problematic when areas of genuine difference arise (such as the treatment of pregnant workers). Conversely, any claim that women are different but equal may appear to play into the hands of misogynists who wish to emphasise women's difference from men as a means of attempting to justify women's subordination. Feminists have also questioned the way in which men appear as the neutral measure against whom women are judged as either the same or different (for example Irigaray 1985a).

I will examine Cornell's characterisation of the relationship between: firstly, legal and moral personhood; and secondly, metaphysical and psychological selfhood and the way in which she responds to the equality/difference problem. I will then highlight the Kantian element in Cornell's work further by comparing it to that of the feminist contractarian, Jean Hampton, whose work I have introduced in earlier chapters. This unlikely juxtaposition of feminist philosophers from different philosophical traditions is employed to examine a further problem: the use of abstract references to "free and equal persons" and whether this can be helpful for feminists. Both feminist philosophers differ from Kant in viewing this idea of the social contract in terms of particular situated acts of imagination and I want to examine the meaning of imagination and its relationship to progressive social change.

In this regard Cornell reworks aspects of Kant's aesthetics, also drawing from the tradition of critical theory, which includes influences of Hegel and Adorno, but her main debt is to Lacan and his view of the "imaginary" as the relationship between the ego and its specular image. The "social imaginary" connotes the images and meanings given to values, symbols and laws in a society. I will argue that Cornell's position does not rely upon her Lacanianism. For both Cornell and Hampton, the picture or image of free and equal persons is to be employed in certain social situations: by judges in Cornell's work and by women and anyone assessing the fairness of their relationships in Hampton's analysis. As Cornell (2008) illustrates, Kant's own position on the imagination changes throughout his work, ranging from the view that ideas of reason such as the categorical imperative cannot be imagined, to a more positive position about the use of the imagination, in his work on aesthetics (Kant 1987). As the imagination is also central to Cornell's reworking of Kant I will look at her view in detail. This can be compared with the Spinozan view of the imagination discussed in chapter 3.

Finally, I consider the problem that Cornell's concepts of the self and of the person may collapse into the Lockean owner of "property in the person", who is viewed as owning his or her imagination, along with rights and their other abilities, as if they are objects that can be alienated. Linked with this problem is the tension between progressive and regressive elements in Kant's view of equal moral worth, on which Hampton also relies. A useful critique, which draws out both the progressive and regressive elements of Kant is that of Victor Seidler (1986, 68–69). Seidler has argued that Kant's view of equal moral worth of all persons is difficult to reconcile with the financial dependency of women and the poor generally. There is also much recent work on Kant's racism (Mills 1997; Battersby 2007). It is more difficult, in positions of financial dependency, for example, to make a decision based upon reason, which is employed by abstracting oneself from one's social situation as Kantian morality demands. It is difficult to "speak truth to power", for example, when the stakes are greater. I could add that this problem is also made more difficult by other psychological factors; for example, the situation may engender empathy with the vulnerability of the person with power, by embracing the image of the supportive wife, as discussed in chapter 2 on Hobbes (see Bartky 1990).

Seidler argues that Kant's ideas about individual independence were threatening to traditional authority relations (thereby highlighting the progressive aspect of Kant) but that these ideas easily work to legitimate capitalist relations of dependency, given that independence and individuality become understood as possessive individualism (see Richardson 2007a). Kant's consideration of the role of gratitude, which appears in *The Doctrine of Virtue* illustrates this tension. He cautions that tact should be shown when giving charity because someone's welfare should not be seen as dependent upon another (Kant 1996, 203). Seidler argues that in a market society in which we compete with others, enlisting their help is experienced as threatening to independence. It is interesting to note the way in which women's emotional and other support within the home has not been viewed as undermining men's independence. This is avoided because it is viewed as both a natural expression of femininity and as part of *consortium*. Hence it is women who are traditionally characterised as "the dependant" because of the male "family wage". (For a discussion of the way in which the meaning of dependency is gendered see Fraser and Gordon 1996.)

Drucilla Cornell's Reworking of Kant's Social Contract

There is not one uncontested way in which to envisage the relationship between legal and moral personhood and the concept of self. Cornell's reading of Kant produces a particular view of this relationship. Historically, legal personhood simply refers to the fact that a human being or company can be treated as having the ability to sue or be sued in the courts. Companies were treated as legal persons in the nineteenth century at a time when this right was denied to married women. The law of coverture meant that if a woman married she was treated as having died in civil terms, so that her property became that of her husband. There were earlier instances of the common law employing the legal fiction of "civil death". Upon joining a monastery, monks were viewed as being dead in civil terms and their possessions distributed according to their will. With the dissolution of the monasteries in England by Henry VIII, they were treated by law as having been brought back to life. In contrast, in an alternative legal fiction in relation to bodies and death, the sovereign was viewed as having two bodies, one being immortal (Kantorowicz 1997; for feminist issues see Richardson 2007a). This fiction allowed for the "disability" of a married queen, such as Mary I, to be remedied. As Jordan describes it, she was,

> two persons politically: a wife who is subordinate to her husband in marital affairs and a magistrate who is superior to every one of her subjects in the affairs of state (Jordan 1987, 440).

So, legal personhood is a legal fiction, which has involved images of dead bodies and sometimes of having two bodies, manipulated according to the needs of powerful parties.

However, it has also been justified by being linked with moral personhood in a manner that has also been detrimental to women, who are positioned as less moral than men and therefore less capable of citizenship. Battersby (1995) has detailed the way Kant's work marks a turning point in modernity, in which aesthetics and morality become viewed as separate to the detriment of women. Women are viewed as incapable of the autonomy required to follow reason, which is demonstrated by the ability to abstract herself from her particular situation to act in accordance with the categorical imperative. For Kant's view of women as passive citizens and the relationship between his political views and his metaphysics, see Battersby (1995; 1998).

In her philosophical and legal framework Cornell brings together personhood as a legal and moral concept with an image of what it is to be a self (with an onus upon the psychology of self-development) in a manner that draws from Kant's social contract, as an idea of reason described in the opening quotation, but not his views of selfhood. She reworks the abstraction required by Kant's morality by dividing legal personhood from her analysis of (and claims for) self-development and situates in a legal context Kant's arguments regarding legitimation. She argues that judges and legislatures should, whenever applying or creating law, ask the question of whether the laws are such that free and equal persons could agree to them – a "test" derived from Kantian contractarianism. Obviously, Cornell is extending this claim to women. In addition, she cites Kant:

> Man's *freedom* as a human being, as a principle for the constitution of a commonwealth, can be expressed in the following formula. No one can compel me to be happy in accordance with his conception of the welfare of others, for each may seek happiness in whatever way he sees fit, so long as he does not infringe upon the freedom of others to pursue a similar end which can be reconciled with the freedom of everyone else within a workable general law – i.e. he must accord to others the same rights as he enjoys himself (Kant 1970, 74; cited by Cornell 1995, 11).

Cornell also remains liberal in the sense that she does not envisage the state as imposing an image of the good life but as giving rights, which protect against the infringement of our freedom by others. However, she extends the meaning of this harm to include, what she terms, "the degradation prohibition", such as the imposition of an oppressive imaginary to evoke sexual shame. This includes, for example, stereotyped images of women imposed upon them by sexual harassers or examples of homophobia, irrespective of gender. She does not think that the state should be involved in what she describes as "the project of becoming a person". This is distinct from the abstract contractarian image of "free and equal persons" in the above Kantian "test". As mentioned above, her analysis of the "project of becoming a person" therefore draws upon Lacanian psychoanalysis but it is not necessarily dependent upon accepting a Lacanian position – with its reliance upon the idea of a childhood "mirror stage" in which we are said to develop an idealised bodily image, the integrity of which may be threatened (as I will discuss further below). What Cornell envisages by this "project of becoming a person" is an idea of self-development in which, as adults, as well as children, we develop "who we are". Importantly, for Cornell, this depends upon an *imaginary* self-image, which can be affected by the way in which we view our bodies but also denotes a broader self-image.

To summarise, there are two different meanings of personhood being evoked by Cornell. The first is the politico-legal person, referenced to Kant and familiar in liberal theory. In this context, the person is envisaged as free and equal (and is traditionally male). As part of a "test" of justice, the question is posed as to whether persons, if they were free and equal and given a choice, would agree to legislation or common law judicial decisions. Those making the decisions or judgements are to ask themselves this question whenever they are trying to make or apply law. Second, Cornell envisages a self who struggles with the "project of becoming a person". As this is a metaphysical and psychological rather than primarily moral/political/legal concept, I will refer to it in terms of selfhood rather than personhood, despite Cornell's reference to the "project of becoming a person". The idea of struggle with self-development (and with "individuating" yourself from others) is particularly relevant to those who are exposed to negative self-images and contradictions (such as the view that their sex or race is incompatible with equal self-worth or citizenship).

Cornell extends Kant's conception of harm by virtue of her debt to Lacanian psychoanalysis. This "project of becoming a person" envisages a self as always developing and vulnerable. This model of self-development also plays a part in her utopian image of the creation of new and more progressive ways of living (that is not necessarily Lacanian). Sexuality is viewed as central to "who we are". Hence, Cornell argues for "sexuate rights" that do not merely legislate against discrimination in relation to sex/gender but also in relation to sexuality viewed more generally, for example in terms of gay rights. She also argues that exposure to violent pornography can force women to view themselves as simply body parts; "a body in bits", which is harmful to their self-images and hence their "projects of becoming a person" (Cornell 1995, 95–163).

At this point Cornell employs the Lacanian idea that we need to imagine our bodies as whole. Therefore, she concludes that, in order to allow us equivalent chances of developing new ways of living, the law should safeguard persons' "imaginary domain", our ideal self-image (which includes, but is not limited to our bodily images). This feeds into her use of Kant's social contract, described above, by employing the following argument. Our self-images should be protected by law as part of our "project of becoming a person" (i.e. self-development), which is undermined by systematic attacks upon our self-image and self-respect. Importantly, the two aspects of personhood and selfhood come together in the following argument. Any legislation that fails to protect self-development (the "project of becoming a person") would therefore fail the Kantian "legal legitimacy test" described in his social contract because free and equal persons would not agree to be ruled by laws that undermined their self-development (by failing to safeguard their self-image and self-respect). The state does not have any say in their actual self-development (which would be to impose upon them an image of the good) but is called upon to allow space for this development. This "space" is envisaged as a way of preventing some individuals (particularly those in dominant positions) from acting so as to impose their negative stereotypes on others, thereby crowding out other ways in which those stereotyped can develop. As I will discuss, the imagination plays a central role in this self-development. Cornell does not argue for "thought crime", of course, and it is only actions such as sexual harassment that constitute such harm. Similarly, she argues for the zoning of pornography, to avoid imposing upon women a particular image such as their bodies in pieces, discussed above (Cornell 1995, 103).

Cornell's reworking of Kant's social contract can be differentiated from that of Rawls. Both use the image of free and equal persons and the question of what they would agree to, given the choice. However, as mentioned above, Cornell wants to keep in play this question (and with it the idea of free and equal persons) and argues that it should be asked *every time* a legal decision is made, either in the creation of laws by the legislature or by judges setting precedents in common law cases. In contrast, Rawls employs the question to decide upon particular rules of justice on one occasion in a hypothetical thought experiment. Cornell does not refer to her move as part of a "social contract" (and as an ex-labour lawyer it will be painfully obvious to her that the contract metaphor is not evocative of free and equal persons). Instead, she refers directly to the question of free and equal persons, in a way that is compatible with Pateman's concerns, discussed in chapter 1.

Cornell is also influenced by Hegel to argue that we are, in modernity, subjects of law:

> Perhaps in the end I am Hegelian enough to think that we are actually constituted in modernity as subjects of right and so, in a sense, we cannot step outside this sphere of law (Florence 1997, 15).

Her work is also an attempt to intervene within particular legal debates with her contemporaries; to argue that if a liberal position is accepted then, in order to be consistent, liberals need to accept the stronger socialist feminist position that she supports.

Whilst there are important concerns that Cornell's position is individualistic (James 2002), to be discussed in detail below, I would argue that this self-development is necessarily social and is treated as such by Cornell. In contrast to a model which entails the discovery of a pre-existing "authentic" self, Cornell stresses that self-development involves acts of creation, in which our ability to imagine ourselves differently is employed to "act up", i.e. to challenge oppressive norms and to produce entirely new ways of living. To illustrate this point, it is useful to contrast very briefly Cornell's image of progressive social change with that of Hannah Arendt.

For Arendt (1958) the creation of something new occurs as a result of human action within the public sphere. Arendt envisages such action by evoking the Ancient Greek image of "the great words and deeds" enacted in the *polis*, which can create new ways of living. This description of change emphasises participation in public. Cornell is concerned with the legitimacy of law but her focus is upon the impact of its actual content rather than the means by which it is passed. She also envisages the self as an ongoing project of development in both public and private in a manner which challenges any clear distinction between the two, whereas Arendt views the self as constituted by its appearance to others through action within the public sphere.

Expanding upon this point, Cornell differs from Arendt with regard to the way in which the public and private are both envisaged as potential sites of change. Cornell's "project of becoming a person", may appear individualised in that it is to be the subject of legal protection and involves *self*-development but it is also acted out with others in different areas of life that could be designated as both public and private. I will return to the question of whether there is a tension in Cornell's work between this social image of self-development and the way in which the law is called upon to protect our individual self-development, below.

Having employed the Kantian social contract as a starting point from which to derive radical conclusions, Cornell is faced with the familiar criticisms that feminists have levelled at this contractarian tradition. Feminists have highlighted that the abstract view of the person has taken the male as the norm in many philosophical theories as well as in practice. Let's break down this concern. First, there is the criticism that the image of "free and equal persons", which purports to be neutral, actually takes male bodies and their (contingent) traditional lives as the norm (which I refer to as a "false universal" in chapter 1). This is tied to the equality/difference debate because women, when faced with this false universal, have the choice of either appearing the same as or different from this male norm.

In response to this objection, Cornell situates Kant's "test" within a social context. She points out that, in practice, it is judges (often male) who are being called upon to think from the position of the woman in the employment of a legal test. This is illustrated by a practical example. There has been some empirical evidence that, in certain cultures and times, men and women have had different views as to what constitutes sexual harassment and what is to be viewed as reasonable behaviour (Fitzgerald and Ormerod 1991; Powell 1986) cited by Cornell (1995, 262). Feminist lawyers have argued that (male) judges will adopt a male view point, whilst perceiving themselves to be objectively reasonable. Some feminist lawyers, for example Monti (1999) have argued that judges should, as part of a legal test of reasonableness in law, be told to imagine the position of the reasonable woman. Leaving aside whether this is possible for male judges whose everyday interactions with women may reinforce traditional stereotypes, Cornell views this approach as wrong in principle. She emphasises the Kantian social contract: that the legislature and judges when proposing any legal decisions should consider whether those decisions are such that free and equal persons could agree to them. This prevents women from being stereotyped as passive victims, who turn to law to protect them. Instead, Cornell argues that they should be envisaged as demanding respect for their equal personhood. More broadly Cornell's approach is framed as a demand that judges, in the operation of law in public, consider women *as if* they were free and equal rather than speculating upon their own stereotypes of what a "reasonable woman" or victim would think and do. This move also has the effect of blocking a demand that judges (a vastly disproportionate number of whom are male and white) impose further stereotypes on the grounds of race and sexuality for example, by asking what the reasonable black, gay woman would do. Obviously, there are strong arguments for increasing the diversity of the judiciary but not for inviting white, male judges to speculate upon stereotypes as part of a legal test.

Further, if judges impose their own stereotypes by, for example, claiming that the victim of sexual harassment was inappropriately dressed, Cornell's reading of Kant allows her to point out that this is an error of public reason. She calls upon judges to behave reasonably by not imposing their own imaginaries upon women but rather to consider them as if they were free and equal persons. This is an important claim and Cornell is right to make it, in contrast to arguments that women should be treated as women in law with separate rights, for example

Irigaray (1992).[2] The difficult question is whether and under what circumstances current judges (when selected from a homogeneous background as in the UK) are capable of standing outside their own experiences to make such a judgement. This is a contingent problem, which would be aided if the selection of the judiciary ensured a greater diversity of judicial backgrounds. However, it also raises a philosophical (and psychological) issue about our ability to abstract ourselves from our social background in order to make a judgement; that is central to Kant's work. It should be noted that Cornell's test is so abstract that it is necessary to flesh it out in order to support some of the (useful) legal proposals that she advocates (Richardson 2004b, 43–62).

In the next section, I will develop this reading of the feminist use of Kant's social contract by looking at Hampton's reading of Kant to consider the political implications of the philosophical move of *abstraction* (of the image of "free and equal persons" removed from social circumstances), which raises other issues aside from that of the "false universal" discussed in chapter 1.

Jean Hampton's Feminist Contractarianism

It may appear to be an odd reading of Drucilla Cornell who has emphasised the use of Lacan, as well as other areas of continental philosophy, in particular Derrida and Adorno and has even denied that the term "contractarian" applies to her (Cornell 1995, 242, fn.16), to juxtapose her work with that of Jean Hampton's contractarianism, which is firmly embedded within analytic philosophy. Nevertheless, as discussed in chapter 1, it is important to recognise that one of the strengths of feminist philosophy is the way in which it draws from a number of traditions in order to understand and attack women's subordination and exploitation. It is this central problem, linked with the use of Kant as a starting position, that results in a convergence between the work of Cornell and Hampton, despite the fact that they start from different traditions in philosophy and do not engage with each others work.

In "Feminist Contractarianism", Hampton (2002) reworks Kant's image of the social contract. Whereas Cornell, like Kant, employs the idea of what "free and equal persons" would agree to as a test of the legitimacy of law, Hampton uses the same image as a test for fairness in relationships, arguing that justice is relevant to all relationships:

2 There have been arguments that this is a rhetorical claim to illustrate the impossibility of such a move (Deutscher 2000). Whilst Irigaray (1985b) provides resources for thinking of a self that does not emerge as a result of a split from the other, her arguments regarding separate treatment of women by law are sadly not impossible to implement as the doctrine of coverture illustrates (Irigaray 1992). This move highlights Cornell's point that liberalism has both a regressive and a progressive side.

> I want to propose that by invoking the idea of contract we can make a moral evaluation of any relationship, whether it is in the family, the market place, the political society or the workplace – namely an evaluation of the extent to which that relationship is just … (Hampton 2002, 350).

She therefore reworks the question in the Kantian social contract of what free and equal persons would agree to, in a new context. As discussed earlier in chapters 1 and 2, a party to any relationship can ask:

> Given the fact that we are in this relationship, could both of us reasonably accept the distribution of costs and benefits (that is, the costs and benefits that are not themselves side effects of any affective or duty based tie between us) if we were the subject of an informed, unforced agreement in which we think of ourselves as motivated by self-interest (Hampton 2002, 351).

As outlined in chapter 1, Hampton argues that she is not assuming that everyone is motivated only by self-interest. She wants to highlight a type of exploitation that is based upon emotional leverage. It is worth looking carefully at this relationship between emotions and reason in her work because it draws from Kant, who has been accused of separating emotions from reason. It is therefore useful to consider whether feminist objections to Kant on this point also apply to Hampton's position. I will consider Kant first then turn to Hampton.

Kneller (1997) argues that moral autonomy, particularly derived from Kant's (1996) *The Foundation of the Metaphysics of Morals* has been associated with the image of a moral "hero" who stands alone and independent of "alien causes", setting aside emotion to obey principles rather than compassion (Kneller 1997, 175). In contrast, she argues that emotional reactions to a situation may be useful in furthering autonomy. If a women is in a relationship with a man who has authority over her as a result of the culture, and finds herself feeling used and frustrated, it may be that she feels uneasy emotionally before actually being able to articulate and reason upon the problem. Nevertheless, this may be a first step to recognising and altering the situation (Kneller 1997, 183). The emotions were a first step towards her autonomy. (Kneller goes on to find resources in Kant's (1987) *Critique of Judgement* for a more nuanced view of emotions than that associated with his earlier analysis.) In this example, she echoes the concerns of Seidler, to question whether,

> the subordination of needs and wants, feelings and desires, actually prepares us to take this kind of control over our lives (Seidler 1989, 245).

The way in which Hampton separates emotion from reason in her Kantian test initially appears to follow Kant in separating emotions and duty. However, Hampton's move is different because she recognises emotions as a potential source of leverage, productive of subordination and exploitation. In contrast to

Kant, Hampton repositions "duty" to think about it in a way that is not opposed to emotional ties. On the contrary, she envisages a situation in which a woman perceives her duty as intimately linked with her emotional commitments to her family. Hampton employs a test in order to illustrate when such a perceived duty is unreasonable. She is suspicious of emotions in this situation but this does not extend to a dismissal of all emotions and there is nothing in her work to suggest any disagreement with Kneller's example in which paying attention to emotions can lead to working out a problem and hence potentially greater autonomy.

Whereas there are arguments that subordination leaves women open to exploitation such that subordination must be analysed as primary (Pateman 1988; 2002), Hampton provides an analysis that works the other way around. Hampton describes how someone who allows himself or herself to be exploited becomes seen (and worse can start to view him/herself) as less worthy of respect than other persons. For example, any woman who continues to act as a servant for her family, without reciprocation, is treated as less than their equal. Whereas this behaviour could be viewed as an example of caring and as morally commendable, Hampton argues that it can have an insidious effect on all parties. In the family, it teaches children that some persons can be treated as if they are subordinate. This behaviour is understood in terms of failure to show respect for equal personhood and does not apply if members of the family are too young or sick to reciprocate.

This last point raises questions about a society in which there are structural reasons for a disproportionate amount of care falling on the shoulders of a particular group. The fact that Pateman prioritises subordination as opening the way to exploitation derives from the fact that she is giving a historical analysis of women's position rather than focusing upon morality. By considering Pateman's position, Hampton can be seen to miss out part of the story. Women's subordination was assumed in the marriage contract with the traditional role of housewife and then could be described as being perpetuated, in part, through the psychological mechanisms that Hampton describes. Hence subordination already preceded exploitation but is also perpetuated by it in the ways that Hampton highlights.

Hampton's work draws out the distinction between the way in which Hobbes and Kant envisage the use of contract. As Gauthier puts it,

> [Hobbes] treats the contract as a deal that each person finds reasonable to accept in order better to advance his or her own interests. [Kant] treats the contract rather as guaranteeing proper respect for him or herself as an end (Hampton and Gauthier 2007, xii).

As discussed in chapter 2, for Hobbes, the failure to treat individuals fairly is in itself wrong, as far as they are concerned, because it stops them from getting what they want and undermines their reputation so they may expect more of the same treatment. In contrast, for Kant, it is wrong because of an additional step: it signals a failure to respect their equal personhood. For Kant, we do not lose equal personhood when this occurs because we always command this respect as persons. Gauthier asks: if we are not actually degraded then how can we appear as such? (Hampton and Gauthier 2007, xiii). He does not develop this question, although, unlike Hampton, Hobbes is the source of his arguments regarding morality (Gauthier 1987). Gauthier's claim could be reversed. If someone's worth is simply to be viewed as his or her value to others (as Hobbes argues) then s/he cannot be viewed as being degraded by an action which fails to respect her/him. S/he is simply being treated in accordance with her/his current worth. So, to be degraded in Gauthier's Hobbesian terms simply refers to the idea of sliding down a league table, which is accurate, based upon others' judgement of one's "market position". In contrast, for Hampton, to be degraded has a different meaning based upon a comparison between how one is treated and how one ought to be treated as a person. Hampton's potential response to Gauthier's question highlights the point that, even when treated badly, one is still a person and so does not actually lose the right to be treated with respect.

Gauthier's concern regarding Kant is similar to Waldron's claim that Locke derived his argument for equality from the idea that God viewed everyone as equal and that this is lost when an external determinant for morality is no longer accepted (Waldron 2007). If it is no longer accepted that there are objective grounds for equal treatment then Hobbes' "sensible metaphysics", with its claim that we are only equal when equally able to defend ourselves is not the only option. Whilst I am not defending any particular view, there are many alternatives. It is possible to argue, for example, for an indirect consequentialism: that we would be happier if we treated each other as if there were objective grounds for equality. There are also attempts to deal with the absence of foundations for ethics and yet maintain an appeal to universal judgement through an extension of Kant's reflective aesthetic judgement to political judgement (Arendt 1989; Beiner and Nedelsky 2001; Ferrara 2008). The diverse approaches to this problem and Hampton's own arguments (1998), which remain closer to Kant by ignoring current critiques of modern foundationalism and attempting to secure grounds for morality, are beyond the scope of this book. However, even without accepting that Hampton can objectively ground her moral theory, she can be viewed as producing a useful psychological analysis of what happens if someone is taught to view herself as less worthy of respect than others. This aspect of her work has much in common with Cornell's extended view of self-development, which draws upon and aims to radicalise the liberal tradition. The common concerns emerge, not only in their employment of the Kantian idea of the social contract, but also their interest in the impact of degradation upon self-image.

Feminist Objections to Kant's Social Contract applied to Cornell and Hampton

Both Hampton and Cornell are potentially subject to objections made against Kant. As well as the concern that the abstract free and equal person is not, in fact, neutral but has characteristics that are traditionally (and contingently) associated with men, there are also broader problems with such an abstraction that need to be teased out. For example, it is a powerful objection that such attempts to ignore a social context allow theorists to attribute actions to the "free will" of the actors, in situations where they actually have little choice. This has applied to both women's historical "consent" to marriage and to workers' "consent" to work. The abstraction of workers from their social context allowed judges to manufacture their consent – if only as a legal fiction – when further attention to their context would have shown that they had little choice but to work in dangerous conditions. Similarly, at a conceptual level, there are feminist criticisms of Rawls' Kantian image (of free and equal persons sitting round a table deciding rules of justice), which have highlighted that he only envisaged (male) heads of household (Okin 1989) and that, as touched upon above, the image of such a person as autonomous neglects the human need for care and the norm of dependency (Kittay 1999).

Hence, the main feminist objection is whether the Kantian social contract with its reference to "free and equal persons" brings with it an image of the self that has (contingent and historical) socialised male characteristics, which have been associated with a preference for principles rather than compassion (Gilligan 1982), discussed with regard to Hampton above. Given that both Cornell and Hampton follow Kant in employing an image of abstract free and equal personhood to provide a test for legitimacy of legislation/legal decisions and of fairness in relationships, the ways in which they understand selfhood therefore need to be examined for gender bias.

For Cornell, what it is to be a self should not be defined by the state and involves a project of developing something new. Even if there is a tendency for judges to think of men as the neutral instantiation of the free and equal person, she is expressly setting up Kant's test with a view to forcing judges to think of women as free and equal persons rather than to impose stereotypes upon them. There may be practical questions as to whether this works in the absence of greater diversity in the judiciary, but she is focused upon the issue.

For Hampton the "image" of free and equal persons is necessary in order to provide "an Archimedean point" outside of society as a means of criticising the current position of women (Hampton 2002, 347). It is this objective claim that she finds lacking in arguments based upon an ethic of care or communitarian appeals to community standards. I have argued (Richardson 2007b) that Hampton's test is a potential tool of consciousness-raising and of political public argument. However, it provides only a starting point in that it can be inferred from the existence of widespread failure of Hampton's test in any society that what is required is major political change, which is critical of material practices. For Pateman's arguments that political theory has been depoliticised by Rawlsian methodology see Pateman (2002, 22), discussed earlier in chapter 1.

Hampton does not question the use of the individual as a starting point for her analysis nor does she stress issues of his/her continuing development, in comparison to Cornell. Nevertheless, Hampton provides a detailed analysis of the way in which someone's treatment as less worthy than a person undermines her/his self-respect. In this she has much in common with Kant's concerns about poverty and equal worth. This can be illustrated by considering Hampton's adoption of Kant's position on retributive justice in the criminal law, to be discussed further in the next chapter. Hampton (1991b) argues that if certain crimes, such as rape or wife-beating, are not properly recognised as such then this should be understood as a public failure of law to recognise women's equal worth as persons. The criminal treats her as less than a person and the law should demonstrate in public that this is incorrect. A public failure of law to do so can lead the victims to (wrongly) view themselves as actually less worthy of respect. They are incorrect because – for Hampton – persons are always equally worthy of respect, irrespective of their evaluation and treatment by others. Hampton therefore recognises the subtle (and less subtle) ways in which self-respect can be eroded. Hampton's demand for respect for women's equal worth covers very similar ground to that of Cornell, despite their different views of what it is to be or have a self.

Interestingly, in common with Cornell, Hampton refers to the "contractarian" Kantian appeal to "free and equal persons" as an image or picture:

> [E]ven though theorists who call themselves "contractarians" have all supposedly begun from the same reflexive starting point – namely what people could "agree to" – these differences and disagreements among people who are supposedly in the same philosophical camp show that contractarians are united not by a common philosophical theory but by a common *image*. Philosophers hate to admit it, but sometimes they work from pictures rather than ideas (Hampton 2002, 342; emphasis in original).

This is an important point that has much in common with Cornell. It replaces Kant's view of his social contract, which asks what free and equal persons would accept as an *idea of reason* and places more emphasis upon this as an "image". This switches the emphasis onto the imagination. Below, in the next two sections, I will consider the role of the imagination in more detail as, for Cornell, it is central to her view of the self as developing, open and experimental and also to the question of what "free and equal persons would agree to", which is to be the focus of the judicial (and legislature's) imagination.

The Role of the Imagination in Cornell's Rereading of Kant's Social Contract

Cornell is eclectic in the way in which she draws from theoretical sources for her own ends. In her analysis of the role of the imagination she employs both Kant and Lacan. Kant describes the imagination as an individual faculty. Lacan (2001, 1–6) describes the mirror stage of development in which a child comes to identify with an image outside of her/himself as part of an analysis of individual development.

In both cases, the imagination mediates between what is external and internal to the individual, associated with images in the mind. This is in contrast to theorists who concentrate upon the "social imaginary", by which they refer to their analysis of images of the world that we are all exposed to through, for example, the media, see Castoriadis (1998). James (2002, 194) argues that there is a problem with the way in which Cornell's work "opens a gap" between the imagination viewed as an individual faculty (and which Cornell also makes the source of individual rights that are to be protected by law) and the social imaginary. I will detail Cornell's position more fully and then turn to the problems raised by James. I aim to tease out different aspects of James' interesting argument in the next section. I will defend Cornell with regard to the relationship between imagination as an individual faculty, which also has social content. This is analogous with the way that the use of language can be described as an individual's ability and yet private language is impossible. However, the question arises as to whether the openness of self, described in terms of the "project of becoming a person" is constrained by the fact that Cornell views us as always subjects of law in modernity. The problem with the image of rights-bearing individuals is the evocation of the fiction of property in the person. I examine the extent to which Cornell's concepts of both personhood and selfhood are able to avoid being interpreted in terms of this politically-regressive legal fiction that may act as a social constraint upon her vision of the openness of the imagination, on which she relies.

James (2002) recognises that the distinction between the individual and social in the different theoretical models of the imagination are a matter of degree. However, she draws a comparison between, what she views as, Cornell's emphasis upon the individual and Gatens' "social" view of the imagination, derived from Spinoza and discussed in chapter 3. As James makes clear, Cornell's position is complex in that her call for law to protect the "imaginary domain" treats the imaginary as something that can be the source of rights. In addition, Cornell's Lacanianism also seems to point in the direction of viewing the imaginary as "individual" in the sense that it is, for Lacan (2001, 1–6). Whilst this is correct, it is also possible to stress that, as James is aware, for Cornell, the imaginary domain is also the potential source of collective experimentation to develop new – more progressive – ways of living and is therefore social. In addition, the decisions of judges, who are called upon to imagine "free and equal persons" are also described by Cornell as potentially acting in accordance with public reason, which is to be assisted by this image, thought experiment or fiction (from Kant's social contract).

Whilst this concern may not lie behind James' position, it may be useful to think about her claim (that Cornell's description of the imaginary is too individualistic, given that it can be viewed as giving rise to rights) in the broader context of some feminist legal theorists' understandable suspicion of rights. This can be illustrated by feminist work that has been influenced by Pashukanis' Marxist view of rights as a commodity (Kerruish 1992). In this work, the main problem that is identified with respect to rights draws from the idea that rights-claims necessarily entail an image of the self as a "possessive individual", i.e. it evokes the legal fiction of property in the person: that we can "own" our rights such that they can be alienated.

As discussed in chapter 4 on Locke, Pateman (1988; 2002) provides a compelling argument that such an image of the self based upon the fiction of property in the person is intimately linked with subordination. The question I want to pose is whether Cornell's work necessarily evokes this fiction of property in the person, with which Cornell herself, as a socialist feminist, would be unsympathetic. Does this image of the possessive individual necessarily haunt all rights claims and, turning specifically to Cornell's work, does it apply to the way in which the imagination features as part of a rights-claim?

To answer these questions, it is necessary to consider both Cornell's view of personhood and of the self in turn. With regard to personhood, it is possible to argue in defence of Cornell that neither the imagination nor rights are viewed as the sort of "things" or "commodities" that can be envisaged by her as being subject to contract or alienated. In other words, the reference to "ownership" of rights, which understandably raises James' suspicions, relies for its sting upon the treatment of such rights through the legal fiction of the property in the person. (Alternatively, there could be practical problems with the enforcement of rights but this is not necessarily always the case (Richardson 1999, 26).)

So, Cornell could deny that this criticism applies to her view of rights because – whilst she calls upon the law to defend self-development and so it is an individual who brings a rights-claim – she does not consider the imagination as either an object or as something that could be treated as if it were alienable. Some work performed in the creation of social images, in advertising for example, *can* be sold in a market but this is not applicable here. Having made this point in relation to Cornell's view of personhood (the "free and equal persons" in her test) it is necessary to consider the same question with regard to her image of self-development ("project of becoming a person"). Does her open creative self-development and experimentation *itself*, irrespective of the role of law, risk collapsing into an image of a "possessive individual?" There have been criticisms from within Foucauldian governmentality literature of the way in which, within neo-liberalism, we are called upon to each view ourselves as an enterprise, which involves working upon ourselves to increase our "human capital". Colin Gordon captures the point when he argues that,

> What cultural critics diagnose as a triumph of auto-consuming narcissism can perhaps be more adequately understood as part of the managerialisation of personal identity and personal relations which accompanies the capitalisation of the meaning of life ... The state presents itself as the referee in an ongoing transaction in which one partner strives to enhance the value of his or her life while another endeavours to economise the cost of that life (Colin Gordon 1991, 44).

It is worrying that Cornell's "project of becoming a person" sounds so similar to this neo-liberal model of "self as enterprise" and contingently may be viewed through this lens (see, for example, Richardson 2004b). However, its openness to interpretation, derived from Kant, does not dictate that this is the case. A more basic problem is the extent to which such creativity of new ways of living can, in fact, be played out given the constraints of current institutions and practices. Are we capable of such leaps of the imagination that Cornell requires of us and, if so, in which circumstances? This will be discussed in the next section when we consider the tension between "the imaginary" and material practices as a way of thinking about social change.

Cornell, the Imagination and Kant's Aesthetics

To outline the central role of the imagination in Cornell's work and the extent to which she relies upon Kant's aesthetics, I will compare her concept of the imaginary with that of Gatens, discussed in chapter 3. Like Cornell, Gatens (1995, 136–141) examines judges' imaginations. Gatens' description of this problem appears to cover the same ground as Cornell in a "different register". It is predicated upon a different understanding of the imagination, which is itself linked with a different image of what it is to be a self. Here, I want to look more closely at their views of the imagination to draw out a different distinction from James' division between Cornell's greater emphasis upon the imaginary as an individual faculty (or central to the development of a bodily self-image) compared with the emphasis upon a social imaginary in Gatens.

Cornell views the imagination as central to social change and also stresses an aesthetic dimension (Cornell 2008). She uses the example of gay activism, which involves "acting up" in ways that shock an oppressive status quo, whilst not threatening others' self-worth. To understand the central role of the imagination and aesthetic acts in Cornell's employment of the idea of free and equal persons, employed in Kant's social contract, it is worth considering Kant's analysis of aesthetics, to which it is intimately related (Cornell 2008, 11–37). In Kant's *Critique of Judgement*, the experience of the sublime can affect the subject in a profound way. Sublime art opens up the experience of our "supersensible vocation." It evokes ideas of freedom, morality and God (Kant 1987, 114–115). Whilst the beautiful, for Kant, is linked with the harmony of the imagination and understanding in a way which is life-enhancing, the sublime is more threatening. The experience of the dynamic sublime, evoked by the might of nature such as the wildness of the sea or storms, threatens us but then (as a result of the use of reason) "we" (i.e. educated white men, not weakened by peace or trade) know that we would stand firm and behave morally even in the face of such a threat. To quote Kant, the sublime calls forth "fortitude" (Kant 1987, 120). We know that, "we would not bow to it if our highest principles were at stake" (Kant 1987, 121). He therefore has an image of a self that is threatened from the outside but then is able to affirm its boundaries – to stand firm – though the use of reason.

Similarly with regard to the mathematical sublime, there is initial discomfort because the imagination struggles and fails to produce an image of the enormity of a natural object, such as a mountain range. This discomfort is followed by the satisfaction of knowing that our failure of imagination is proof that our attempt to visualise it was at the behest of reason. The striving to imagine such greatness arouses in us feelings of "ideas of reason", those ideas, such as freedom (and the Kantian social contract described at the start of this chapter) which cannot be conceptualised. As Kant expresses this,

> Hence the feeling of the sublime is a feeling of displeasure that arises from the imagination's inadequacy, in an aesthetic estimation of magnitude, for an estimation by reason, but is at the same time also a pleasure, aroused by the fact that this very judgement, namely, that even the greatest power of sensibility is inadequate, is (itself) in harmony with rational ideas, insofar as striving towards them is still a law for us. For it is a law (of reason) for us, and part of our vocation, to estimate any sense object in nature that is large for us as being small when compared with ideas of reason; and whatever arouses in us the feeling of this supersensible vocation is in harmony with that law (Kant 1987, 114–115).

It is noteworthy that when Kant talks about the sublime, he limits the experience to a certain section of the population. It is important to avoid conflating Kant's description of the autonomous self with that of the economic man. Kant excludes from the experience of the sublime men who have a "commercial spirit", arising from prolonged peace and which produces "selfishness, cowardice and softness" (Kant 1987, 22). Whilst the stereotype is still masculine, Kant's appeal to an earlier notion of heroic valour fits with the way in which warriors themselves are viewed as sublime in the pre-critical, *Observations on the Feeling of the Beautiful and Sublime* (Kant 1991a).

For Kant, women are excluded from the experience of the sublime, which is important because of its moral implications in that it is an experience of using reason to stand firm against an external force. However, he does not view women as actually incapable of having this experience. This is despite the fact that he views courage as a masculine virtue (Kant 1974, 124–125; see Battersby 2007). Kant employs the weak argument that women should be afraid of nature and therefore should not experience its threatening aspect because they may be pregnant and jeopardise the foetus.[3]

3 This is similar to Kant's argument that women are also capable of thinking deeply but should not do so because it is not charming to men (Kant 1991a, 78). Women are to hold back from developing these abilities because of their natural role. This is in contrast to his more positive comment in *What is Enlightenment?* in which he comments sarcastically, "The guardians who have kindly taken upon themselves the work of supervision will soon see to it that by far the largest part of mankind (including the entire fair sex) should consider

Cornell (2008) states that she draws upon Kantian aesthetics and that aesthetic acts can bring about progressive social change. In this way, Cornell positions herself as part of a tradition in critical theory that starts with Kant and acknowledges a debt to both Kant, whose description of aesthetics has been sketched in part above, and to Adorno's reading of Kant that influences the way in which she views aesthetics as having a role in social change. To expand upon Adorno's position involves relating it to Kant. For Kant, information about the world is brought together and understood through the way in which we categorise it. If an object were to fall outside of the categories then it is not perceived at all. Adorno argues for a different view of the perceiving subject (the human being) and the object: that it is possible for an object (a specific work of art) to shock us into a different conceptual framework. At different historical times it is possible to re-evaluate an object. The main example of this, for Adorno, is the possibility of viewing objects as no longer commodities within a capitalist mode of production, Hence, autonomous art raises the possibility of an experience that is not commodified, that is no longer viewed in terms of its price (for an analysis of this move in a feminist context see Battersby 1998, 125–147). It is this conceptualisation of the imagination that lies behind Cornell's image of "acting up" by public demonstrations of new ways of living. However, she also envisages other uses of the imaginary in her arguments, which I will now discuss in detail.

As outlined above, Cornell envisages a legal system which does not impose its image of the good but can allow space for individuals to open up progressive and diverse ways of living by constraining those whose behaviour (understood through their own imaginaries) threatens to enforce an unjust status quo. For example, the sexual harasser with his stereotyped views of women is to be constrained by law from acting in such a way that interferes with women's freedom. The law is to prevent the harm of having stereotypes imposed such that they appear to be the only way of thinking about oneself; thereby stultifying self-development. This concern regarding oppressive imaginaries extends to an analysis of the (male) judicial imagination. As discussed, Cornell therefore expresses her claim that judges must resist imposing their imaginaries upon women in the court room in terms of a demand that they employ public reason. In this context, judges' imaginations are viewed as producing a stereotyped fiction, whereas the imagination that law is called upon to protect (the "imaginary domain") has a positive role in the creation of new social relations. It is a mistake of judges (and others) to assume that a negative stereotype of a woman represents an unchangeable essence of her nature rather than, for example, a possible reaction to the way in which she is positioned within a contingent historical network of power. In its negative role, Cornell's view of judicial imagination seems to have much in common with Gatens' (1995) analysis of the imagination derived from Spinoza (discussed in chapter 3). It is a form of knowledge that is inadequate (to employ Spinoza's term) and often linked

the step forward to maturity not only as difficult but as highly dangerous". He is here arguing in favour of this step forward that involves thinking for yourself (Kant 1970, 54).

with emotion – a point that James (2002) illustrates is a common understanding of the imagination within different models. In its progressive, creative usage Cornell's imagination may also be linked with strong emotions but Cornell does not see it as forming the basis of an action that is contrary to public reason or of being based upon knowledge that is in some way inadequate. As discussed in chapter 3, Gatens seeks to analyse why I find it difficult for judges to reject stereotypes by employing a Spinozist rather than psychoanalytic framework.

I suggest that the major split between Cornell and Gatens on the imagination is not the degree of emphasis upon the individual compared to the social – as both employ both individual and social analysis – but upon the role of the (always both social and individual) imagination in social change. This is intimately linked to a metaphysics in which Cornell emphasises our imagination whereas contemporary readings of Spinoza prioritise the body, and what it can do, along with our daily habits. As discussed in chapter 3, this emphasis upon the body has been popular amongst continental philosophers, such as Althusser (1997), Balibar (1998), Montag (1999) and Deleuze (1988). Part of this move is motivated by Marx's view that, "It is not consciousness that determines life, but life that determines consciousness" (Marx and Engels 1998, 42). The way in which we imagine the world is viewed as stemming from our daily activities and bodily habits, which exposes subordination in contrast to an emphasis upon rights claims. Again, this should not be overstated and may be a matter of emphasis. Cornell would recognise the importance of bodily habits and seeks to extend experimentation, understood as imaginative leaps that are also acted out physically.

Whilst Gatens' Spinozist analysis covers similar ground to that of Cornell, when Cornell aims to curtail the negative imposition of imagination in her call for judges to be reasonable, Cornell's discussion of the positive aspect of the imagination differs from Gatens' approach. This difference takes two forms: one linked with personhood and one with selfhood. On personhood, judges are to be asked to employ the image of "what free and equal persons would agree to" in a positive way to help them to employ public reason – a move that brings together reason and imagination as a heuristic device or technique to try to get judges to imagine women differently. For Cornell, the development of the self occurs through acts of imagination, which are creative and aesthetic. This can be contrasted to the progressive social change envisaged by Spinoza in terms of increased powers of acting of both individual and social bodies through the encouragement of greater uses of reason. However, as illustrated in chapter 3, Gatens, Lloyd and James emphasise ways in which the (Spinozan) imagination plays a major role in social change. Similarly, Cornell also moves away from the Kantian emphasis upon reason to envisage a more positive role for the imagination.

I have juxtaposed Cornell's work with Gatens' Spinoza in order to explore how she envisages the imagination, its link with personhood, selfhood and progressive social change. Finally, it is possible to make some tentative suggestions with regard to fleshing out Cornell's model of the imagination, whilst recognising that the Kantian framework employed differs greatly from that of Spinoza in both its politics and metaphysics (and the fact that Cornell does not remain faithful to Kant, particularly with regard to the role of the imagination). I want to defend the view that instead of employing a Lacanian analysis of the self in relation to the imagination, a more useful approach would be to employ the way in which imagination is envisaged by Spinoza, as that which is linked with emotion as part of, what he calls the, "first type of knowledge" and still affects us when this knowledge is superseded. When this is applied to Cornell's concerns the role of the imagination is slightly altered but can perform the work she wants within a progressive framework, which is derived from the Kantian social contract. For example, consider a woman who is thinking about engaging in, for example, a choice of sexual behaviour that is portrayed negatively. Initially, if she has little experience of this activity, the images that will come to mind are those from popular stereotypes – often from portrayals in the media. These images will often be linked with negative emotions and stereotypes about women. However, it is possible to examine and challenge these, in a move akin to "consciousness-raising", corresponding to Spinoza's second form of knowledge. The initial emotions and image will potentially remain but could also be superseded.

This very simple model no longer relies upon a Lacanian notion of the *imago*, or idealised bodily image *per se*. In addition, metaphysically, it is not based upon the idea of defining oneself in terms of lack (or what one is not) in comparison with a positive model of desire, as demonstrated by Gatens (1995) or Deleuze's (1988) reading of Spinoza. One way of illustrating this point is to consider the way in which Judith Butler (1993, 8) employs Lacan to describe the idea that the identity of a heterosexual is secured by defining him/herself against homosexuality. Here, the self is viewed as that which is cut off from others by defining itself against what it is not; what is excluded as "less than human" – albeit that in Butler's work this cut from the constitutive outside may be portrayed as unstable. In contrast, metaphysical models of self derived from Spinoza involve thinking about the self in terms of both human bodies and connections with others, in complex ways that are not predicated upon the need to envisage such a cut nor in terms of understanding oneself as defined against what one denies or lacks.

Whereas "poststructuralist theory" has argued that there is a break between Kant as modern and Lacan, Battersby (1998, 81–102) argues that this position derives from a focus upon epistemology and neglects the similarities between these writers when their metaphysics is considered. In particular, she argues that both Kant and Lacan are characterised by the idea of the self as constituted by its outside, or what it is not. This allows her to develop a relational metaphysics by reworking Kant. This, she contrasts with the position of Woman in Lacan, who is viewed as symbolic of otherness. This move closes down discussion of actual women's reactions to the ways in which they have been positioned historically. (For an application of Battersby's work to a legal context see Richardson (2000, 119–134; 2004b, 28–42; 2007c).) I will return to this point in the final chapter.

Conclusion

Cornell's response to the equality/difference problem is to reject calls for "reasonable woman" tests in law but to insist that judges focus upon the image of free and equal persons, to be applied to both women and men. This represents a demand that judges should not impose their imaginary stereotypes upon women. Whilst Cornell relies upon a psychoanalytic framework to understand such judicial imaginary, Gatens employs an account from Spinoza, in which the imagination is treated as the first form of knowledge, detailed in chapter 3.

Cornell's appeal to Kantian personhood in law (as something which is distinct from self-development for which the law is to leave space) involves an abstraction. Whilst feminists have illustrated how such a move is often problematic in that the "neutral" person of philosophy can often be seen to have male bodies or traditional (contingent) male characteristics, it can also be useful in trying to shift the imagination away from the current situation. In this respect her aim is the same as that of Hampton. Both employ Kant's social contract to claim reasonableness, which can prompt us to imagine freedom and options available to women that do not currently exist.

Cornell's approach to personhood and the open idea of self-development both depend upon the imagination. James has argued that there are problems in viewing this as something that can be owned; that is the subject of legal rights. In contrast, I have argued that the main problem with rights-claims is that they evoke the fiction of property in the person, discussed in chapter 4. Cornell does not envisage the imagination or rights as alienable and therefore does not rely upon this fiction. However, the image of the "possessive individual" haunts Cornell's image of self-development in that it fits neatly within the neo-liberal notion of "the self as an enterprise". Whilst there is this danger, her image of self-development is so open that it need not always collapse into this image.

Whereas James understandably points to a tension between the individual and social when comparing Cornell with Gatens, I am interested in considering the tension that comes to light when analysing their different understandings of the role of the imagination in social change. To express the difference crudely, Gatens, in common with other continental philosophers influenced by Spinoza, stresses the role of bodies whereas Cornell stresses the mental aspect of imagination. However, this material/ideal distinction – like that between the individual and social imaginaries – can be overstated and may be a matter of emphasis. Rather than separate mental leaps of imagination and bodily habits, it is possible to think, with Spinoza, of the mind and body together as attributes of the same substance. This emphasis upon the psychological impact of physically acting out a role, dwelt on at length by Pascal, is summarised by Althusser in the following way, "Kneel down, move your lips in prayer, and you will believe" (Althusser 2008, 42). It may be possible to read Cornell in such a way that her demand that we "act up" is given greater emphasis. This would take her conception of thc imagination closer to Gatens. The openness of her conception of self can be viewed as resonating with Spinoza's evocative comment that,

> For no one has so far determined what the body can do (Spinoza 2000a, 2, P2, S, p.167).

Chapter 7
Conclusion: The Social Contractarians and Contemporary Images of Women

The Fiction of the Social Contract

In Pateman's ground-breaking work on the social contractarians, she highlights a problem: that any evocation of this fiction will invite a view of the self as owner of property in the person. Her aim is to promote both practical proposals, such as a basic income, whilst also showing how the fictions that we use to think about contract justify subordination. This concern with the use of the image of the contract can also be expressed in a different form. It is also the case that images of what it is to be an autonomous self risk collapsing into an image of the property-owning individual, who views himself as free when able to protect himself from the threatening outside, whether conceived of as nature, other individuals or the state, by drawing behind his property. As I will illustrate, this conception of the bounded individual is historically and contingently gendered. Whilst Taylor (1997) draws a distinction between metaphysical individualism and advocacy individualism, I want to conclude by looking at the way Jennifer Nedelsky's (1991) analysis in this area illustrates how different metaphysical images of "who we are" affect judges' imaginations, a point discussed by both Gatens and Cornell, drawing upon different frameworks, as illustrated in chapters 3 and 6.

The way in which Pateman refers to the social contract, together with the marriage contract and employment contract is important in showing why such a progressive idea failed to live up to its potential. It is the image of the contract – the thought experiment of individuals sitting round a table that Hampton finds so useful for thinking about free and equal persons – that Pateman rejects. As she notes, it is not necessary to think of this image of contract in order to analyse free and equal personhood and – as Mills argues (Pateman and Mills 2007, 84–92) – to that extent their work is not in conflict. I have highlighted how Pateman's work can be used to illustrate the political limits of Hampton's moral analysis. I have also argued that Pateman is misread when she is viewed as assuming that the sexual contract has already happened such that women are somehow trapped as a result. Contentiously, I have supported my claim that her work can be viewed as compatible with aspects of Foucault's middle period. What it means to be a housewife or an employee involves daily habits and rituals but it also has meaning historically by virtue of the way in which we think about contract and the fiction of property in the person. As Pateman argues, contract creates housewives and employees.

I want to conclude by illustrating some of the ways in which the arguments made by the classic social contractarians have stayed with us and to highlight some of the (contingent and historical) ways in which women (and in particular women's traditional work of childcare) trouble these frameworks themselves. It is therefore of interest to see how the courts struggle to ascribe a value to the cost of care work to a mother in ways that draw from both Locke and Kant, although not their views on women *per se.* These provide alternative ways of conceptualising a problem compared to, what I will refer to as "pre-modern" views, which are dependent upon the idea of natural status. I outline a contemporary type of legal case, which has taken place in common law. Whilst the example is from the UK and has also arisen in other common law jurisprudence, the illustration is not sketched in order to give a particular legal analysis, nor to raise questions about the efficacy about this type of loss distribution, but to examine the use of the concepts arising from contractarian thought, as discussed in earlier chapters. The aim is to see how they are put to work today. I will then consider the meaning of autonomy, that arises from these cases and end by looking at the political role of images and fictions.

The Example of the Wrongful Conception Cases

In the so-called "wrongful conception cases", parents took negligence claims usually against a health authority or trust, on the basis that a faulty sterilisation operation lead to the birth of an (initially) unwanted child. The main case in the area is the House of Lords' decision in *McFarlane v Tayside Health Board* (1999),[1] the first case of this type to come before the Law Lords. They decided that, provided a child is born healthy, awarding compensation for the costs of bringing up a child would not be "fair, just and reasonable".[2] However, the pain and suffering and inconvenience associated with the pregnancy and birth plus loss of earnings and any medical expenses associated with the pregnancy were awarded (with Lord Millett dissenting). This overturned a Court of Appeal decision[3] from 1985 in which damages had been granted based upon the upkeep of the child. It also overturned the lower court's judgement.

In his dissenting judgement Lord Millett agreed with counsel for the Health Board's defence that the pain and suffering in relation to pregnancy could not constitute a head of damage because pregnancy is a natural event and not an injury to the body. However, he would have awarded damages of £5,000 to represent the harm that was done to both parents in losing their right to choose the size of their family, which he describes in terms of "loss of autonomy". The Lords in *Rees v*

1 *McFarlane v Tayside Health Authority* H.L [1999] 3 WLR 1301; [2000] 2 AC 59.

2 *McFarlane v Tayside Health Board* [2000] 2 AC 82 (Lord Steyn).

3 *Emeh v Kensington and Chelsea and Westminster Area Health Authority* [1985] QB 1012 CA.

Darlington Memorial NHS Trust[4] take up this new head of damage. Curiously, Lord Millett treats both parents as being equally situated with respect to this loss of autonomy.

Locke: Property in the Person

A Lockean approach, as discussed in chapter 4, would be to view women as owners of their abilities or property in the person. If they risk suffering a loss, such as loss of earnings, the question arises as to whether or not, as prudent owners, they can insure this property, including loss of earnings or the work carried out in childcare. In cases of wrongful conception, it is the doctors who are in the only position to evaluate the risk of faulty sterilisation and hence to insure. Indeed, it is a feature of the case that if the claimants had been made aware of the risk then they could easily have used other methods of contraception. One of the Lords' worries is that they could be forced to offset the benefits of having a child (despite the fact that such an offset is not usually viewed as necessary, for example you do not reduce a miner's accident compensation on the grounds that he can spend time in the sunshine). This is described as a problem of putting a value on human life and hence commodifying it, which the Lords conclude is impossible.

If the work involved in childcare itself is considered then it is clear that such personal matters have already been "commodified" by the courts. The traditional work of women in the home including: the provision of housework, companionship and sex has been given a price in common law. For example, in the UK, prior to its abolition by the Administration of Justice Act 1982 there was a head of damages in negligence that allowed men to be compensated for the "loss of *consortium* of a wife". In 1952, the Lords refused to extend this common law claim to a wife whose husband had become impotent as a result of the defendant's negligence. Lord Goddard made the historical position clear when, in turning down the wife's claim, he stated that,

> The action which the law gives to the husband for loss of *consortium* is founded on the proprietary right which from ancient times it was considered the husband had in his wife. It was in fact based on the same grounds as gave a master a right to sue for an injury to his servant if the latter was thereby unable to perform his duties. It was an action of trespass for an invasion of the property right which, arising from the status of villeinage or serfdom, the master had over his servant. *Best v Samuel Fox and Co. Ltd.* [1952] AC 731–732 (Lord Goddard).

There have also been cases in which childcare has been given a value in the courts. Under the Fatal Accidents Act 1976 a child can claim for "non financial dependency", i.e. the lost care as a result of the death of the carer, usually the

4 *Rees v Darlington Memorial NHS Trust* [2004] 1 AC 309.

mother. The courts initially took the logical step of calculating this sum upon the diminishing need for childcare calculated upon the cost of a nanny.[5] They later rejected such calculation.[6] The judge now directs himself or herself, as if directing a jury, to the question of what an award for a loss of a mother should be. This has resulted in lower payments than those based upon mathematical calculations. In a move not guaranteed to comfort the bereaved, a qualitative assessment of the replacement care has been made and used to offset the claim. So, for example, when the Court of Appeal decided that the new carer was providing better quality care than the mother in *Stanley v Saddique* (1992)[7] the damages were reduced as a result. The courts have been willing to put a figure upon the cost of childcare but have not been willing to view wrongful conception cases as a situation in which someone has to provide such care (as extra work).

The fact that the Lords were willing to ignore the usual principles of tort law in the wrongful conception cases is consistent with the devaluation of childcare in the Fatal Accident cases. Lady Hale notes that,

> It is, perhaps, an indication of the reluctance of the common law to recognise the cost of care to the carer that claims for wrongful conception and birth of healthy children have not previously been analysed in this way: thus in McFarlane's case, no claim was made "in respect of any care or trouble undergone by the pursuers in the course of bringing up their child". *Parkinson v St James and Seacroft University Hospital NHS Trust* [2002] QB 287 (Lady Hale).

I want to consider the political antecedents of this way of characterising motherhood. A Lockean approach could be characterised as moving women from being defined in terms of natural status to being defined in terms of their property in the person. So crudely (married) mothers move from being serfs (albeit entered into by contract) to workers. However, as I have discussed throughout the book, Carole Pateman has relentlessly argued there are problems with the Lockean fiction of property in the person in which we are treated as the owners of our abilities, which can be alienated. She (rightly) shows how this legal fiction of property in the person justifies subordination within the workplace, taking up the Marxist point that, because you cannot actually separate yourself from your labour power in fact the employment contract is one of subordination, i.e. you have to turn up and be told what to do for a limited number of hours. She argues further that the absence of workplace democracy undermines the possibility of a participative democracy because it means that the social skills, knowledge and confidence, let alone the expectation of having a voice, is undermined.

Motherhood can be distinguished from paid employment, of course, as Pateman illustrates. It is not limited in terms of time and may take place in the home

5 *Spittle v Bunny* [1988] 3 All ER 1031.
6 *Stanley v Saddique* [1992] 2 WLR 459.
7 *Stanley v Saddique* [1992] 2 WLR 459.

alone, without supervision – save in extreme circumstances when supervision is implemented by the state to safeguard the child. There are now many mothers who are not wives, some of whom are supported by the state, which has been described as "the husband" in their lives (Brown 1995). Where mothers are wives there is no longer a difference in formal legal status between them and workers, given that wives are no longer subject to the doctrine of coverture after rape in marriage become illegal (for example this occurred in 1991 in the UK).[8] The fiction of property in the person is so prevalent that it is an obvious move for claimants to make, especially within tort law, to claim either childcare expenses, if this is "outsourced", or to claim the loss of earnings if this is performed by the mother, who was the person subject to the negligence.

The courts are used to putting a price upon injuries and death to decide compensation, without being squeamish about thereby commodifying the body. It may be that it is a better approach to argue that they are the owners of their abilities and gain compensation than to be viewed in a pre-modern manner. However, my concern, following Pateman's analysis of property in the person, is that embracing such a framework may come at a price. It is one of the fictions that we employ in everyday life and in legal cases that is associated with subordination, even if its use in this case would not set up such a relationship. It is therefore an empirical question as to the effect of appealing to such a fiction for pragmatic reasons in court. On the other hand, it could be argued that failure to do so would not be disruptive to the way the fiction operates in everyday life and would simply affirm a pre-modern view of women, to be discussed below.

Pre-modern Approaches

This approach highlights what is radical about modernity and the priority that the social contractarians (and their image of the individual) gave to the idea of choice rather than a fixed natural status in society. Whilst, from Locke onwards, this was applied to men, it is useful to consider what happens when it is applied to women in a practical legal situation, employing some of the arguments made by contemporary feminists discussed in this book.

In *Physical Damage in Negligence* a legal academic Christian Witting (2002) supports Lord Millett's dissenting position in *McFarlane* by arguing that the women in the wrongful conception cases should not be compensated for pain and suffering in relation to the birth because pregnancy is "natural" (although he raises some arguments in favour of awarding compensation for such pain and suffering as "socially constructed harm" (Witting 2002, 195–196)). I am not going to discuss his specific legal arguments but want to focus upon this element of the argument alone and its political rather than legal implications. It is of interest that this argument is still raised today. The argument is that the pain and suffering associated with the

8 *R v R* [1991] 4 All ER 481.

pregnancy is not associated with deleterious change to the body and that this is a prerequisite to describing it as "natural harm". It has to be said that it is not usual, in legal practice, to question whether the head of damage of pain and suffering is related to an actual injury because it is only in the wrongful conception cases that such a nice differentiation can be raised. Usually it is obvious that the pain and suffering has arisen from an injury. The majority of the Law Lords simply argued that the negligent treatment to which Mrs McFarlane had been subject had resulted in pain and suffering and that was enough on which to base the claim.

What is interesting in this position is the way in which the appeal to what is "natural" can operate as the basis of an argument that no harm has been done as a result of negligence which produced a result clearly unwanted by the woman. Witting comments:

> In *McFarlane*, the mother's conception was an entirely natural event that her physiological condition was designed to induce and to accommodate …
>
> Most women are only too glad to avail themselves of the opportunity to conceive and give birth at some stage in their reproductive lives …
>
> Her organs continued to function in the way that "nature intended" (Witting 2002, 192–193).

In this appeal to nature, "nature's intentions" are relevant but Mrs McFarlane's very clear intentions are not. I characterise this as "pre-modern" because it appeals to an image of women as defined by natural status and not by their own choices.

Lord Millett, whose dissenting conclusion in *McFarlane* (that damages could not be awarded for pain and suffering unrelated to bodily injury) is being supported and explained, argues that the harm of an unwanted pregnancy is merely "subjective". He states,

> If the law regards an event as beneficial, plaintiffs cannot make it a matter for compensation merely by saying that it is an event they did not want to happen. In this branch of law at least, plaintiffs are not normally allowed, by a process of *subjective* evaluation, to make a detriment out of a benefit. *McFarlane v Tayside Health Authority* [2000] 2 AC 112. (Lord Millett) Italics added.

So, if this "pre-modern", status-based approach had been adopted, the state would impose its view of "the good" against the clear wishes of Mrs McFarlane; viewing the fact that the doctors had treated her with a lower standard of care than was reasonable, which produced a result she expressly did not want, as *objectively* beneficial. Any perceived harm was therefore merely subjective.

I want to juxtapose this approach with a Kantian perspective, employed by Hampton and discussed in the last chapter. Whilst this is a case in the civil law of tort I want to consider some of the arguments by Hampton about crime and then discuss their applications to civil claims. The aim is to show how a Kantian perspective can be used today to produce a different view of the individual, whether or not this particular application is accepted. As explained in chapter 5, in *A New Theory of Retribution* Hampton (1991b) argues that we feel more hurt by a crime (for example if someone intentionally breaks our legs) than by any equivalent pain that occurs by accident because we feel that the criminal has treated us as of less worth than we deserve. For Hampton, we have been degraded by the crime. The criminal has held him/herself above us and by his/her actions indicated that we are not worthy of respect. The statements in court (and the legal outcome, punishment in the case of the criminal law) should therefore serve the purpose of demonstrating public recognition of the fact that the victim is not actually worth less than the criminal. This argument is predicated upon the Kantian view, discussed in the last chapter, that there is no natural hierarchy and so everyone should be treated as (objectively) equal in terms of self-worth and the right to have his or her life plans respected. Whilst it is necessary to recognise the ways in which Kant's work is gendered (as discussed in the last chapter) this one aspect of Kant's work that shapes Hampton's approach is important.

Hampton discusses objectivity and subjectivity in a different context from Lord Millett. She distinguishes between the objective injury (of being treated as unworthy of respect as a person) and that person's subjective evaluation of the injury. For someone who (rightly) recognises her/his own self-worth (who has not been taught that s/he is unworthy of equal treatment because of her gender or race, for example) a crime will be demeaning. The victim is stung by the failure of the criminal to respect her/him as a person. However, those who have learned (wrongly) that they are not worthy of such respect would not feel demeaned by the criminal act. In other words, in this case, the criminal accords the victim worse treatment than is (objectively) deserved (based upon the assumption that all persons are of equal worth) but the victim (subjectively) does not appreciate this fact because of her/his low sense of self-worth. Hampton describes the victim in such a situation as being 'diminished'.

There is another possible reaction to a crime in which the victim is diminished. This situation occurs if the victim initially felt that s/he was of equal worth with all other persons but then, as a result of the crime, stops believing that this is the case. For Hampton, following Kant, this is a *subjective* view because the victim again fails to recognise the objective fact of her/his equal worth. The harm of the crime in this instance is two fold. First, objectively, the criminal has treated the victim as of lesser worth than s/he should be accorded as a person; and, second, this has caused the victim to feel diminished in her/his own eyes. This way of thinking about the harm of crime can be used to think about the harm of rape, which has been associated with shame in many cultures and a reduction in a woman's value or price (in the Hobbesian sense, as discussed in chapter 2). This is why, Hampton argues, there must be public recognition of this harm, which serves the purpose of acknowledging the victim's equal worth, which was under attack as a result of the crime. The punishment of the crime is part of this public recognition of the victim's objective worth. Hence a derisory penalty fails in this task.

Whilst there is a clear distinction between crime and tort, which I will discuss below, this analysis helps explain why I find the classification of harm in this case as "merely subjective" so disturbing. The view that Mrs McFarlane suffered merely "subjective" harm is incompatible with respect for women as equal persons; as an end in themselves. It appears that Lord Millet recognises this problem because he also creates an entirely new head of damage based upon loss of autonomy, for which there was no previous precedent. So, this approach means that he is pedantic regarding one usual head of damage but then is forced to make up law without precedent to deal with the move.

Whilst the defendant doctor in the wrongful conception actions did not intend to harm the claimants, his actions still fell below a reasonable standard of care. In her discussion of criminal law, Hampton briefly mentions the application of her concept of harm to tort law. She states,

> A person wrongs another if and only if (while acting as a responsible agent) she treats him in a way that is objectively demeaning (Hampton 1991b, 395).

She then comments in a footnote,

> This definition needs refinement … [T]he definition does not adequately distinguish between intentional harming that counts as wrongdoing, unintentional harm that counts as wrongdoing (negligence) and unintentional harming that does not count as wrongdoing (e.g. accidents). Presumably the first two involve 'objectively demeaning' treatment but not the third; however more analysis is needed to explain why this is so (Hampton 1991b, 395 fn. 19).

I think that the answer to this appears clear in Hampton's own analysis. If someone is an unwitting participant in an accident then s/he does not hold herself/himself out as on a higher footing than the victim. In contrast, failure to take reasonable care may carry with it the implication that the claimant was not worth the effort of carrying out treatment to a reasonable standard. Whilst the "objectively demeaning treatment" in tort law is obviously not as great as in crime because it is not intended, I would agree that it is still wrong doing. The closer this action is to just being an accident the less demeaning it is, of course. Imagine if a doctor had been drunk compared with one who was lacking sleep because of an emergency, for example. There is something of a sliding scale in negligence. The harm here is not simply described as the consequences of the low standard of care but relates to the implications of not being treated as worthy of respect. This is exacerbated if the existence of the harm is not acknowledged publically. Where the negligence is closer to the criminal end of the scale, to claim that there is no harm because there is no injury to the body (or that it is only subjective and not really harm) fails to recognise that Mrs. McFarlane is a person, in the moral and political sense of the term, whose intentions matter. In such circumstances, *contra* Lord Millett, it is adding insult to injury for the defendant to argue that his negligence, which significantly altered both Mrs McFarlane's body and her life plans against her will, was a "blessing" upon the claimant. This move imposes upon Mrs. McFarlane the state's view of her own interests rather than respecting her ability as a person to set her own ends and goals.[9] In other words, for the law to fail to recognise that harm has occurred would itself be degrading. Whilst Lord Millet's judgement recognises this in part in a confused manner, it is perhaps most clearly spelt out in Lady Hale's judgment in *Parkinson v St James and Seacroft University hospital NHS Trust* when she states,

> To cause a woman to become pregnant and bear a child *against her will* was an invasion of that fundamental right to bodily integrity. *Parkinson v St James and Seacroft University Hospital NHS Trust* [2002] QB 284 (Lady Hale) Italics added.

This shift towards bodily integrity to deal with this type of case makes us focus upon the woman's intentions. Whilst I want to emphasise that we are discussing tort law, an analogy could be drawn with regard to rape without physical injury. Here, there are familiar arguments that sex is "an entirely natural event that women's physiological condition was designed to induce and to accommodate", that sex is natural and that she wanted it really etc., given that the appeal to nature marginalises women's intentions. So, a useful way of viewing the harm is in terms of bodily integrity but the reason that this is useful is because it focuses upon (rather than marginalising) women's intentions – the overriding of which is in itself an objective harm

Kant and the "Loss of Autonomy" Head of Damage

In his dissenting judgement in *McFarlane* Lord Millett would have awarded damages for "loss of autonomy" set at £5,000. Both these awards were, of course, much smaller than the costs of bringing up a child. I want to explore the way in which the Lord Millett's reference to "autonomy" is understood in these cases and then consider the meaning of autonomy, drawing upon Hampton's Kantian analysis.

---

9 For a useful discussion of this aspect of Kant in the context of personal relationships, see O'Neill 1989, chapter 6. I am trying to hold apart the legal assumption of equal respect for persons from other aspects of Kant's gendered metaphysics and recognise that this may produce a point of tension. However, a strong Kantian notion of autonomy that has been subject to feminist critique is not required in order to argue that McFarlane's stated goal of having no more children should be respected in order to respect her as a person. For a discussion on the progressive use of Kantian personhood, see Cornell (1995, 4–27).

In *McFarlane* Lord Millett said that,

> [Mr. and Mrs. McFarlane] have lost the freedom to limit the size of their family. They have been denied an important aspect of *their personal autonomy.* Their decision to have no more children is one the law should respect and protect. They are entitled to general damages to reflect the true nature of the wrong done to them. *McFarlane v Tayside Health Authority* [2000] 2 AC 114 (Lord Millett) Italics added.

Whilst the reference to autonomy is very useful, to refer to the "autonomy" of a married couple rather than an individual is odd. Given the legal history of the doctrine of coverture, feminists are right to be suspicious (Priaulx 2004, 329). Indeed, Lord Millett's position on the naturalness of birth, which marginalises women's intentions, illustrates the extent to which the woman's ability to have her own ends/goals respected is precisely the point at issue. It could be argued that in recognising "loss of autonomy" Lord Millett is explicitly answering these concerns about the need to recognise the harm that has occurred, albeit in a contradictory manner. However, as discussed above, the derisory sum fails to give this its due accord. It fails to recognise the cost of childcare to the carer and hence to acknowledge the carer's worth. I also want to consider why this confusion about autonomy appears less than innocent by looking further at its historical context.

Kant (1991b) distinguishes autonomy (in which you are able to self-legislate) with heteronomy, the position of being under another's tutelage. The (rather contradictory) move of subsuming women's autonomy within the family is a dangerous (and familiar) one for women. Whilst this may not have been Lord Millett's intention, to subsume women's "autonomy" within the family historically has meant its opposite (a relationship of dependence). This traditional position of women is in direct contrast with the Enlightenment ideal of someone willing to think for his or herself as a person. It is consistent with Kant's own personal ambiguity as to whether women could be viewed as "persons" (see Battersby 1998 for more detail on this).

Therefore, applying Hampton's ("Kantian") analysis to the wrongful conceptions cases, the (objective) harm in these cases is based upon the fact that Mrs McFarlane was not treated as if she were a person, whose intentions mattered. She should not be treated with less than reasonable care that resulted in an unwanted pregnancy and is in a different position to this than her husband. This is well expressed in Lady Hale's characterisation of the harm as being one of bodily integrity but only because this brings to centre stage the issue of Mrs McFarlane's intentions. If these were denied in court by focusing upon the idea that pregnancy is natural and so there was no harm done, her status as a person is further undermined and the harm is perpetuated.

Autonomy and the Boundaries of the Self

There are different ways of thinking about autonomy that are suggested by the social contractarian tradition, particularly if this is to include Spinoza. Feminists have recognised the need to examine the meaning of autonomy and to highlight the ways it has been historically gendered but may not be so in future. The question of how to think about autonomy can be informed by the frameworks of the social contractarians, whose central concern involved conceptualising the inter-relationship between individuals and examining the relationship between individuals and the state, given that they do not envisage individuals signing up to an actual contract. This relationship between ourselves and others raises a question as to how we envisage the "distance" between individuals and how they are imagined as either individuals coming together or being individuated from others, depending upon the starting position. The question of social distance can also be viewed psychologically as well as ontologically in terms of an individual needing to avoid the extremes of isolation, on the one hand, and of being overwhelmed by others, illustrated by the claim for "a room of one's own", on the other hand. Gilligan (1982) has shown that amongst both children and adults (in a specific part of Western culture in 1982) men preferred the risk of isolation and women the risk of being overburdened by relationships. To put this more negatively, men expressed anxiety about the risks inherent in relationships whereas women were more concerned about isolation. The contingent genealogy of this claim and the image of the self as bounded is obviously complex but there are elements of it that can be traced to the work of the social contractarians.

One way of thinking about how we associate with others is demonstrated by Battersby's (1995; 1998; 2007) reading of Kant's *Critique of Judgement* in a manner that demonstrates the link between this issue of social distance from others, an image of self as "bounded" and morality – along with the way in which this has become historically gendered. This is of interest at a time when some women (depending upon, amongst other factors, class, race, sexuality and disability) have sufficient opportunities to be able to leave unsatisfactory sexual relationships and to regard relations with others as a source of pleasure. As outlined in the previous chapter, Kant (1987, 114–115) describes the experience of both the dynamic and mathematical sublime, the might of nature and its enormity, as initially threatening to overpower the self. This initial disturbing experience of the sublime is then recovered as "we" (i.e. men who have not been weakened by peace or trade) recover ourselves though the use of reason, as the final aspect of the experience. We know that we would be able to stand up to the might of nature to employ reason and behave morally. Similarly, with regard to the mathematical sublime, we realise that our attempt to imagine the size of a mountain range (and the disquieting failure of the imagination to do so) was carried out because our reason demanded it. This second element of the experience gives us an awareness of our "supersensible vocation" that can elicit ideas, such as that of God and freedom and the idea of the social contract itself. As discussed in chapter 1, Battersby

(1996) illustrates that women artists, who were discouraged from working within the canon of the sublime, produced art that challenged the canon. The "female sublime" elicited the idea of a self that is – like Kant's self – disturbed by the idea of being overwhelmed by what is external to it. Its boundaries are threatened. However, these artworks of the "female sublime" do not portray an image of a self that simply recovers its boundaries against the outside. They evoke a sense of a self that avoids both being overwhelmed and also avoids isolation, both of which are potential threats. This is not an appeal to the idea that artists illustrate some essential insight of women but that they give expression to a gendered experience which is historically contingent. Kant's image of the self that experiences the sublime is clearly linked with morality as described above. As Battersby points out, it is also one that he denies to women, arguing that they should be timid in the face of nature because they may be pregnant. This is akin to Kant's arguments about women's intelligence. They are viewed as being capable of experiencing the sublime, just as they can fill their heads with Greek and be less appealing to men, but they should stop themselves from doing so (Kant 1991a, 78).

Kant's image of the self that is threatened by its outside but then recovers its boundaries against it is not the familiar *homo economicus* but a more warrior-like character. Nevertheless, in terms of its "boundedness against others", it bears more than a passing similarity with that of Locke, in which the self-owning individual and his property can set a boundary against the external world. Again, there is a link with morality. Nozick expresses this well with the comment that,

> A line (or hyper-plane) circumscribes an area in moral space around an individual. Locke holds that this line is determined by an individual's natural rights, which limit the action of others (Nozick 1974, 57).

Nedelsky discusses how this image of the self as "bounded" against its outside (this time other people and the state) fits within the development of US law. It is an image associated with the view of property as a source of security and a limit upon government power. The framers of the US constitution viewed such economic inequality as natural and sought to protect the minority of property owners against the majority. So, liberty became linked with property rights. She illustrates this with a quotation from Charles Reich, which is evocative of both Kant's "bounded" image of the self discussed above and, in particular, Locke's view of the self as holder of property,

> The institution called property guards the troubled boundary between individual man and the state … Property draws a circle around the activities of each private individual or organization. Within that circle, the owner has a greater degree of freedom than without. Outside, he must justify or explain his actions, and show his authority. Within, he is master, and the state must explain and justify any interference.

Whilst Cornell argues that women must be treated as persons in law, (and I accept that this is right in the limited context in which she is writing, as discussed in the previous chapter) Nedelsky's work raises the question as to whether law relies upon a bounded conception of self being employed, that is contingently historically gendered. This draws upon a view of the self and its property in isolation from others that also fits with the Hobbesian image of freedom as the absence of impediments. Autonomy is achieved through the ability to exclude others. I have extended Nedelsky's arguments with regard to the way this question is relevant to the current development of privacy law (Richardson 2007c).

Nedelsky considers the way in which children learn autonomy to argue that human relations can be a source of autonomy, which is fostered by positive interventions to teach children rather than by simply leaving them alone. There is common ground between Nedesky's description of autonomy as something that is developed in concert with others and Battersby's understanding of the "female sublime" in which artists conveyed a sense of self that exists between the extremes of isolation from others and being overwhelmed by others. As discussed in the previous chapter, Battersby draws upon this image to think about a self that is not defined against its "outside" or, as envisaged, as in psychoanalysis, as cut from the other.

Whereas Hobbes, Locke and Kant produce images of such a bounded self, both Rousseau and Spinoza explore ideas about our relationship with others that trouble this image in different ways. Rousseau's model is completely gendered, such that women are trapped, never to have autonomy but only to be subservient to men. There is a tension in the position of Rousseau's men, who are caught between being natural man and citizen, which are considered mutually exclusive. This is illustrated by Emile who automatically becomes a citizen when taking on the duties of being married to Sophie, but then, rejects her to become an isolated natural man. Just as Hobbes views individuals as competitive, requiring the sovereign to maintain peace, so Rousseau argues that men's *amour propre* sets them in competition. Nevertheless, Rousseau's arguments for the existence of the general will allows him to envisage self-interested individuals making decisions in the best interests of the whole. His image of the republican state in which men are "forced to be free", and a woman rejoices at the state's victory in war despite the death of her children, rejects the concept of self as a bounded individual, demonstrated by the isolation of Emile as a natural man. This is not in order to think about emergence of selfhood in terms discussed by Battersby and Nedelsky, but in favour of the subsumption of individual interests to the fatherland. He is closer to Hobbes, Locke and Kant than is Spinoza in that, rather than thinking how an individual can develop and emerge, his starting position is that of the self-interested individual and he tries to imagine what can mould them together into a collective. As discussed in chapter 5, there are built in tensions in this way of viewing associations, which are exacerbated by the role allocated to women. These include not only the conflict between the natural individual compared to the citizen but also both the romantic heterosexual couple and the patriarchal family, whose interests will both clash with those of the state.

Spinoza provides a model that is much closer to that of Nedelsky and Battersby in which there are never isolated individuals. In addition, the essence of an individual is not envisaged as a fixed underlying quality but depends upon what the individual does to survive and thrive. In other words, it is defined by "its becoming" rather than "its being". This gives rise to a different view of autonomy that is based upon an increase in rationality – not envisaged as mere calculation of interests, as in Hobbesian inspired game theory, nor a Kantian faculty – but as the second form of knowledge that is intimately linked with a (bodily) imagination. It means that, as Balibar puts it,

> (against "individualism") … the autonomy or power of the individual is not reduced, but enlarged, by the constitution of a State or Civil Society, and (against "holism") ... the sovereignty or power of the State is not reduced, but enlarged, by the growing autonomy of the citizens (especially their freedom of thought and expression) (Balibar 1997, 10).

This view of what it is to be a self does not assume that our autonomy is based upon our ability to draw behind boundaries and isolate ourselves from others but to enter into richer and more complex relations with other things in the world, including other persons. Hence, freedom is not the absence of external impediments or the ability to keep others out of our property in which we are free, but involves the increase in our powers of acting that occurs when we understand what produces joyful encounters. In chapter 3, I argued that Spinoza's final comment, denying women citizenship, is contradicted by his thought that it is in the interests of everyone to allow others to enrich their experience so as to increase their knowledge. This is not like increasing books in a library but is a discernment of the reasons why some things in the world agree with us, thereby increasing our powers of acting.

Whilst there is some very exciting and productive feminist work on the imagination, I do not believe that this is in conflict with emphasising the importance of this view of reason that Spinoza offers. There is research within the philosophy of cognition that is in keeping with such a view of cognition, which stresses that we use, not only our bodies but also other things in the world in order to help us think; that cognition is embodied and does not occur just "in the head" (Clark and Chalmers 1998; Clark 1997). As Gatens points out,

> [For Spinoza] knowledge is more a mode of being than of having, not something we possess but something we *are* or *become*. As Monique Schneider notes, in attaining knowledge we do not gain an acquisition, as if something new were added to an inventory of our possessions, but rather we exist differently (Yovel 1992, 159; cited by Gatens 1995, 127).

This applies to both imagination and reason as productive of knowledge, necessary to increase our freedom and to find different ways of entering into relations with others.

Bibliography

Althusser, L. 1997. "The Only Materialist Tradition, Part 1: Spinoza", in *The New Spinoza*. Montag, W. and Stolze, T. eds, Minneapolis: University of Minneapolis Press.

Althusser, L. 2007. *Politics and history – Montesquieu, Rosseau, Marx*. Trans. Brewster, B. London: Verso.

Althusser, L. 2008. *On Ideology*. London: Verso.

Althusser, L. and Balibar, E. 1977. *Reading Capital*. London: New Left Books.

Anderson, B. 2006. *Imagined Communities: Reflections on the Origin and Spread of Nationalism*. Revised. London: Verso Books.

Arendt, H. 1958. *The Human Condition*. Charles R. Walgreen Foundation lectures. Chicago: University of Chicago Press.

Arendt, H. 1989. *Lectures on Kant's Political Philosophy*. Paperback ed. Chicago: University of Chicago Press.

Ashcraft, R. 1995. "Lockean Ideas, Poverty, and the Development of Liberal Political Theory", in *Early Modern Conceptions of Property*. Brewer, J. and Staves, S. eds, 43–61. London: Routledge.

Atiyah, P. S. 1985. *The Rise and Fall of Freedom of Contract*. Corrected ed. Oxford: Clarendon Press.

Auchmuty, R. 2005. "The Rhetoric of Equality and the Problem of Heterosexuality", in *Feminist Perspectives on Contract Law*. Mulcahy, L. and Wheeler, S. eds, 51–74. London: Routledge Cavendish.

Axelrod, R. M. 1990. *The Evolution of Cooperation*. Harmondsworth: Penguin.

Balibar, E. 1997. *Spinoza: From Individuality to Transindividuality*. Delft: Eburon.

Balibar, E. 1998. *Spinoza and Politics*. Trans. Snowdon, P. London: Verso.

Bartky, S. L. 1990. *Femininity and Domination Studies in the Phenomenology of Oppression*. London: Routledge.

Battersby, C. 1989. *Gender and Genius: Towards a Feminist Aesthetics*. London: Women's Press.

Battersby, C. 1995. "Stages on Kant's Way: Aesthetics, Morality, and the Gendered Sublime", in *Feminism and Tradition in Aesthetics*. Brand, P. Z. and Korsmeyer, C. eds, 88–114. University Park, PA: Penn State Press.

Battersby, C. 1996. "Her Blood and His Mirror: Mary Coleridge, Luce Irigaray and the Female Self", in *Beyond Representation: Philosophy and Poetic Imagination*. Eldridge, R. ed, 249–272. Cambridge: Cambridge University Press.

Battersby, C. 1998. *The Phenomenal Woman: Feminist Metaphysics and the Patterns of Identity*. London: Routledge.

Battersby, C. 2007. *The Sublime, Terror and Human Difference*. London: Routledge.

Beck, U. 1999. *Risk Society: Towards a New Modernity*. Trans. Ritter, M. London: Sage.

Beiner, R. and Nedelsky, J. 2001. *Judgement, Imagination, and Politics: Themes from Kant and Arendt*. Lanham, MD: Rowman & Littlefield Publishers.

Bittner, R. 2007. "A Horse in the Basement: Nietzschian Reflections on Political Philosophy" presented at the Society for European Philosophy, Brighton.

Boucher, D. and Kelly, P. J. eds. 1994. *The Social Contract from Hobbes to Rawls*. London: Routledge.

Brennan, T. 2004. *The Transmission of Affect*. Ithaca, NY: Cornell University Press.

Brown, W. 1995. *States of Injury: Power and Freedom in Late Modernity*. Princeton: Princeton University Press.

Butler, J. 1993. *Bodies that Matter on the Discursive Limits of "Sex"*. New York: Routledge.

Butler, J. 1999. *Gender Trouble*. 10th ed. New York: Routledge.

Butler, M. A. 1978. "Early Liberal Roots of Feminism: John Locke and the Attack on Patriarchy", *The American Political Science Review* 72(1) (March): 135–150. doi: <http://www.jstor.org/stable/1953604>.

Butler, M. A. 2002. "Rousseau and the Politics of Care", in *Feminist Interpretations of Jean-Jacques Rousseau*. Lange, L. ed, 212–228. University Park: Pennsylvania State University Press.

Butler, M. A. 2007. "Afterword: Roots and Shoots-Revisiting Locke's Attack on Patriarchy", in *Feminist Interpretations of John Locke*. Hirschmann, N. J. and McClure, K. M. eds, 123–130. University Park, PA: Pennsylvania State University Press.

Castoriadis, C. 1998. *The Imaginary Institution of Society*. Minneapolis: The MIT Press.

Cavarero, A. 1995. *In Spite of Plato: A Feminist Rewriting of Ancient Philosophy*. Cambridge: Polity.

Caverero, A. 2002. *Stately Bodies: Literature, Philosophy, and the Question of Gender*. The Body, in Theory: Histories of Cultural Materialism. Ann Arbor: University of Michigan Press.

Caygill, H. 1995. *A Kant Dictionary*. Oxford: Blackwell.

Chapman, R. A. 1975. "Leviathan Writ Small: Thomas Hobbes on the Family", *The American Political Science Review* 69(1) (March): 76–90.

Clark, A. 1997. *Being There: Putting Brain, Body, and World Together Again*. Cambridge, Mass: MIT Press.

Clark, A. and Chalmers, D. 1998. "The Extended Mind", 58 *Analysis* 7–19.

Cohen, G. A. 1995. *Self-ownership, Freedom, and Equality*. Cambridge: Cambridge University Press.

Constant, B. 1988. "The Liberty of the Ancients Compared with that of the Moderns", in *Political Writings*, Trans. Fontana, B. ed, 307–328. Cambridge: Cambridge University Press.

Cornell, D. 1995. *The Imaginary Domain: Abortion, Pornography and Sexual Harassment*. London: Routledge.

Cornell, D. 1998. *At the Heart of Freedom: Feminism, Sex, and Equality*. Princeton, N.J: Princeton University Press.

Cornell, D. 2000. *Just Cause: Freedom, Identity, and Rights*. Lanham, MD: Rowman & Littlefield Publishers.

Cornell, D. 2008. *Moral Images of Freedom: A Future for Critical Theory*. Lanham, MD: Rowman & Littlefield Publishers.

Darwall, S. L. 2003. *Contractarianism / Contractualism*. Oxford: Blackwell.

Deakin, S. 2002. "The Many Futures of the Contract of Employment", in *Labour Law in an Era of Globalization Transformative Practices and Possibilities*. Conaghan, J., Fischl, R. M. and Klare, K. E. eds, 176–196. Oxford: Oxford University Press.

Dean, M. 1992. "Pateman's Dilemma", 21(1) *Theory and Society* 121–130.

Deleuze, G. 1988. *Spinoza, Practical Philosophy*. Trans. Hurley, R. San Francisco: City Lights Books.

Deleuze, G. and Guattari, F. 1994. *What is Philosophy?* Trans. Tomlinson, H. and Burchill, G. London: Verso.

Den Uyl, D. J. 1983. *Power, State and Freedom*. Assen: Van Gorcum.

Den Uyl, D. J. 1987. "Passion, State, and Progress: Spinoza and Mandeville on the Nature of Human Association", 25 *Journal of the History of Philosophy* 369–395.

Dennett, D. C. 2004. *Freedom Evolves*. London: Penguin.

Descartes, R. 1996. *Descartes: Meditations on First Philosophy*. Trans. Cottingham, J. ed. Revised. Cambridge: Cambridge University Press.

Deutscher, P. 2000. "The Declaration of Irigarayan Sexuate Rights: Performativity and Recognition", in *Feminist Perspectives On Law & Theory*. Richardson, J. and Sandland, R. eds, 71–87. London: Routledge Cavendish.

Durkheim, E. 2008. *The Elementary Forms of Religious Life*. Cladis, M. C. ed. Trans. Cosman, C. Oxford: Oxford Paperbacks.

Dworkin, R. 1989. "The Original Position", in *Reading Rawls: Critical Studies on Rawls' A Theory of Justice*. Daniels, N. ed, 16–52. Stanford series in philosophy. Stanford, California: Stanford University Press.

Ferrara, A. 2008. *The Force of the Example: Explorations in the Paradigm of Judgment*. New York: Columbia University Press.

Filmer, R. 1991. *'Patriarcha' and Other Writings*. Sommerville, J. P. ed. Cambridge: Cambridge University Press.

Fitzgerald, L. F. and Ormerod, A. J. 1991. "Perceptions of Sexual Harassment: The Influence of Gender and Context", 15(2) *Psychology of Women Quarterly* 281–294.

Florence, P. 1997. "Towards the Domain of Freedom: Interview with Drucilla Cornell", 17 *Women's Philosophy Review* 1, 8–29.

Foucault, M. 1977. *Discipline and Punish: The Birth of the Prison*. Trans. Sheridan, A. London: Allen Lane.

Foucault, M. 1990. *The History of Sexuality: An Introduction*. Trans. Hurley, R. London: Vintage.

Foucault, M. 1991. *Remarks on Marx: Conversations with Duccio Trombadori*. Trans. Goldstein, R. J. and Cascaito, J. New York: Semiotext(e).

Foucault, M. 1998. *Technologies of the Self: A Seminar with Michel Foucault*. Gutman, H., Hutton, P. H. and Martin, L. H. eds. Amherst: University of Massachusetts Press.

Foucault, M. and Faubion, J. D. 2002. *Power*. London: Penguin Books Ltd.

Fraser, N. 1996. *Justice Interruptus: Rethinking Key Concepts of a Post-socialist Age*. 1st ed. London: Routledge.

Fraser, N. and Gordon, L. 1996. "A Genealogy of 'Dependency': Tracing a Keyword of the U.S. Welfare State", in *Justice Interruptus: Rethinking Key Concepts of a Post-socialist Age*. 1st ed. 121–150. London: Routledge.

Fricker, M. 2007. *Epistemic Injustice: Power and the Ethics of Knowing*. Oxford: Oxford University Press.

Gatens, M. 1995. *Imaginary Bodies: Ethics, Power and Corporeality*. London: Routledge.

Gatens, M. and Lloyd, G. 1999. *Collective Imaginings: Spinoza, Past and Present*. Routledge.

Gauthier, D. P. 1987. *Morals by Agreement*. New ed. Oxford: Clarendon.

Gauthier, D. P. 2006. *Rousseau: The Sentiment of Existence*. Cambridge: Cambridge University Press.

Gilligan, C. 1982. *In a Different Voice: Psychological Theory and Women's Development*. Cambridge, Mass.: Harvard University Press.

Goldman, E. 2006. *Living My Life*. Abridged. London: Penguin Books.

Gordon, C. 1991. "Governmental Rationality: An Introduction", in *The Foucault Effect: Studies in Governmentality: With Two Lectures by and an Interview with Michel Foucault*. Gordon, C., Miller, P. and Burchell, G. eds, 1–51. Chicago: University of Chicago Press.

Hacking, I. 2002. *Historical Ontology*. Cambridge, Mass.: Harvard University Press.

Hampton, J. 1988. *Hobbes and the Social Contract Tradition*. Cambridge University Press.

Hampton, J. 1991a. "Two Faces of Contractarian Thought", in *Contractarianism and Rational Choice – Essays on David Gauthier's Morals by Agreement*. Vallentyne, P. ed, 31–55. Cambridge: Cambridge University Press.

Hampton, J. 1991b. "A New Theory of Retribution", in *Liability and Responsibility: Essays in Law and Morals*. Frey, R. G. and Morris, C. W. eds, 377–414. Cambridge: Cambridge University Press.

Hampton, J. 1992. "Correcting Harms Versus Righting Wrongs: The Goal of Retribution", 39 *UCLA Law Review* 1659–702.

Hampton, J. 1997. "The Wisdom of the Egoist: The Moral and Political Implications of Valuing the Self", 14 *Social Philosophy and Policy* 21–51.

Hampton, J. 1998. *The Authority of Reason*. Cambridge: Cambridge University Press.

Hampton, J. 2002. "Feminist Contractarianism", in *A Mind of One's Own: Feminist Essays on Reason and Objectivity*. Antony, L. M. and Witt, C. eds, 337–368. 2nd ed. Boulder, Colorado: Westview Press.

Hampton, J. 2007. *The Intrinsic Worth of Persons: Contractarianism in Moral and Political Philosophy*. Farnham, D. ed. Cambridge: Cambridge University Press.

Hampton, J. and Gauthier, D. 2007. "Foreword", in *The Intrinsic Worth of Persons: Contractarianism in Moral and Political Philosophy*. Farnham, D. ed, ix–xii. Cambridge: Cambridge University Press.

Hinton, R. W. K. 1968. "Husbands, Fathers and Conquerors", 16(1) *Political Studies* 55–67.

Hirschmann, N. J. 2007. "Intersectionality before Intersectionality was Cool: The Importance of Class to Feminist Interpretations of Locke", in *Feminist Interpretations of John Locke*. Hirschmann, N. J. and McClure, K. M. eds, 155–186. University Park, PA.: Pennsylvania State University Press.

Hirschmann, N. J. and McClure, K. M. 2007. *Feminist Interpretations of John Locke*. University Park, PA.: Pennsylvania State University Press.

Hobbes, T. 1991. *Man and Citizen: De Homine and De Cive* Indianapolis: Hackett Publishing Co, Inc.Hobbes, T. 1994. *Leviathan: With Selected Variants from the Latin Edition of 1668*. Curley, E. ed. Cambridge: Hackett.

Hobbes, T. 1999. *Human Nature and DeCorpore Politico*. Gaskin, J. C. A. ed. Oxford: Oxford University Press.

Hutchings, K. 2001. "Feminist Philosophy and International Relations", 27 *Women's Philosophy Review* 1, 31–55.

Irigaray, L. 1985a. *This Sex Which Is Not One*. Trans. Porter, C. and Burke, C. Ithaca, N.Y: Cornell University Press.

Irigaray, L. 1985b. *Speculum of the Other Woman*. Trans. Gill, G. C. Ithaca, N.Y: Cornell University Press.

Irigaray, L. 1992. *Je, Tu, Nous: Towards a Culture of Difference*. Trans. Martin, A. London: Routledge.

James, S. 1996. "Power and Difference: Spinoza's Conception of Freedom", 4 *Journal of Political Philosophy* 207–228.

James, S. 1997. *Passion and Action: The Emotions in Seventeenth-Century Philosophy*. Oxford: Oxford University Press.

James, S. 2002. "Freedom and the Imaginary", in *Visible Women Essays on Feminist Legal Theory and Political Philosophy*. James, S. and Palmer, S. eds. Oxford: Hart.

James, S. 2006. “The Politics of Emotion: Liberalism and Cognitivism”, 81 *Royal Institute of Philosophy Supplements*, 58, 231–244.

James, S. 2007. “Repressed Knowledge and the Transmission of Affect”, in *Living Attention: On Teresa Brennan*. Jardine, A., Lundeen, S. and Oliver, K. eds, 45–56. Albany, N.Y: State University of New York Press.

James, S. 2008. “Democracy and the Good Life in Spinoza’s Philosophy”, in *Interpreting Spinoza*. Huenemann, E. ed. Cambridge: Cambridge University Press.

James, S., Lloyd, G. and Gatens, M. 2000. “The Power of Spinoza: Feminist Conjunctions”, 15(2) *Hypatia* 40–58.

Jordan, C. 1987. “Woman’s Rule in Sixteenth Century British Political Thought”, 40(3) *Renaissance Quarterly* 421–451.

Kant, I. 1965. *Critique of Pure Reason*. Trans. Kemp Smith, N. Unabridged ed. New York: St. Martin’s Press.

Kant, I. 1970. *Kant: Political Writings*. Reiss, H. S. and Nisbet, H. B. eds. Trans. Nisbet, H. B. 1st ed. Cambridge Texts in the History of Political Thought. Cambridge: Cambridge University Press.

Kant, I. 1974. *Anthropology from a Pragmatic Point of View*. Trans. Gregor, M. J. The Hague: Nijhoff.

Kant, I. 1987. *Critique of Judgement*. Trans. Pluhar, W. S. Indianapolis: Hackett Publishing Co, Inc.

Kant, I. 1991a. *Observations on the Feeling of the Beautiful and the Sublime*. Trans. Goldthwait, J. T. Berkeley: University of California Press.

Kant, I. 1991b. “An Answer to Question: ‘What is Enlightenment?’” in *Kant: Political Writings*, 325. 2nd ed. Cambridge Texts in the History of Political Thought. Cambridge: Cambridge University Press.

Kant, I. 1996. *The Metaphysics of Morals*. Sullivan, R. J. ed. Trans. Gregor, M. J. 2nd ed. Cambridge Texts in the History of Philosophy. Cambridge University Press.

Kant, I. 1999. *Metaphysical Elements of Justice: Part One of The Metaphysics of Morals*. Trans. Ladd, J. 2nd ed. Indianapolis: Hackett Publishing Co, Inc.

Kantorowicz, E. H. 1997. *The King’s Two Bodies: A Study in Mediaeval Political Theology*. Princeton: Princeton University Press.

Kennedy, H. 1992. *Eve was Framed: Women and British Justice*. London: Chatto & Windus.

Kerruish, V. 1992. *Jurisprudence as Ideology*. Sociology of Law & Crime Series. London: Routledge.

Kittay, E. F. 1999. *Love’s Labor: Essays on Women, Equality, and Dependency*. New York: Routledge.

Kneller, J. 1997. “The Aesthetic Dimension of Kantian Autonomy”, in *Feminist Interpretations of Immanuel Kant*. Schott, R. M. ed, 173–190. Pennsylvania: Pennsylvania State University Press.

Lacan, J. 2001. *Écrits: A Selection*. Trans. Sheridan, A. London: Routledge.

Laslett, P. 1999. "Introduction", in *Locke: Two Treatises of Government – Student edition*. Laslett, P. 3rd ed. Cambridge: Cambridge University Press.

Le Dœuff, M. 2002. *The Philosophical Imaginary*. Trans. Gordon, C. London: Continuum.

Lefebvre, A. 2008. *The Image of Law: Deleuze, Bergson, Spinoza*. New York: Stanford University Press.

Levin, I. 2004. *The Stepford Wives*. London: Bloomsbury.

Lloyd, G. 1994. *Part of Nature Self-knowledge in Spinoza's Ethics*. Ithaca, N.Y: Cornell University Press.

Locke, J. 1999. *Locke: Two Treatises of Government*. 3rd ed. Cambridge: Cambridge University Press.

Lukes, S. 2006. *Individualism*. Reprinted Ed. Colchester: ECPR Press.

Macpherson, C. B. 1962. *The Political Theory of Possessive Individualism: Hobbes to Locke*. Oxford: Clarendon Press.

Mansbridge, J. 2008. "Carole Pateman: Radical Liberal", in *Illusion of Consent: Engaging with Carole Pateman*. O'Neill, D. I., Shanley, M. L and Young, I. M. eds, 17–30. Pennsylvania: Pennsylvania State University Press.

Mansfield, H. C. 1979. "On the Political Character of Property in Locke", in *Powers, Possessions, and Freedom: Essays in Honour of C. B. Macpherson*. Kontos, A. ed, 23–38. Toronto: University of Toronto Press.

Mark, T. C. 1979. "Spinoza's Concept of Mind", 17(4) *Journal of the History of Philosophy* 401–416. doi:10.1353/hph.2008.0753.

Marx, K. 1992. *Capital: Volume 1 – A Critique of Political Economy*. Fowkes, B. ed. Trans. Mandel, E. London: Penguin Classics.

Marx, K. and Engels, F. 1998. *The German Ideology: Including Thesis on Feuerbach*. Amherst, N.Y: Prometheus Books.

Matheron, A. 1969. *Individu et communauté chez Spinoza*. Paris: Ed. de Minuit.

Mill, J. S. 2008. *On Liberty and Other Essays*. Gray, J. ed. Oxford: Oxford Paperbacks.

Miller, D. 1982. "The Macpherson Version", 30(1) *Political Studies* 120–127.

Mills, C. W. 1997. *The Racial Contract*. Ithaca, N.Y: Cornell University Press.

Mills, C. W. 2008. "The Domination Contract", in *Illusion of Consent: Engaging with Carole Pateman*. O'Neill D. I., Shanley, M. J. and Young, I. M. eds, 49–74. Pennsylvania: Pennsylvania State University Press.

Montag, W. 1995. "'The Soul is the Prison of the Body': Althusser and Foucault", 1970–1975. 88 *Yale French Studies* 53–77.

Montag, W. 1999. *Bodies, Masses, Power: Spinoza and His Contemporaries*. London: Verso.

Monti, G. 1999. "A Reasonable Woman Standard in Sexual Harassment Litigation", 19(4) *Legal Studies* 552–579. doi:10.1111/j.1748-121X.1999.tb00639.x.

Murphy, J. B. 1992. "The Workmanship Ideal: A Theologico-Political Chimera?" 20(2) (May) *Political Theory* 319–326.

Nedelsky, J. 1991. "Law, Boundaries and the Bounded Self", in *Law and the Order of Culture*. Post, R. ed, 162–189. Berkeley: University of California Press.

Negri, A. 1991. *The Savage Anomaly: The Power of Spinoza's Metaphysics and Politics*. Trans. Hardt, M. Minneapolis: University of Minnesota Press.

Neuhouser, F. 2007. The Critical Function of Genealogy in Rousseau's Second Discourse presented at the Society of European Philosophy Annual Conference, Brighton.

Nietzsche, F. 2006. "On Truth and Lies in a Nonmoral Sense", in *The Nietzsche Reader*. Ansell, K., Pearson, A. and Large, D. eds, 114–123. Revised. London: Wiley-Blackwell.

Nozick, R. 1974. *Anarchy, State and Utopia*. New York: Basic Books.

O'Donovan, K. 1997. "With Sense, Consent, or Just a Con? Legal Subjects in the Discourse of Autonomy", in *Sexing the Subject of Law*. Naffine, N. and Owens, R. J. eds, 47–64. 1st ed. North Ryde, NSW: LBC Information Services.

O'Neill, O. 1989. *Constructions of Reason: Explorations of Kant's Practical Philosophy*. Cambridge: Cambridge University Press.

Okin, S. M. 1982. "Women and the Making of the Sentimental Family", 11(1) (Winter) *Philosophy and Public Affairs* 65–88.

Okin, S. M. 1989. *Justice, Gender, and the Family*. New York: Basic Books.

Okin, S. M. 2002. "The Fate of Rousseau's Heroines", in *Feminist Interpretations of Jean-Jacques Rousseau*. Lange, L. ed, 89–112. University Park, PA: Pennsylvania State University Press.

Pateman, C. 1970. *Participation and Democratic Theory*. Cambridge: Cambridge University Press.

Pateman, C. 1979. *The Problem of Political Obligation: A Critique of Liberal Theory*. Chichester: Wiley.

Pateman, C. 1988. *The Sexual Contract*. Polity Press: Cambridge.

Pateman, C. 1989. "'God Hath Ordained to Man a Helper': Hobbes, Patriarchy and Conjugal Right", 19(4) *British Journal of Political Science* 445–463.

Pateman, C. 1995. *The Disorder of Women: Democracy, Feminism and Political Theory*. Cambridge: Polity Press.

Pateman, C. 1996. "A Comment on Johnson's: Does Capitalism Really Need Patriarchy?" 19(3) *Women's Studies International Forum* 203–205.

Pateman, C. 2002. "Self-Ownership and Property in the Person: Democratization and a Tale of Two Concepts", 10(1) *The Journal of Political Philosophy* 20–53.

Pateman, C. 2003. "Freedom and Democratization: Why Basic Income is to be Preferred to Basic Capital", *The Ethics of Stakeholding*. Dowding, K., De Wispelaere, J. and White, S. eds. 130–148. Palgrave.

Pateman, C. 2004. "Democratizing Citizenship: Some Advantages of a Basic Income", 32(1) *Politics & Society* 89.

Pateman, C. 2007. "Why Republicanism?" 2(2) *Basic Income Studies* 1–6.

Pateman, C. 2008. "Afterword", in *Illusion of Consent: Engaging with Carole Pateman*. O'Neill, D. I., Shanley, M. L. and Young, I. M. eds, 231–244. Pennsylvania: Pennsylvania State University Press.

Pateman, C. and Mills, C. W. 2007. *Contract and Domination*. Cambridge: Polity.

Patton, P. 2006. *Deleuze and the Political*. London: Routledge.

Pettit, P. 1996. "Freedom as Antipower", 106(3) (Jan) *Ethics* 576--604.

Phillips, A. 2000. "Survey Article: Feminism and Republicanism: Is This a Plausible Alliance?" 8(2) *The Journal of Political Philosophy* 279–293.

Phillips, A. 2008. "Free to Decide for Oneself", in *Illusion of Consent: Engaging with Carole Pateman*. O'Neill, D. I., Shanley, M. L. and Young I. M. eds, 99–118. Pennsylvania: Pennsylvania State University Press.

Powell, G. N. 1986. "Effects of Sex Role Identity and Sex on Definitions of Sexual Harassment", 14(1) *Sex Roles* 9–19.

Priaulx, N. 2004. "That's One Heck of an 'Unruly Horse' Riding Roughshod over Autonomy in Wrongful Conception", 12(3) *Feminist Legal Studies* 317–331. doi:10.1007/s10691-004-4989-y.

Pyle, A. and Hampton, J. 1999. "Jean Hampton", in *Key Philosophers in Conversation: The Cogito Interviews*, 231–239. London: Routledge.

Rawls, J. 1999. *A Theory of Justice*. 2nd ed. Oxford: Oxford University Press.

Rice, L. C. 1990. "Individual and Community: Spinoza's Social Psychology", in *Spinoza Issues and Directions: The Proceedings of the Chicago Spinoza Conference*. Curley, E. M. and Moreau, P. eds. Leiden: E.J. Brill.

Richardson, J. 1999. "'A Burglar in the House of Philosophy': Theodor Adorno and Drucilla Cornell and Hate Speech", 7(1) *Feminist Legal Studies* 3–31. doi:10.1023/A:1009285602918.

Richardson, J. 2004a. "Feminist Perspectives on the Law of Tort and the Technology of Risk", 33(1) *Economy and Society* 98–120.

Richardson, J. 2004b. *Selves, Persons, Individuals: Philosophical Perspectives on Women and Legal Obligations*. Aldershot: Ashgate Publishing.

Richardson, J. 2007a. "Contemporary Feminist Perspectives on Social Contract Theory", 20(3) *Ratio Juris* 402–423. doi:10.1111/j.1467 9337.2007.00367.x.

Richardson, J. 2007b. "On Not Making Ourselves the Prey of Others: Jean Hampton's Feminist Contractarianism", 15(1) *Feminist Legal Studies* 33–55.

Richardson, J. 2007c. "The Law and the Sublime: Rethinking the Self and its Boundaries", 18(2) *Law and Critique* 229–252. doi:10.1007/s10978-007-9010-x.

Richardson, J. and Sandland, R., 2000. *Feminist Perspectives on Law & Theory*. London: Routledge Cavendish.

Rousseau, J. 1968. *Politics and the Arts: Letter to M. D'Alembert on the Theatre*. Trans. Bloom, A. Ithaca, N.Y: Cornell University Press.

Rousseau, J. 1987. *La Nouvelle Heloise: Julie, or the New Eloise – Letters of Two Lovers, Inhabitants of a Small Town at the Foot of the Alps*. Trans. McDowell, J. H. Abridged. University Park, PA: Pennsylvania State University Press.

Rousseau, J. 1992. *Discourse on the Origin of Inequality*. Trans. Cress, D. A. Indianapolis: Hackett Publishing Co, Inc.

Rousseau, J. 1993. *Emile*. Trans. Foxley, B. London: Everyman.

Rousseau, J. 2004. *The Social Contract and the Discourses*. Trans. Cole, D. G. H. London: Everyman's Library.

Ryan, A. 1988. "Hobbes and Individualism", in *Perspectives on Thomas Hobbes*. Rogers, G. A. J. and Ryan, A. eds. Oxford: Clarendon Press.

Sachs, A. and Hoff Wilson, J. 1979. *Sexism and the Law: A Study of Male Beliefs and Legal Bias in Britain and the United States*. New York: Free Press.

Schochet, G. J. 1998. "The Significant Sounds of Silence: The Absence of Women from the Political Thought of Sir Robert Filmer and John Locke (or 'Why Can't a Woman Be More Like a Man?')", in *Women Writers and the Early Modern British Political Tradition*. Smith, H. L. ed. Cambridge: Cambridge University Press.

Schochet, G. J. 2007. "Models of Politics and the Place of Women in Locke's Political Thought", in *Feminist Interpretations of John Locke*. Hirschmann, N. J. and McClure, K. M. eds, 131–154. University Park, PA: Pennsylvania State University Press.

Seidler, V. J. 1986. *Kant, Respect and Injustice: The Limits of Liberal Moral Theory*. London: Routledge & Kegan Paul.

Seidler, V. J. 1989. "Kant, Respect, Individuality and Dependence", in *Kant's Practical Philosophy Reconsidered: Papers*. Yovel, Y. ed, 235–254. Boston. Springer.

Shapiro, I. 1992. "Workmanship Revisited: Reply to Professor Murphy", 20(2) *Political Theory* 327–331.

Skinner, Q. 2008. *Hobbes and Republican Liberty*. Cambridge: Cambridge University Press.

Smith, D. W. 2003. "Deleuze and the Liberal Tradition: Normativity, Freedom and Judgement", 32(2) *Economy and Society* 299–324.

Smith, H. L. 1998. *Women Writers and the Early Modern British Political Tradition*. Cambridge: Cambridge University Press.

Sorell, T. 2007. "Hobbes's Moral Philosophy", in *The Cambridge Companion to Hobbes's Leviathan*. Springborg, P. ed, 128–156. Cambridge: Cambridge University Press.

Spinoza, B. 2000a. *Ethics*. Parkinson, G. H. R. ed. Trans. Parkinson, G. H. R. Oxford: Oxford University Press.

Spinoza, B. 2000b. *Political Treatise*. Trans. Shirley, S. Cambridge: Hackett.

Spinoza, B. 2001. *Theological-Political Treatise: Gebhardt Edition*. Trans. Shirley, S. 2nd ed. Cambridge: Hackett.

Spinoza, B. 2002. *Spinoza: Complete Works*. Morgan, M. L. ed. Trans. Shirley, S. Cambridge: Hackett.

Strauss, L. 1963. *The Political Philosophy of Hobbes*. Chicago: University of Chicago Press.

Taylor, C. 1992. "Atomism", in *Communitarianism and Individualism*. Avineri, S. and De-Shalit, A. eds, 29–50. Oxford: Oxford University Press.

Taylor, C. 1997. "Cross-Purposes: The Liberal-Communitarian Debate", in *Philosophical Arguments*, 181–203. Harvard: Harvard University Press.

Taylor, C. 2004. *Modern Social Imaginaries*. New title. Durham: Duke University Press.

Teeven, K. M. 1990. *A History of the Anglo-American Common Law of Contract*. London: Greenwood Press.

Thompson, E. P. 1977. *Whigs and Hunters: The Origin of the Black Act*. 1st ed. Harmondsworth: Penguin.

Tronto, J. C. 1993. *Moral Boundaries: A Political Argument for an Ethic of Care*. New York: Routledge.

Tully, J. 1993. "After the Macpherson thesis", in *An Approach to Political Philosophy: Locke in Contexts*, 71–96. Cambridge: Cambridge University Press.

Tweedie, J. 1979. *In the Name of Love*. London: Cape.

Waldron, J. 2007. "Locke, Adam, and Eve", in *Feminist Interpretations of John Locke*. Hirschmann, N. J. and McClure, K. M. eds, 241–268. University Park, PA: Pennsylvania State University Press.

Witting, C. 2002. "Physical Damage in Negligence", 61(1) *The Cambridge Law Journal* 189–208.

Wollstonecraft, M. 1996. *A Vindication of the Rights of Woman*. New edition. Mineola, N.Y: Dover Publications Inc.

Yovel, Y. 1992. *Spinoza and Other Heretics 1: The Marrano of Reason*. Oxford: Princeton University Press.

Index